T0248169

Praise for
Original Love

"This is one of the rare books destined to inspire new and seasoned meditators alike. Drawing on his own deep experience and years of teaching, Henry Shukman brings a lucid and refreshing cast to the fundamentals of practice, and reveals how the loving we yearn for is always, already here; love is intrinsic to what we are. Please gift yourself with this powerful, poetic, transformative guide to awakening our hearts."

—Tara Brach, author of *Radical Acceptance*

"Henry Shukman is one of the wisest and most poetical teachers of dharma we have today. In an increasingly fragmented world, he is unusually good company."

—Sam Harris, *New York Times* bestselling author of *Waking Up* and host of the *Making Sense* podcast

"This is a book the world has been waiting for—one that speaks clearly and eloquently to the reality of love as the foundational energy of this world. I can't think of a more important project for humankind than all of us finding this love as a matter of urgency. Of all the books on meditation I've read, none have so clearly laid out the finding of love as its central project. It's also unusual for a book like this to come from the hand of a poet; it's a beautiful book, but more important, it's one we all need, and we need it now." —Richard Rohr, author of *Falling Upward*

"[Shukman's] writing is gorgeous, funny, fascinating, and audacious."

—Rick Hanson, bestselling author of *Buddha's Brain*

"Henry Shukman has a natural, contagious, and enlightened enthusiasm, which his fine writing style carries so beautifully to the reader through every page. This is a book for breaking the spell of the 'me,' not in the sense of erasing ourselves but in taking the journey of awakening where we can come out from behind the surface, defended self and appear fully and transparently and even lovingly in this difficult world. A book to carry to some quiet place every day so that you can journey with a companion who has walked a good part of the way before you and who will become a very good friend to you, page by revealing page."

—David Whyte, author of *Consolations* and *The Sea in You*

"A fascinating and beautiful contribution to the world of meditation by an adept in the practice."

—Roshi Joan Halifax, abbot and founder of Upaya Zen Center

"*Original Love* is a lively compendium of all you want to learn about meditation, mindfulness, suffering, non-suffering, joy, coming home, and being whole. All that is in this book is hard-earned, on the ground, and clearly explained. Shukman so much wants to share his understanding that you can feel the excitement and longing right in the center of the still page. This book is a great friend, one who tells the simple, obvious truth that is right in front of our face. And on top of all this, Shukman knows how to write, like an angel."

—Natalie Goldberg, author of
Writing on Empty and *Three Simple Lines*

"Henry is a masterful teacher. His insight, compassion, and wisdom combine to provide some of the best meditation teaching out there."

—Kelly Boys, author of *The Blind Spot Effect* and director of
the Foundation for a Mindful Society and the Mindful Cities Initiative

"Take a break. Fall in love with your life. Breathe in the rich fragrance of mindfulness as taught by a master Zen teacher who is also a superb poet. For beginning or advanced students of meditation, Henry Shukman will lead you seamlessly into your own original love for life as it is, and you as you are. Extraordinary in its freshness and replete with all kinds of wisdom, this book illuminates waking up naturally, aimlessly, in your own time. Enjoy it."

—Polly Young-Eisendrath, bestselling author of
Love Between Equals and *The Present Heart*

"This book, like Henry himself, is wise and deep and filled with heartfelt meditation advice and beautiful, powerful stories. You will be very glad that you've read it."

—Michael W. Taft, author of *The Mindful Geek*

Original Love

Original Love

THE FOUR INNS ON THE
PATH OF AWAKENING

Henry Shukman

HarperOne

An Imprint of HarperCollinsPublishers

For Stevie and Saul and Clare

Contents

Part One: The First Wheel-Rut

THE FIRST INN:
Mindfulness

THE SECOND INN:
Support

THE THIRD INN:
Absorption

Part Two: The Second Wheel-Rut

THE FOURTH INN:
Awakening

Foreword

BY RICK HANSON

"All sickness is homesickness." I first heard that from Tara Brach, perhaps quoting Dianne Connelly, and it's been a guide for me ever since.

When the body is ill, it's no longer in its healthy resting state: its home base. When the mind is stressed or upset, it too has been driven from home. The signposts of this exile are feelings of pressure, anxiety and sadness, frustration and irritation, hurt and loneliness. Because the brain evolved a "negativity bias" to keep our ancestors alive in harsh conditions, these experiences get hardwired quickly into the nervous system. Over time, this can become the new normal, a kind of chronic inner homelessness.

If all sickness is homesickness, the reverse is also true: all health is coming home.

What is our true home? We know it when we find it. You can feel at home in your kitchen, in the woods, in the arms of your mate. Sometimes under the stars or on the edge of the sea. There is also the sense of home deep inside ourselves, the most reliable home of all, the one we take with us wherever we go.

In these pages, Henry Shukman shows us how to come home again. And with a little skillful effort, we never need to leave.

I first met Henry through his revelatory memoir of despair and awakening, One Blade of Grass. *He's been a teacher for me, opening doors of insight and inner freedom, and also a friend. We've tramped through the snow together in Santa Fe, New Mexico, and shared meals and sorrows when talking about our families. Henry is many things, to name a few: a father and husband, a poet and scholar, a Zen master with a wicked sly sense of humor, and an exuberant cook. He is an extraordinary writer who brings you into the immediacy of his own realization, his own experience of the real home that lives through each of us, breath after breath.*

For it is the love in the origin of all arising that is his subject here.

To live in the sense of this, he provides a clear step-by-step exploration of meditation practices that takes readers through establishing stable mindfulness and self-nurturance, and then easing into blissful absorptions and the openings of awakening. He shows us new possibilities in what may be familiar practices of self-awareness, contemplation, even prayer. He offers many experiential activities that are effective invitations into the wordless states of being that are the true gold of the journey. Because he has walked these paths so much himself, and in a variety of traditions, he's extremely skillful at dealing with each twist and turn, including for individual needs. Throughout, he is the kindest of teachers, encouraging and commiserating and coaching with both the light touch of his natural sweet spirit and the fearless penetrating oomph of someone who's experienced the dissolution of his ego and come back with nothing left to lose.

Henry also provides an important, fresh framework for understanding the confusing complexity of psychospiritual tools

*and teachings. Educated at Oxford, yet modest and unpreten-
tious, he is quietly brilliant in his overview of the seemingly
many paths that are actually one path . . . or no path at all,
since in truth we are all always already home.*

That is the real genius of this book.

*Woven through his practical guidance, personal examples,
and conceptual clarity is a single bright joyful thread: You are
already home. The foundation of your psyche is an indestructible,
unstainable love. In simple biological terms, humans evolved to
live together based on "caring and sharing"—compassion and
justice—since that promoted surviving and thriving for both in-
dividuals and bands. We are naturally moved by suffering, and
we long to give and receive kindness, respect, and comfort. Sure,
much like the sun can be obscured by clouds, we can lose sight
of this inner light. But it is always shining, and Henry shows us
how to disperse the mind's clouds while knowing, and knowing
again, the heart's true home.*

*Even more deeply, "beneath" the contents of awareness—the
thoughts and feelings and other flotsam and jetsam in the stream
of consciousness—Henry reveals the nature of that inner light:
continually giving itself in the present, like a fountain spreading
out into and disappearing into the moment while being continually renewed. The givingness of presence is love, even when the
contents of that giving seem far from it. What a reassurance to
know this! In the midst of stresses and quarrels, and when reckon-
ing with mistakes and regrets and remorse, in this book you can
find the sure refuge of really knowing the rising, shining, inher-
ently loving generosity in consciousness itself.*

*And deepest of all, as someone who has had the bottom fall
out in the most radical of awakenings, Henry invites us into the*

emergingness of reality itself, its own endless givingness as it originates into the present. A plausible theory of time—why is there always something new?—is that it is simply the expansion from the big bang of our four-dimensional space-time universe. The expansion of space in its three directions is so vast we don't notice it, but as time expands into the next moment, leaving the current one behind, we live always in creation. What a gift! With his own offerings of eloquence, clarity, and realization, Henry Shukman helps us appreciate, surrender into, and find our most fundamental home in the continual appearing of something from nothing, living in the giving that is love.

RICK HANSON, PHD
Wellspring Institute for Neuroscience
and Contemplative Wisdom
San Rafael, California, USA
On the unceded lands of the Miwok
and other Native people
October 21, 2023

An Invitation

Imagine you're alone in a quiet room. No one can disturb you. You're comfortable, you're still, and gradually you're getting the sense that a greater quiet surrounds you and holds you. The more you feel this quiet, the more you know in your bones that you can trust it. It's beautiful and precious, and you find yourself letting go of your plans. Your to-do list evaporates, your agenda disappears like vanishing ink. Now there's only the quiet, which feels almost like a presence, and it brings on a deep sense of well-being.

You bask in it and feel you're touching something familiar yet also mysterious and potent. Your heart opens, as if this spell of quiet contains a secret, primordial love, outside time, that has always been here, an unseen bedrock of life. It's as if a pervasive love underlies everything you experience, as if the whole world floats on a lake of ineffable love.

In a while, you take a deeper breath and end the period of meditation. You go downstairs, make coffee, and enter your day, feeling not just replenished but as if you have just touched something wider, an unnameable mystery, a secret side to your life that has reset your priorities.

This is meditation—a clear, deep stillness that can meet our most profound spiritual yearnings exactly and fully. No special buildings. No rituals, priests, doctrines, or dogmas. No machineries of institutional power. Just you, your own space, and a commitment to be quiet and still for a while. Yet you emerge from it feeling spiritually fulfilled. Right in the middle of your ordinary life.

This is the taste of "original love." It's real, and I believe it's accessible to all of us. I hope this book will inspire and help you to find it.

The Question

There is a Buddhist scripture that consists of only one letter. That single letter is both the title and the entire contents of the teaching.

A.

It is considered by some to be the supreme expression of all Buddhism—its whole teaching, all its wisdom and compassionate engagement with life—summed up in a single letter.

A. (Pronounced "Ah.")

How on earth could one letter, all on its own—without subject or object, without a word to which it belongs—signify, suggest, or encapsulate an all-pervasive wisdom? How could it represent an all-inclusive love?

That's my challenge: to solve that riddle, and to your complete satisfaction. So it's clear not just to your mind but also your heart. So you know how it feels. So you feel the "original love" that is hidden within it. And, actually, within you.

The Universe's Garden

This is a work of unabashed advocacy. It seeks to persuade you that a radical reversal in our ordinary understanding of self and world is available. And that it matters because it not only brings us closer to reality, but also has far-reaching benefits, both for an individual and for society at large.

This book is about *the* best subject. It's about the single most astounding fact you will ever come to know. It's about you. You yourself are the most astonishing reality in the whole universe. You—right where you are, right now, whether you are reading these words while standing at an airport newsstand, slouching in a subway car rattling under the streets of a great city, sagging behind the wheel on a gridlocked freeway, or sitting at a lamp-lit desk at night scrolling down the Amazon home page—are not what you have taken yourself to be.

Yes, you are the person with the history, hopes, relationships, physiology, aptitudes, and fallibilities that help to define who you think you are. But you are also both much more, and much less. When we get right down to it, our sense of self is an illusion, like a mirage over a hot road, no more substantial than a reflection on the surface of a lake. To "awaken" is to realize this, and this book is a guide to catching glimpses of what that means.

If this book succeeds even a little, it will open a crack in your sense of self—a chink in the armor of your certainties, of your confidence in the basic assumptions we all make about life—that will allow a revelation to begin to unfold in your life, as well as in the lives of those around you, and ultimately, perhaps, in the whole human family, and through it, in the great family of all animate beings.

This book is about joining wholeheartedly in the play of this cosmos, which bursts forth in a spectacular array of life on this planet. Here, the bare mineral desert of the galaxy, in its vast, austere beauty, explodes in the wild play of life. This is the universe's garden. This right here is its treasured hothouse. Right here is where the cosmos *blooms*. And among the many forms in which it blooms, here is the creature—you—that has enough consciousness to be cognizant of its situation, to know how it evolved to be what it is, and to be aware of its own awareness. And to discover in its very bones that it is part of the whole of creation. The universe is blooming right now as *you*.

Somehow, however crazy it sounds, the universe *loves* you. So much that it is making you, giving you life and awareness. To experience this love in our hearts is what it takes to unwrap the gift this life can be, even in the midst of its challenges and difficulties.

The proposition of this book—and of the deep meditation traditions from which it draws—is that it is possible to see through our sense of ourselves as separate entities, and to break an enchantment we didn't know we had been caught in. Far from this risking a dissociative tumble into a vortex of nihilism, breaking the spell that separates us from the universe can be the single most healing, positively life-transforming event that can happen to us, with massive beneficial impacts on our priorities, orienting us away from self-protection and self-promotion and toward concern for the well-being of others, arising from a deep sense of connection. And the reason awakening can accomplish all this is that it opens up a boundless love—the "original love" of this book's title.

This is not a romantic love, or a selfish love that craves what it wants. Instead, it's a deep sense of appreciation, of cherishing, of caring, of compassion, of joy, and of being beloved. It's unconditional.

A deft, light touch of grace, an unexpected gust of feeling beloved, a tiny tap on the heart like a drop from a leaking faucet, a raindrop of coolness on a hot brow, or the relief of a single tear—the one right touch releases love from within, bringing with it the true flavor of being alive that our hearts yearn for. Only to love is the fulfillment of our life. We human beings are made to experience love. When we feel love, we feel alive. The path of our life, whether we recognize it or not, is paved with love. The trail may be graveled or mossy or grassy or rocky, but whatever its apparent surface, just beneath it lies love.

A REVERSAL

This may all sound quite bizarre or improbable. Bear with me. Most of us carry around more unquestioned certainties than we realize, and reappraising them can lead to unexpected discoveries.

In his groundbreaking work on evolution, *The Selfish Gene*, Richard Dawkins invites biologists, and a wider public, to think about organisms in a new way, in the manner of a Necker cube. The Necker is a series of lines on paper that represent a cube. The image of the cube can "flip" in a viewer's mind from having its lower left face seem "nearer" the viewer, to its upper right face seeming closer, and vice versa.

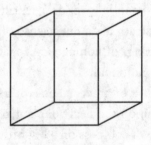

A Necker cube

Dawkins offers the possibility that in a comparable kind of flip, our view of organisms could shift. We could observe and study how the organism itself is functioning, from the perspective of its needs and purposes. Or we could shift our view to the functioning of the genetic material that generates the organism, and see how the genes accomplish their purposes by means of the organism's life. Neither vantage is exclusively correct, but to see only one is to have an incomplete view.

The matter in this case is our view of self. We commonly feel we have, and are, a separate, fixed entity, something within us that uses the labels "I, me, mine." This view can also "flip." Normally, we cling to an intuitive sense of being "me," but we can come to see that the sense of *me* is nothing more than a set of stories in the mind. Together they conjure up a kind of genie—"Me." That is to say, the sense of *me* is not as stable or solid as we take it to be, and depends on an implicit narrative repeatedly generated by our thinking— namely the story of "my life," with its memories, events, relationships, activities, and imagined futures. Whereas in point of fact, all that is actually present at any time is the content of one particular moment—*now*—which may well include memories and imaginings, but these too are merely thoughts arising here and now.

To have our view flip in this way, to break through the spell of separateness and see through the genie of self, to realize that it has never been more real than a mirage, to grasp that it has not been what it has seemed to be—that I do not constitute a fixed, stable core or nugget or entity that is who I am—is to undergo a revolution and a liberation.

That alone is good. But the Necker cube is not a sufficient analogy for this shift. In another analogy, it's more like flipping from a geocentric worldview to a heliocentric one. Rather than continuing to believe that the sun, moon, and stars revolve around a flat earth, as they appear to do to the naked eye, we realize our planet is in fact a rotating sphere that revolves around the sun, as do the other planets in our solar system. We might still sometimes "feel" that Earth is at the center of our solar system, but that feeling no longer fools us into believing that we really are.

To "wake up" from the dream of the separate self is like that. Awakening releases us from a belief in a core, isolated "me," distinct from all else, around and outside which an environment exists. We see through the construction we have made, of being a self moving through a world that is apart from us.

This sense of things is so deeply intuitive that it is hard to believe it could be an incomplete view. Yet it is. Anyone who has glimpsed awakening can attest to that.

But what are we once the spell of "me" is gone?

This is the best part. We find we are part of an indivisible whole. We are not separate from anything. There is a level of our experience, of our very consciousness, wherein we and all things are "one." That "one" has been given many labels throughout the centuries by the meditation traditions: Luminous Mind; Buddha Nature; *Sunyata*, or Emptiness; the Dharma Body; Non-dual Awareness; the *Turiya*; the true Self; *Nirvana*; God. It has been described as the "one mind," the "great heart," the "single body," "one dream," "radiant nature," reggae's "one love," and so on. How we might attempt to describe it, the name we might want to give it, probably depends on how it happens to be experienced at any given time. It can be sensed as any or all of the preceding, and likely in many more ways too. But whichever it is, we discover, most remarkably, that there is a level of our reality in which we are inseparable from all else.

This, as we will see, is why waking up matters. This is

why it is worth our time and effort to shake off our slumber of separateness, and why it has such potential for the beings of this planet.

Richard Dawkins also writes that if "superior" aliens ever reached planet Earth, the first question they'd ask of humanity would be: Have you discovered evolution yet? In other words, do you know how you got here?

We might add a second question the aliens could ask: Have you discovered who you are? Have you awakened from the illusory, separate sense of self? Have you found the boundless consciousness that connects you with all things?

AWAKENING HAS A potential like nothing else to heal the destructive divisions of this world. And it's not too late. The Dalai Lama says that if every eight-year-old on the planet were to learn meditation, then we would eliminate violence in a single generation.

In a few short decades, we could turn armaments into museum displays, reminding us of the brutalities of earlier epochs, much as cities in Germany and other parts of Europe have "stumbling stones" built into their sidewalks today— small brass plaques on which a passerby might stumble, as reminders of the horrors of the Second World War. Each one is inscribed with the name of a Jewish person who once lived nearby, before dying in the Holocaust.

Likewise, we might place decommissioned tanks and guns, missiles and bombs, around our cities, to remind us of earlier times of violence and destructiveness that as a species we will have outgrown.

To wake up into the union of all things, to find the single

community of all creation that we are truly part of, might be the one thing that could actually accomplish this.

THE CART TRACK
AND THE FOUR INNS

So how do we get there?

Basically, we learn to meditate. And we learn to love meditating. That's what this book aims to help with.

An ancient Chinese document, recently unearthed from a vast cache of old scrolls found in the Dunhuang caves of China, describes the path of meditation as a cart track. The track has two wheel-ruts worn in the earth, one for each wheel. The first rut is "mindfulness practice." The second is "awakening."

The point of the analogy is that on the path of meditation, we need both wheel-ruts. We are fallible, erring, and suffering creatures who need the wheel-rut of practice—of gradual growth and healing through mindfulness—which helps us develop in wisdom, kindness, and patience, in incremental ways. At the same time, the second rut, awakening, is always here too—the awakening we may seek is actually already within us, waiting to be seen.

We need both wheel-ruts: neither on its own can support us. The main body of this book is an exploration of the journey along this two-rut track. It maps out this track in greater detail, and parses the first rut into three critical areas of attention, before moving to the second rut.

But now let's adjust the picture. Imagine that the track

leads up a valley deep into a mountain range. As the path snakes up the gorges and river valleys, farther into the highlands, it passes by four inns—four refuges at which the pilgrim in search of peace and well-being, and perhaps the deeper truths of life, can stay for a while, and learn what each inn has to offer.

Think of this book as a trail that leads you to these four roadside inns. Each inn offers shelter along the route, with dormitory windows offering different vistas. From the first, there are views of meadows and aspen groves; from the second, of wooded hills, where insects, birds, and blossoms flourish; from the third, of a river rushing through a gorge, and a distant lake; and from the fourth, of far-off mountains, which blush at sunset and whose peaks are sometimes wrapped in cloud, a sublime picture in late light.

The first inn is *Mindfulness*, where we come home to our life right now, again and again. We learn to love ourselves— that is to say, to have compassion for the ways we suffer, which helps us to love others, and to appreciate our life.

The second inn is *Support*. Meditation may seem like a solitary pursuit, something that's all up to us, like doing reps at the gym. Or we may have some ideal of an adept meditating alone on a mountaintop. But really, it's just as much about support *and* connection. We all need support, encouragement, guidance, and connection on the path of practice. This inn is where we learn ways of finding more support, and of opening up to connection of various kinds that may already be here without our recognizing it. We learn to trust more. We open to forms of love we're already receiving. We discover how connected we really are. This helps to make us more tender, more vulnerable, and therefore all the more ready to connect with others and receive help.

The third inn is *Absorption*. Absorption is akin to flow states, in which we get so engaged in an activity that we lose all sense of time and self, and find deep fulfillment in what we're doing. It is one of the hidden treasures of meditation. When it happens, we start to fall in love with this very moment, and become absorbed in the beauty of simply sitting still.

The fourth inn is *Awakening*, where we get flooded with an infinite love that includes all things. We'll be unpacking what that means down the road, and exploring ways all of us can get a taste or glimpse of it.

We explore these four inns in the four main sections of this book, where we taste the flavor of "original love" that each one has to offer.

ORIGINAL LOVE

So what is "original love"?

The great Indian sage Yogananda, sometimes dubbed the twentieth century's first "superstar guru," was one of the first teachers of yoga and meditation in America. He once said that life is a movie, and that a person's true purpose is to turn around and see the projector from which it comes. When we see that, and see the beams of light making the images, we discover the origin of everything, arising out of boundless love. We find that love is the origin of creation.

The good news is that it's possible to see this for ourselves. The even better news, however, is that there are intermediate, incremental steps we can take, without having to have the kind of breakthrough experience that reveals the "projector." These intermediate steps can make our lives in this ordinary world a whole lot easier and richer. They can inspire us to live more kindly and wisely, and make us happier than we ever thought possible, even before we've turned around to see the projector, the source of the movie that is each person's life.

The Buddha himself seems to have realized that although a few adepts "got" his deepest teaching almost on the spot, many, many more did not. He therefore laid out step-by-step approaches for everyone to follow.

In one sense, the program of meditation is gradual: it helps to have the basics of one inn before moving on to the next. But from another perspective, it is not gradual, because in every moment of our lives, the miracle of awakening is always here. (Hence, once again, the parallel wheel-ruts of the cart track.) It's possible to recognize at any time that in the heart of each moment, somehow, against all the odds, there is an infinite goodness. Each moment of life is a kind of goodness incarnate—no matter how hard life may be, or how far from goodness it may seem.

No matter what, we are the universe blooming, shining with awareness of itself. To become able to savor this in even a small way opens up the original love deep in our own nature—unconditional, indiscriminate, a love that bestows limitless well-being in our hearts and minds, which can grow and spread ever wider.

And above all, we can feel this original love through meditation. The purpose of this book is to persuade you of that as a possibility, and to map out a practical path to it— the path of meditation—and to help you follow it.

It suggests nonreligious, evidence-based approaches to understanding the benefits of meditation, and offers practices to help us integrate them into our lives, as we work toward building a more compassionate and loving society for all.

It presents the full sweep of meditation—the "royal road," as the Buddha called it—from mindful regulation of a rattled nervous system, where we recover the balance needed for wholesome lives of creativity and harmony in household and community; to gradually opening up to the many kinds of support and connection that sustain us; to tasting the wonder of meditative absorption, where our sense of separateness diminishes; and finally, it leads to astounding existential discoveries of our boundless unity with all.

This book hopes to lead us back into what we most long for—a world of love. The true trail of practice is love all the way, from start to finish. The trail of breadcrumbs that guides us through the territory of the heart is love itself. Meditation is a path of love.

And it's for everyone. If mindfulness and the search for awakening sound like rarefied pursuits, perhaps reserved exclusively for a privileged few, please remember this: the features of our own consciousness that we unearth through practice are already here, within us. Meditation is *the* most accessible way to find them. All it costs is a little time each day. A daily pause.

Meditation is not really anything separate from being human. In a sense, it's not really even an activity. True, we follow simple instructions that guide and support our paying attention. But fundamentally, it is always simply about being quiet and still. About simply being.

Who are we when we are not doing anything? Who are we when we are simply alive? When we simply *are*?

WHO IS THIS BOOK FOR?

Meditation is for everyone. Parents who ache for their children's well-being, some of whom may have come to dread the telephone, because they know the kind of news it can bring. Young people quietly traumatized by the lifestyle displays on their social media. Hardworking families longing for a break. Caregivers offering their hands and hearts day after day, hoping to stave off a burnout they fear may be coming. Anyone alone and isolated in the heart of a teeming city. Anyone facing a major diagnosis—and we all face the ultimate diagnosis, though it may feel remote.

Who among us would not benefit from a little pause, a little peace, and a taste of a boundless love that asks nothing of us—no beliefs, no dogmas—but offers itself freely, if we just learn to sit still and release ourselves into silence?

One of the core planks of the approach to life and meditation this book offers is that we don't need blinding revelations or massive enlightenment experiences (though they may come) to encounter an unconditional love waiting to be touched in the heart of even ordinary moments. Truly, my hope is that this book may serve as a place of healing, nourishment, hope, and encouragement for anyone who picks it up.

Each of us can use this life to uncover our true nature, to discover who we are at a deeper level. It kind of *is* like the movie *The Matrix*. There *is* an illusory aspect of the way we experience life. But unlike in the movie, in the real, live, actual matrix of this life, when we peel back the layers of illusion, we don't find giant alien insects. Instead, we find an unimaginable, boundless source of love, creativity, and generosity. We find infinite stillness. We find a silent awareness that holds all things and unifies them. We find an ultimate healing, or better, an innocence that never even needed healing. We come home to who we truly are. In a sense, who *doesn't* need that?

My Story

One evening when I was nineteen years old, I found myself alone on a beach in Ecuador, gazing over the Pacific Ocean, five thousand miles away from my hometown of Oxford, England. The sun was lowering toward the horizon, and something extraordinary was about to happen to me.

I had grown up in an unhappy, broken home, cared for by our brilliant, troubled mother, and my skin was ravaged by severe, chronic eczema. The affliction began when I was an infant, and it often flared up in infectious impetigo, which would land me in the hospital for several days at a time.

But for the past six months I had been far away from all that, working and backpacking in South America, where my skin had miraculously healed, and I felt I had become myself at last.

While I stood on that beach before the marvel of the sun setting over the Pacific Ocean, a deep happiness overtook me. Nothing held me back, and I fell into an intimacy with the scene unlike anything I'd known. Something amazing happened. Somehow I let go of myself, and fell into the midst of all creation. I discovered my unity with the whole cosmos.

I belonged on this earth in a way I had never dreamed of before, and felt I touched the real purpose of my existence.

Whatever happened in that marvelous moment, it changed the course of my life. It was as if suddenly I had fulfilled a secret purpose it had been my life's mission to fulfill—though I'd had no inkling of having had such a mission until then. I could have died happily that night.

It would be years before I realized that I'd had a bona fide "awakening" experience. But the name didn't matter. For days after, for weeks, I walked about in a daze of relief, feeling light as a feather, with a fire of love pouring up through my chest.

Then I flew home to England.

Back home, almost as soon as I walked through my door, it all changed.

It's a complicated story. But in a nutshell, no sooner did I get home than I had a nervous breakdown. If I had discovered my cosmic unity with all things on that South American beach, back home under a rain-soaked Oxford rooftop, while lying in a bathtub, I felt as if I had fallen down through the bath's plughole into some kind of hell, into a despair from which I thought I would never escape. From infinite love I had condensed into an infinitesimal dot of misery.

That's what my struggle for the next several years was about: the awakening on that beach—what it had been, what it meant, and above all, how to find it again. And the breakdown afterward—what *that* had been, why it had happened, and how to heal from it. My life has been about coming to terms with both the trauma and the awakening. Is there a way to deny neither, to grow from both?

This book presents the ways and means—the trainings, the therapies, and the years of meditation—that helped me most, and that now, after fourteen years of guiding others, I feel confident do offer a dependable trail, both through the dark forests our lives can take us into and up into the breathtaking mountains of awakening it is our birthright to discover. And after all that, it leads us right back down into the "marketplace," as Zen calls it, of ordinary life.

THIRTEEN YEARS AFTER that moment on the Pacific beach, I found myself back in South America on a writing assignment, during which I stayed in a fishing village on the Venezuelan coast while I got some work done.

The village was a huddle of tin-roofed homes, which nestled among palm trees around a curving bay. On the beach, small fishing boats lay tethered by long ropes to the palms. At night you had to be careful not to trip over them.

I started a habit. Each evening as the sun was about to set, I found my way to a quiet stretch of beach, where I would dig a little mound of sand with my hands to form a seat, and do my evening meditation, listening to the nearby waves.

After I got over the slight embarrassment of doing this strange thing out in the open, in front of anyone who might stroll by, I began to relish the ease and quiet of the evening calm, sitting bathed in the warm air as the light faded.

On the third evening, I heard some children's voices nearby, calling out, "*Señor, Señor.*" After a few moments I realized they were calling me. I looked up to see three boys in shorts.

They asked what I was doing, and when I told them I

was meditating, they asked if I would teach them how to do it.

As they got settled, I explained how to position their bodies, how to count their breaths, and how to relax, not try too hard. Soon they were sitting still and quiet.

After five minutes I told them they'd done great, and that was plenty. But they all wanted to do more, so we sat for another five.

After that, they came and joined me each evening. Sometimes other kids came, and occasionally an adult or two, curious about what the children were up to. It became a regular thing. One night I didn't show up, and the boys came and found me the next morning, to ask where I had been. I was there for six weeks, and didn't miss another night after that.

Whenever there was someone new, I went over the instructions again, and the others seemed to listen in happily enough. I realized it was actually nice to feel like a beginner again and again. It freed my companions and me of any sense that we ought to be getting better at it. Every time, it could be as if we'd never done it before.

I thought back to the daunting, austere practice I had done at the Zen monastery where I had trained. The atmosphere there had been undeniably powerful but intimidating too. No one made a sound. No one moved.

This was basically the same sitting, but it felt so different. There was an ease in the air. Whatever little huddle of us it might be, sitting there by the quiet bay, under the palms as the light dissolved, we were there only to rest. To unwind. We made no demands on ourselves. We were just *being*. As day gave way to night, so we gave way to being. We slipped loose from whatever agenda we might have had, and let the evening hold us.

In years to come, I often thought about sitting on that beach with those young people. After completing years of rigorous training in Zen, practicing Mindfulness-Based Stress Reduction and other mindfulness systems, and taking a deep dive into Absorption (or "Jhana") training, I remembered that time on a beach in Venezuela, with young people looking for a simple way to appreciate the fading of each day. It occurred to me that in all the practices I had done, there was a common ground. In all of them, there was a kind of bedrock they would bring you to, which was always about ease. Not trying, not striving, but knowing in your bones that at some deeper level of your being, all was well. And when I inquired further as to what that wellness was about, and why it was there, the answer always came back the same. Whatever the practice, and whatever the time or place in which we did it, what each practice uncovered was love. Love for life, love for self, love for others, love for this world. Love was the basis.

This basic love had different faces. It changed according to the angle of light, so to speak, that a particular practice shone on it. The angle of approach varied, and gave it a different complexion. In *Mindfulness*, it had a flavor of self-compassion, and of love for this world and for others. Sometimes we felt a deeper kind of *Support* holding us and loving us, as if we were embedded in a wider connectedness. Sometimes we settled into an intimacy with the moment at hand as we entered *Absorption* and fell in love with the fabric of experience here and now. And an all-embracing love seemed to fill the whole of existence when we tasted *Awakening*.

That was the origin of this book. *Original love* was the treasure that all flavors of practice opened up in their different ways.

So come and sit with us on the beach. Get settled, close your eyes, and relax, don't try too hard. Right now, there's a great ocean gently lapping at the shore of our lives, waiting for us to notice it. Peace and joy are always here. You're invited. You're welcome. Come on in.

GUIDED MEDITATION

A Visualization

(Feel free to record yourself reading this passage aloud—and any of the other exercises in this book—so you can listen back to it and focus on the meditation.)

Come into a comfortable position, and let yourself be still. Feel yourself becoming still. Feel what it's like to be still. Feel stillness gently infiltrating your body.

Just for a few moments, let yourself drop everything.

Let your shoulders, arms, and hands become limp, like old ropes. Let your face soften, and your throat also. Let your jaw relax and sink a little. Allow your chest to become warm, along with your belly. Feel your weight in your seat, and let your hips be at ease. Your legs, ankles, and feet are becoming limp.

Rest like this for a moment.

Notice that you're giving yourself some time and some space in which all you have to do is come home to yourself. Just be with yourself. You don't have to be in any special state. Nothing needs to be different right now because you're coming home to you, giving yourself a chance to simply be you.

Now imagine that you're sitting on a warm beach on a quiet evening. Nearby hills encircle a small bay, and the sea is gently stirring against the sand.

You're sitting near some palm trees. The day is ending. The sun has just set, the air is rich, the light is turning powdery, and the whole atmosphere of this place and this time has a special peacefulness.

You're alone, with a kind of solitude that feels friendly. You can feel it like a mild pressure in your chest, a tenderness. It feels like a privilege to be in this warm, secluded place. It touches and meets some old yearning inside you just to be sitting here quietly, with the sea lapping nearby and the sand warm beneath you.

Enjoy this peace. Let yourself bask in it. Steep in it. Let the evening air soften and become absorbed into your very flesh, so the fabric of your body becomes warm, relaxed, almost as if it were dissolving into the atmosphere around you.

There's a village nearby. You can hear the sounds of its inhabitants—children playing, voices calling, families chatting as they prepare the evening meal. Sweet smells of cooking drift on the air.

You notice all this and continue to sit in quiet stillness, listening, basking in peace and ease, as if the evening's peace were pervading your skin, and for a moment it's as if you sense some kind of greater awareness holding the whole scene.

There's a sense of promise too, as if you were glimpsing a kind of goodness in the world, and you are on a path to getting to know that goodness better. It feels like the right path, a path just for you.

Bask in this feeling of goodness for a little while.

When you're ready, let movement come back into your body. Open your eyes and continue with your day.

Part One

The First Wheel-Rut

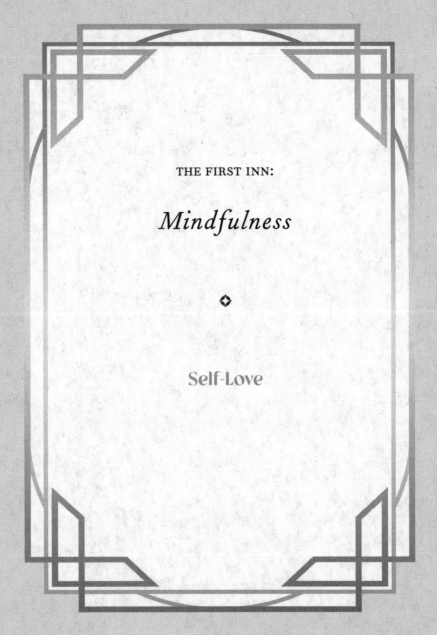

THE FIRST INN:

Mindfulness

❖

Self-Love

CHAPTER ONE

Coming Home to Mindfulness

To illustrate what mindfulness means, the twentieth-century Chan meditation master Sheng Yen told a story about a condemned man in China being given his last supper, which consisted of tofu with roasted peanut sauce. After the meal, he was led to the place of execution, where the guard asked if he had any last words.

The man thought for a moment and then said, "Yes, I do. Please convey a message to my son. Tell him that roasted peanut sauce goes very well with tofu, and that he should be sure to try it. And I love him very much." Then he calmly went to his death.

Most of us think we are aware of the here and now, when in fact we are aware of it only to a limited degree. We so commonly have a habitual internal chatter going on, through which we filter our present-moment experience, that we rarely even notice it going on. Nor do we recognize the extent to which it compromises our awareness of what is happening around us and within us, here and now.

The man in the story took the time to notice and appreciate the food before him, even at the hour of his death. That appreciation, along with his love for his son, eclipsed what was about to happen to him just a few moments later—namely, the end of his life.

To discover and develop mindfulness is to learn to inhabit and occupy the present moment in ways that can certainly help greatly with stress and anxiety. But it can also do much more. It can awaken us to the richness of experience being granted us at any moment, and open our hearts in gratitude and awe to the incomparable gift of being alive and aware.

A VALLEY

Imagine you're walking up an old track in a long valley. Tufts of grass grow by the roadside, and you notice them. Stones underfoot embedded in the dirt of the track impress themselves on the soles of your feet, as do the edges of puddles and potholes that lie here and there. Even through your shoes you feel the variations in texture.

Sometimes you're in the shade of trees. Other times you move through sunshine. Clouds gather, and the surface you're walking on becomes dull. Then the clouds part. The little rocks in the track glint once again, and smooth patches of mud gleam.

You hear birdsong. You hear insect sounds. Little creatures whir by your face and zing past on their way from hedge to hedge. It's a rich sensory experience, full of detail.

Now imagine you're riding down the same track on a bicycle. The texture beneath you is muffled and uniform. You mostly feel the ongoing smoothness of the rubber tires, which absorb the finer variations in the texture of the surface beneath you. Potholes become nothing more than a uniform bump. Likewise, the rocks you ride over get converted into a uniform muffled bump that could be caused by any object of roughly the same dimensions.

You whiz in and out of shade, unaware of the differences between the kinds of shade shed by different trees. You probably don't notice the insects, unless one happens to knock against your face. And birdsong becomes more of a general tapestry, with the melodic lines of individual birds indistinguishable from each other.

Now imagine the track has been paved over and become a road, and you're traveling down it in your car. Even if you have the windows open, you'll hear very little besides the sounds of the engine and the rush of the wheels over the asphalt. Trees become a green blur. The sensory details of being in the valley are little more than a dim awareness of land rising on either side of the road.

Perhaps there's a vague impatience to get to the end of the valley and into the next area of topography, where you'll know you're that much closer to your destination.

Now imagine the road has become a freeway, and you're traveling at high speed. The salient features are the mile markers that roll by and the digital clock in the car. You simply want to get to your destination. To make the journey more interesting, you're listening to a podcast or an audiobook. As far as possible, you might even prefer not to be present at all. Where you are is simply an inconvenient distance to be crossed in order to get to where you want to be.

BECOMING A MEDITATOR, opening up to a path of meditation, could be viewed as slowing down the car, parking it, getting out of it, and walking—going through life at a pace where we can experience the sensory details of the trip.

We sit still every day in order to come home to this moment. Now. A most ordinary moment can become a treasure composed of one beauty after another. To see the shadow of a plant on a wall or the shaded blur caused by a particular angle of sunlight coming through a window; to hear the soft notes in the soundscape of this moment; or to feel the components of body sensation as we sit still—all of these are rich experiences if we just slow down and settle enough to be open to them.

The problem is that in our pursuit of goals, we tend to get distracted from the richness of our actual life. It's not wrong to have goals and aspirations. It's healthy, and inspires and motivates us. But what if we could let them be simply the valley track we've chosen to walk down? We're going in a certain direction. Fine. But as we go, we're going to experience each step of the journey—each moment, *this* very moment—so that the goal is our chosen direction, not something we're obsessing about reaching as quickly as possible, to the exclusion of all current experiences here and now. Otherwise, what will happen once we reach the goal? We'll very likely set another goal, and speed off toward that one as fast as we can. And so on.

By slowing down, by deciding that each moment is worth

experiencing for itself, we can broaden our life. It's not that life has no direction. It's that paying attention to what happens along the way makes life richer and fuller. Even though we're moving in a chosen direction, it actually matters more to us how it is here and now than how it might be down the road. And some even say there is a curious law of nature, by which we'll fulfill our goals sooner and more amply if we savor the journey toward them.

This very moment, right now, as it is—somehow we start to recognize it as already complete. Already the world is fulfilled. That's not to say there aren't problems and immense challenges—as well as cruelty and suffering, and injustice and oppression. We must call out these issues and devote serious, sustained effort to their resolution. At the same time, we can appreciate the wealth given to us in any moment, by the moment itself. And we trust that the positive orientation that appreciation arouses will help us to better play our part in making this world a kinder place.

Try This

Come into a comfortable seated position. Feel the support beneath you, whether it's a chair, a couch, or a bed.

Explore what it would take to move into comfortable stillness and to enjoy being still. Give yourself time to find your way into stillness.

Rest. Let your body be at ease. Relax your arms. Relax your legs. Let your hands be slack. Let your feet release any tension, any activation that is in their muscles—let it go.

Let your throat become relaxed and soft.

Listen. Listen to the whole tapestry of sounds around you.

Don't do anything. Just be at rest and let sounds be present. Let your resting body be present too, just as it is.

Great: a first little taste of the hospitality of our first inn, Mindfulness.

PRACTICE AS THE HEART'S HOME

The beginning of practice is to settle down, and to see more clearly what's going on. And it turns out we can't do either without opening our hearts to the here and now, even just a little.

So we sit down, and are still, and quiet, and learn to surrender a piece of ourselves—whatever piece it is that is in haste to be elsewhere, that resists being right here, right now—so that we can open up to *now*.

The object is to begin to take stock of what is going on. There are many methods. A classic one in various traditions, including Zen and Vipassana, is to watch the breaths come and go. It can help to count them. Breaths are both a lifeline for our attentiveness, to which we can return again and again through a period of meditation, and our actual lifeline. Of all the tried and tested anchors for mindfulness, the breath is the most widely practiced and esteemed.

In the Buddhist formulation of practice known as the "four foundations of mindfulness," the first "pasture" in which to pen the unruly "cattle" of our wandering minds is the body. And among body sensations, breath is paramount.

The body, naturally, is always here, in present-moment

time. The mind, however, is inclined to jump away and get lost in thought—"lost" in the sense that it loses its awareness of being here, where the body currently is.

There may be times when we want to be less aware of where we are, and seek to be "lost" in what we're doing. Artists, musicians, athletes, or people writing reports, developing new projects, or working at long, repetitive tasks or crafts that require skill and judgment—in all these, too self-conscious an awareness might get in the way of what we're doing. Rather, we might want to get so absorbed in the task that we are hardly aware of anything else. We glance at the clock and see an hour has flown by. Lo and behold, under our hands the project has advanced as if by itself, by the grace of our absorption in the task, and come out better than we could have hoped.

Mindfulness is similar but different. The similarity is that mindfulness often takes us to a comparable place of calm energy like that we find when absorbed in a task. But on the other hand, rather than being engaged in an outward task, we're seeking not to lose ourselves, but to stay present and aware. We hear sounds, we feel body sensations, and we become more aware of the coming and going of thoughts, while simply sitting quietly with ourselves.

This is not so easy to do in meditation. Most of us find that as soon as we sit down and "do nothing," our minds commonly engage us in one thought after another.

In some early sutras, this phenomenon is likened to a monkey swinging through the trees, grabbing hold of branch after branch—the branches being analogous to thoughts. No sooner does "monkey mind" let go of one thought than it grabs another.

In the West, this phenomenon was first observed in 1924 by the German psychiatrist Hans Berger, who used his invention of electroencephalography to measure electrical activity in the brain. He expected to find that when people were at rest, doing nothing, their brains would be inactive. But he observed that this was not the case. Instead, during times of not being engaged in a task, their brains were very active. Later, in the 1970s, the term "default mode" was coined for this phenomenon, followed by "default mode network," some two decades after that, when the parts of the brain active during the operation of the default mode were first pinpointed by new neuroimaging technology.

Our resting condition, or "default," is not very restful after all. Not only do we get caught up in thoughts, but also these thoughts tend to be about the past or future, and often generate regret or anxiety. They trigger our sympathetic nervous system, and we get uncomfortably hyped up and uneasy.

(The relationship between thought and feeling is subtle and close. Some commentators say that whenever there is thinking, there is also feeling. But even if that's not always the case, thoughts frequently engender feelings, and feelings commonly provoke thoughts.)

The first practice in meditation, then, is generally *sati*, or mindful awareness of the here and now, with an attitude of welcome toward whatever arises. It turns out that this is a great way to start.

THESE DAYS, "MINDFULNESS" is the standard translation of the ancient Pali word *sati* (*smrti*, in Sanskrit). *Sati* actually carries an implication of recollection, of remembering—perhaps something like "remembering that we are actually here, alive and aware in this very moment." Or else "remembering to bring our awareness practice to bear on experience here and now." Some have tried translating it as "recollective awareness"; others translate it as "present-moment awareness." So far, for now, "mindfulness" has stuck.

There are many methods for developing mindfulness, but they all boil down to this: becoming more aware of what is going on in this moment, both inside and outside us, and accepting it. That's not the end of it, but it's a necessary start.

Broadly speaking, there are two main styles of practice: having a single focus and endeavoring to keep our attention on it; and not having a single focus, and instead endeavoring to track whatever is salient in awareness at any given moment. The first is often known as *focused attention*, and the second as *open presence* or *choiceless awareness*. Most of the contemplative schools of Buddhism, and other traditions, have at least some variants of both styles.

Because the grand project of meditation begins with our becoming more aware of the sensorium we are living in, our "box" of experience, you might think that the first step would be any method that helps us know it better in the here and now. But actually, it's hard to do anything deliberate with our attention when we are feeling restless, agitated, anxious, impatient, or uneasy. So the first step is to settle down. And there are different approaches to that.

MINDFULNESS OF BODY

In early Buddhism, there are "four foundations of mind-fulness," and the first is "mindfulness of body." We know when we are developing mindfulness of body because it feels like we're coming home to our bodies.

For many, a movement practice, such as qigong, or a stretching practice, such as yoga, will be invaluable in the adjustment to meditation. When I first began sitting regularly, in the focused attention style of Transcendental Meditation, in which you keep your attention on an internally voiced "mantra," the instructors taught a brief yoga routine we were encouraged to do before each sit. When I later switched to Zen meditation, I also started participating in longer yoga classes. Coming home to my body, being aware of what my body was feeling, experiencing how it felt to live in my body, and feeling it becoming limber and loose, fluid and strong—all this was a heartwarming rediscovery of a sense of myself as an embodied being. It was a kind of healing unto itself just to be more present in my body.

In *Yoga and the Quest for the True Self*, the psychologist and yoga teacher Stephen Cope writes, "As we begin to re-experience a visceral reconnection with the needs of our bodies, there is a brand-new capacity to warmly love the self. We are able to experience an immediate and intrinsic pleasure in self-care." I was starting to discover that for myself.

I didn't know it at the time conceptually, but I was growing in "mindfulness of body"—the first of the four foundations of mindfulness. It meant that my meditation deepened. Sometimes I would find myself so absorbed in the breath that there seemed to be nothing else in the field of awareness. It became entrancing, beautiful, and even purifying. I would emerge from a sit with a sense of having been scrubbed and rinsed, as if my mind and heart were purer.

I was starting to love life again, in a way I hadn't for a long while. I could feel my heart, like a zone of warmth in my chest that was alive with a subtle, soft eagerness to taste experience, and with a gratitude too, simply for being able to be *me*. For being alive. The part of me that loved life was itself coming back to life.

It was the meditation that was resurrecting it. And it was a renewed mindfulness of body that was breathing life into the meditation.

WHY SHOULD AWARENESS of the body be the first foundation of mindfulness? Why is it that to come to know the body, and learn to inhabit it, is apparently as pertinent a piece of guidance today as it was in fifth century BCE India?

In a nutshell, our large hominin brains are well equipped for rehearsing future scenarios and for rehashing past events. Some speculate that our thick prefrontal cortex evolved to run simulations—to model the outcomes of possible courses of action. Apparently, it was also to rerun past events, presumably in order to learn from them. When we're involved with outward tasks that occupy our attention, we tend to feel okay. We're engaging what some researchers call the task positive network. When we're having downtime, or "idle time," the default mode network is activated, whereupon we spend more time lost in thoughts of the past and of imagined futures than we do experiencing the moment at hand.

This leads to unhappiness. Why? Because we tend to regret the past and fear the future. Our brains evolved to have a strong negativity bias, meaning they react more powerfully and persistently to perceived threats than to perceived rewards. After all, if we neglect a genuine threat just once, then we might die. So our brains not only "fire" at threats but also "wire" the threat response more strongly, in order to prompt that response again more readily if necessary. So we have work to do just to get to a more balanced state vis-à-vis the world.

On top of that, we dislike feeling negative affective states. They in themselves often alarm us, producing an additional layer of negative feeling. So we tend to distract ourselves from them in all manner of ways. Some of these distractions may be constructive; others may be destructive. Either way, as long as we are unable to be at rest in the present when it includes difficult feelings—making it impossible to tend to those feelings—it will be a challenge to find ease in the simple fact of being alive.

To tell ourselves *not* to dwell on the past or future seldom works. The mental habit is too strong, reinforced by a million years of evolution. If we offer our attention an alternative area of focus, then this shift makes it easier to break the spell of rumination. Hence anytime we shift our attention to our body experience, we are necessarily focusing on the here and now. The body lives in the present tense. It doesn't have the capacity to "live" anywhere else. Only the mind can do that. To discover that we always have body experience going on, like a marvelous submarine seascape just beneath the glittering surface that captivates our attention, is a wonderful thing. It takes a shift in perspective, and in interest, but it is entirely possible. For many, it feels like a homecoming.

As children, we tended to live in awareness of our bodies more than we do as adults. To reconnect with the vividness of present-moment experience that we knew as a child, to the richness of body sensation going on all the time, can be moving—as if we were returning to some lost homeland of the soul, like wandering Odysseus finding his way back to Ithaca.

But this may not be so true if we had traumatic experiences in childhood, or indeed later. Trauma can leave us disconnected from our bodies, in effect disembodied or dissociated. In that case, it can take some careful, tender work to gently relearn how to inhabit our bodies, and to accept, allow, and release old feelings and energies that have become locked inside body tissue. We may also need supportive work to activate and become aware of positive sensations in the body. According to leading trauma researcher Bessel van der Kolk, dance, yoga, ball games, and other sports can all help with this.

Once again, a hallmark of developing this area of attention is that we start to feel a blossoming of self-love. For some, this may happen quite naturally. We sense the goodness and relief that practice is bringing into our life, and we bask in them. For others, it may take a little adjustment to sense this more clearly. We find the flavor in our body kindled by this homecoming, and allow ourselves to be warmed by it, like someone pulling up a chair to the hearth of an old farmhouse kitchen. We let the warmth reach us, as it wants to do. As we let it into our awareness, we recognize that to receive this kind of warmth is natural and good. We let it melt away any lingering feelings of inadequacy. What's left is a deep self-acceptance. And on closer inspection, we find it's very much like self-love.

Some of us may not realize how much we have been missing this until it starts to rekindle within us. Like an early-morning sun, self-love starts to break in through the cloud cover, and to slant up the valley of our life, warming the atmosphere and allowing things to glisten and shine. It renews our love of life.

And it may go deeper still. As meditation teacher James Baraz has taught in his Awakening Joy classes, at a certain point in learning to swim, we go from flailing in the water to floating. The water, which we had been fearful of and fighting against, when we trust it and relax, and lay our body out on it, turns out to have been here, ready to support us, all along. Likewise in meditation practice, at a certain point we find it's not just about loving ourselves but also about *being* loved, by a deeper innate tenderness intrinsic to awareness itself.

Either way, we know that mindful awareness is developing when a sense of love for life, for our bodies, for ourselves, and for this moment, starts to melt our hearts. As Ram Dass says, mindfulness is "loving awareness."

Try This

A Brief Body Scan

Get into a position that requires no effort at all to be maintained. Be comfortable. Now be still.

Feel your feet. Sense a mild warmth within your feet.

Let your attention move into your ankles, your lower legs, and your knees. Feel a gentle warmth in them, as if your attention itself were a sunshine that warmed whatever it attended to.

Let it spread to your upper legs. Feel a mild warmth envelop them.

Let that warmth now move into your buttocks and your hips. Feel it spread into your lower back and your belly. Now it moves to your midback and midriff (the center of your torso, between your belly and your chest).

Let the warmth spread into your upper back and chest, and all the way up your body to your shoulders and clavicles.

Bring your attention to your hands. Let them be slack and warm. Allow the warmth to seep into your forearms, upper arms, biceps, and triceps.

Now let the warmth spread through your shoulders and into your neck. Let your neck be warm and soft. Allow your throat to melt and become warm. Feel your lower jaw soften and sink just a little.

Let your face be slack. Let the sides of your head feel warm, and the back of your head too, and also your cranium (the dome of the top of your head).

Let your whole body rest in a single cloud of warmth for as long as you like.

Excellent. Thank yourself for giving this kind attention to your body.

THE OTHER THREE FOUNDATIONS OF MINDFULNESS

Beyond mindfulness of the body, the other three foundations of mindfulness are further ways of parsing out the strands of our experience here and now. They are as follows:

mindfulness of feelings
mindfulness of mind
mindfulness of dharmas

"Mindfulness of feelings" does not refer to emotions or affective states, but rather to whether sensations are pleasant, unpleasant, or neither. To be aware of this "valence" of sensations—pleasant or otherwise—is a great way for us to notice our moment-by-moment experiences more acutely. Most sense experiences tend to be neutral. But some are distinctly pleasant and some are unpleasant. Noting their valence can make it easier for us to stay aware in the here and now. It can also make the unpleasant easier to bear and the pleasant more delightful. And sometimes sensations that seemed neutral will become mildly pleasant when we examine them more closely.

"Mindfulness of mind" refers less to what is going on in our minds and more to our *state* of mind—including emotions, feelings, disposition, moods, temperament, and attitudes. To know whether we're feeling calm, joyous, anxious, or envious, or are craving something or hoping one thing won't happen and something else will, is very helpful, both in meditation and in life. It's about becoming aware of the conditions of our minds and hearts.

This is actually essential for meditation. By turning the gaze of welcoming, impartial, nonjudging awareness on our emotional state, we right away help it. We have a built-in capacity to give ourselves a compassionate inward "hug" if we learn how to turn it on. In a way, this is the heart of what meditation practice is about on the level of "mindfulness."

Let's say we're feeling anxious. In our sitting, the first step is to acknowledge that. Then we let our attention move from our thoughts and bring attention down into the area of the body where the emotion is active. There will be a zone, most likely around the heart or midriff, where some kind of tension or contraction or agitation is physically palpable. We bring our awareness to that, let it rest there, and give whatever is present a warm welcome.

As soon as we manage to do that, we have accomplished several things. First, we have disengaged from the emotion. We have dis-identified from it. We are no longer completely caught up in it. Instead, without having had to push it away or ignore it, we have rediscovered another level of our awareness, one in which we have the capacity to give ourselves and our emotional life a loving welcome.

It's a clever move. It means we are now in a different emotional state—a compassionate, gently loving one, which likely brings with it some peace and even a quiet joy. Yet we didn't have to either manage or banish or contort what we were feeling. Rather, it's as if we found a way to expand ourselves, so that the feeling state could stay as it was but become included within a broader awareness. It's as if we grow just a tiny bit—just enough to encompass the difficult emotion. It's a little like the difference between gripping a small, hard stone in our hand and opening the hand and letting the stone rest on our palm, so we can sense the stone's weight, as well as the softness and warmth of our palm. The stone is still there, but we can appreciate it now.

Not only that, but we have also established that there is another level of consciousness wherein the things that ordinarily matter to us are not quite so important. We have in effect become a bit more philosophical about life, simply by finding this more accepting dimension to our awareness, which we may not have known prior to starting to practice or which we may have forgotten.

PERSONALLY, THIS MOVE was hugely important for me on my meditation journey. I was in my midtwenties, and since the age of nineteen, when I'd suffered a breakdown, I had been caught in repeated maelstroms of worry. There were childhood factors behind this—chronic, disfiguring eczema and a difficult parental divorce and remarriage—but I saw my inability to live in a positive frame of mind as a personal failing for which I lambasted myself, believing that any human being should be able to keep themselves in good emotional order. I plunged again and again into shame, berating myself for being so unhappy. It was meditation that gradually helped me gain some perspective and recover a much more positive attitude toward life.

BUT SIMPLY BECOMING more aware and accepting of life isn't the end of the path. In traditional Buddhist thought, mindfulness is where meditation begins, and it's the basis that allows our practice to develop. Over time, what it can naturally develop into is states of greater concentration, or deeper mindfulness. This is where the fourth foundation of mindfulness, "mindfulness of dharmas," begins to kick in.

"Mindfulness of dharmas" means becoming aware of certain teachings—*dharmas*—that offer ways of examining present-moment experience more exactly and precisely. Doing this can lead to deeper, more blissful states of mind.

Among these teachings (*dharmas*), I want to touch on just one, which is perhaps the most useful of all. It's about becoming aware of our senses separately.

When we sit, the most active senses are usually hearing, body sensation, and seeing, in that order. Naturally, we can't close our ears as we can our eyes, and even in the quietest places, our hearing will detect at least some inner ear hiss or hum. When sitting, it can be very helpful to note to ourselves that we are indeed hearing. We can say to ourselves silently, *Hear . . . hear. . . .* We use the word as a label every few seconds to remind ourselves that hearing is going on. This can be very grounding.

(There are various "noting" or "labeling" methods. This one is adapted from meditation teacher Shinzen Young's Unified Mindfulness system.)

We can also use the word, *Body . . . body . . .* again silently voiced in the mind, to bring our awareness into the body. We'll feel the seat, our feet on the floor, perhaps the warmth of clothing, and the coolness of skin against air. We may also sense a gentle tingle or warmth in an area within the body, or within the body as a whole. Using the label "body" like this can again help us be more grounded and present, here and now.

Likewise, if our eyes are open, we can silently say, *See . . .*

see . . . to remind ourselves that seeing is happening. It's good to relax our vision, and let sight become more receptive—more about "receiving" sights and less about "looking at" things. This can become quite relaxing and calming, and again, the label will help us be more aware of the sense of sight.

We can also do this even if our eyes are closed. The gray scale behind closed eyelids can be interesting to gaze into. We may detect gradations of light and dark, and subtle shades of color. We may also sense a depth of field in the semidarkness, as if we're gazing into the middle distance of a misty landscape at late dusk.

We might think that this would cover most of our sense experience during a typical meditation. But we also have a kind of inward sense system, in which we see images and hear talk in the mind. These two inner sense phenomena are what we normally call "thinking." It can be tremendously helpful to break our experience of thoughts down into what they are actually composed of—namely, images and "inner talk."

Here, we can say, *Talk* . . . and *Image* . . . to help us be aware when speech and images are indeed arising in the mind. By using the labels, we become less caught by our own thinking, and learn to be more aware of it when it arises, rather than getting lost in long trains of thought. Not that this will come about easily or quickly. Thoughts tend to be quite "sticky," and we do easily get caught by them. Anytime we find we have been lost in thought, the key thing to note is that we have come back to the here and now. Otherwise, we would not have noticed that we'd been thinking. At this point, we can say, *Talk* . . . or *Image* . . . or both retroactively, to help us recognize more clearly what had just been going on.

There is a third branch of the system of inward experience: emotion-sensation. Emotions show up in the body as
a form of sensation in the chest or belly, usually consisting
of tightness, heat, heaviness, or agitation, if negative; and of
warmth, spaciousness, or expansiveness, if positive. If we
notice emotion-sensation arising in the torso, we can say,
Feel . . . feel . . . The particular help of labeling like this, especially when it comes to negative feelings, is that the label
can make it easier to be neutrally aware of what is going on,
without adding an additional layer of dismay or resistance.
Generally, we don't like negative emotions, and to use a label
in this way can take us a step closer to being able to observe
them without reacting against them. This can greatly help in
learning to welcome and even love them.

We already explored this important area somewhat, in
the preceding paragraphs on "mindfulness of mind," and
we'll be returning to it again in the next chapter. Meanwhile,
we can note that learning to manage, allow, welcome, and
even love our negative feelings is one of the greatest gifts
that regular, repeated meditation practice can bring.

REASONS TO MEDITATE

It's often said that the purpose of mindful meditation is to
become more present to our lives as they are happening. And
this is an excellent reason, and a great project to commit to.
But why?

Here I want to explore two key fruits of being more present.

1. SELF-IMPROVEMENT

There is an ancient method of categorization in the Zen tradition that recognizes four kinds of meditation practice. Mindfulness is known as the "first kind of Zen." The old masters called it "ordinary Zen," meaning that it's about ordinary benefits, such as feeling less anxious or rushed, enhancing our concentration, or improving our health through reducing stress.

But even though it may be "ordinary," it is very valuable. In fact, it just may be the best "kind of Zen." After all, this is where practice begins for most of us. It's here that we start to become more content in ourselves. We are learning to *be* ourselves and finding that this can be enough.

We start to enjoy who we are. This is not to say that we don't work on shortcomings in our behavior or performance, but rather that we are less down on ourselves, we don't get on our own case so much. We start to appreciate small things, such as making a good cup of coffee. We start to enjoy being who we are and doing what we do. We learn to trust our inclinations, to accept our temperament, and not to second-guess ourselves. We can even savor our likes and dislikes, welcome our moods, and tend to our emotional woundedness, if we are aware of any. We are learning to cherish even what ails us. We start to love ourselves just for being who we are.

This is a deep self-improvement project, yet it's a different mindset from normal notions of "improvement." It begins with self-acceptance and self-cherishing.

Self-cherishing is different from self-serving. It's different because we are not seeking to feed a hungry, grumbling lack in ourselves that can never be fed enough. Rather, in this mode, by contrast, we take a step back and learn to love ourselves as we are. Once the love is tapped and begins to flow, life as it is becomes sweeter and something to be loved, and we are no longer so hungry.

And actually, this is an "improved" state, although no big "self-improvement" goals have been met. The love itself is an improvement we might be surprised by.

2. SELF-LOVE

As we develop in our mindfulness, we start to feel more anchored in our lives, more grounded and centered. But although many of us come to practice with stated aims, such as less anxiety, better sleep, enhanced relationships, or improved concentration at work—all of which are viable reasons to meditate—often the greatest need that brings people in goes unstated.

It's to have more self-love.

Our modern Western culture has led to a dearth of self-love. Blame the Protestant work ethic or industrial-scale utilitarianism, whereby our value is measured by our productivity. Or hold Puritan shame to account, or Calvinist shame, or Catholic guilt, or the misunderstanding of the needs of the infant that some commentators point to in Western culture—whatever the cause, few people seem to allow themselves much self-love.

Basic self-acceptance is something to be attended to by all of us. We must do our psychological healing, and a key pivot point is learning to love ourselves.

The British psychologist Robert Holden, PhD, puts two statements forward in his book *Loveability*:

1. I must love others *before* myself.
2. I can't love others *until* I love myself.

He asks us which we believe to be true—hoping we'll find that it must be the second. If we think we can truly love others without loving ourselves, then we can test it by seeing what happens if we do decide to start with self-love. Try it for yourself.

You're here. You're alive. All these trillions of cells with their multiple components have come together to let you be you. And it will never happen again. Don't we owe it to this incredible conjunction to enjoy it, to appreciate it?

The more our basic awareness allows us to be present to what is, the more we heal. The more we let love in, the richer and more treasurable this moment becomes. And the less we will be pinning our hopes on something that is not present here and now.

Some people might think mindfulness practice—as its name suggests—is a matter of the mind. But it's not. It's a matter of the heart. As long as the heart remains closed, practice will be an uphill struggle. As soon as a ray of warmth lands on us, and the heart opens just a crack, practice finds its true home and becomes much easier—in fact, becomes a treasure house of warmth and love. And that all begins with self-love.

The stronger our mindful awareness grows, the more it expands, so that we can find ourselves sitting in a broad experience of a tender, gently scintillating awareness—a soft awareness that seems to reach as far as we can feel or see. It may pervade the entire field of our sitting.

But this can arise even while we are feeling distress. For example, we might become aware of some anxiety, perhaps manifesting as a tightness in the chest. While keeping that in awareness, we can also become conscious at the same time of a broad context of a larger awareness—sometimes seeming velvety, sometimes wide and clear, spacious, bright, smooth, or oceanic—but always present all around. As our awareness naturally gravitates into this broader field, the "difficult" feeling in the chest simply becomes a phenomenon that is free to arise as it wants. It is free to be there, fully welcome.

And because we are now more identified with the sense of spaciousness, we are getting a double whammy of well-being: first, the intrinsic goodness of the wider awareness, which is always peaceful, and is sometimes a delicious experience; and second, because we haven't tried to banish the knot of anxiety, it too is receiving the treatment it most needs, namely, to be held in loving, kind attention, so it can unbind itself in its own good time.

A TASTE OF MINDFULNESS
IN ACTION

Winter in the Black Forest, Germany. January. A damp cold, as if the air were filled with frigid dew that hung like an invisible mist, and made itself felt in your bones.

Low, gray skies. It was as if the steep valley where I was staying had a lid on it, a ceiling of gray tin. It would have been easy to calculate the volume of the valley with elementary trigonometry.

I had been coming to a retreat center here for a couple of years now to lead Zen retreats. Recently, on this trip, I had been feeling a buzz of energy in my chest that wasn't very comfortable. It was disturbing, in fact, both in and of itself, because it felt bad, but also because of what it represented: a loss of the peace I had been able to enjoy through my practice pretty much anytime I stopped and looked for it. What had happened to my beloved practice? Why had this usurper of comfort smuggled itself onboard?

I wasn't sleeping well either, what with jet lag, and when I woke at 2:00 a.m., as I often did, soon enough the buzzing chest contraction would wake up too, like a stranger in my rib cage. I tried my best to let it be there, without fretting, and often I would forget all about it. Then it would show up again all of a sudden.

One evening I was out walking around the hamlet where the retreat center stood. The steep roofs of the houses were sheets of white snow, all leaning at various odd angles, and beyond them the vertiginous sides of the valley were steep planes of white too, marked by lines where tracks traversed them. Dark masses of trees hung high up on the hills. It was all so beautiful. But in my sense of its beauty, I noticed just a little fear too. Somehow the scene was scary. It stirred a vague sense of the forests of Central Europe, and the menaces they contained, which my Jewish forebears who lived in Poland and Ukraine must have known. Many of them died in the Holocaust.

When I had first been invited to lead a retreat in Germany, I had feared coming here. Germany had been a place of horror and darkness during my childhood. Now that I'd completed several heartwarming retreats in this valley, I'd forgotten that earlier primal response. I thought I'd left it behind. What if I hadn't? Then this anxiety—if that's what it was—made perfect sense. Once again, my body had been calling out to me, and I hadn't been listening.

As soon as I thought of it that way, something like a dam broke, and a flood of warmth washed through me. My mind relaxed, my heart opened, and I felt a tenderness well up. That was it. An old anxiety, perhaps a remembered or intuited trauma from my forebears, or from my parents' wartime childhoods, had reawoken.

It was helpful just to state it to myself. Once again, I was paying attention to how my body was actually feeling, and honoring it. Once I did, I knew that I could allow the feeling to be present in my chest. And once I allowed it, I could see that in a sense it was beloved. All it had been wanting was to be recognized, and now it was.

My gait became light, energy flowed palpably through my body, and I felt well again. All it had taken was mindful attentiveness, backed up by mindful allowing. Perhaps the real problem hadn't been a feeling but an unacknowledged resistance to it.

Practice Tips

HOW LONG AND WHAT TIME OF DAY?

When starting to meditate daily, two things can help a lot. First, don't do it for too long. Five minutes is a fine starting dose. Once you have done two weeks of five minutes every day without missing a day, if you like, you could try going up to seven minutes a day. After two weeks of that, if you want, try ten minutes a day.

If you start finding you are missing days, then drop back to the previous level that allowed you to maintain consistency. At this point, we value daily consistency over duration. Really, consistency is the key.

A target level of duration would be twenty minutes, but it's way better to do five minutes every day than twenty minutes twice a week.

Second, try to establish a regular time for it each day. The ideal, mostly for pragmatic reasons, is to meditate first thing upon arising. It's actually easiest to do it first thing, before the demands of the day have started to encroach on us and clamor for our attention (with the exception of bladder relief and maybe brushing the teeth—and for some, a cup of coffee).

If first thing is hard—for example, if you have young kids to take care of—then try to grab the earliest opening you can. One nice alternative time is right before a meal, if possible—perhaps before breakfast or lunch. This can take a little more self-discipline because we will already find ourselves being carried by the momentum of daily activities, but the feel of the sit coming right before the pleasure of a meal can help.

Some other good options for time of day:

- After exercising and taking a shower: We are already more aware of the experience of the body.
- Dusk: To sit just before supper, approximately in the twilight hour, when day is over and the magic of night is starting to cast its spell over the world, can feel great.
- Last thing at night: Finally, a sit right before bed, in the quiet stillness of a house or an apartment, can be lovely.

One challenge, at this later time, can be the allure of the pleasure of lying down between the sheets. But to defer a pleasure can be pleasurable in itself. It can awaken another kind of pleasure—one that is a combination of the anticipation of the pleasure to come and the exercise of self-control. It can be a lovely thing to feel that we have that degree of self-control. It reconnects us with part of ourselves that is attuned to something calmer, that is larger than our desires, and that knows how to choose what is most aligned with our deeper purpose. And that feels good.

Other helpful points:
- Don't meditate soon after eating. Leave it for an hour, unless that would mean missing your sit for the day.
- Keep pen and paper near you when you sit. If you think of something you don't want to forget, then jot it down. Don't write too much—just enough to remind you later.
- Use a timer and set it to your chosen duration for the meditation. There are many apps for meditation timers available. It's also fine to use the timer on your phone, though you might want to set it to a soft-

toned sound for the end of the period. Get comfortable and hit start. Consider the time to be running, even while you're finding the right posture and starting the process of settling down.

GUIDED MEDITATION

Getting Grounded in the Here and Now

Come into a comfortable seated position for meditation. Let the body relax, all the way from the skull and lower jaw, down through the arms, and down through the chest and belly. Allow the hips to be slack. Let the upper legs be soft, and let the lower legs be at ease. Allow the ankles to be loose and the feet to be at rest.

Nice. Relax. Be entirely at ease.

Let's give some attention to the body. Without trying to do this at all perfectly, let yourself be aware of whatever parts of the body present themselves. Be very easy about this, not striving at all in any way.

Now listen for a moment—whatever sounds are most salient in the moment, simply hear them. Let them be present. Perhaps there is a constant hum of some kind in the background or a light hiss. Perhaps some household sounds or office sounds. Allow yourself just to receive the tapestry of sound.

Now notice the sense of sight. The soft lamplight in your room or the bright daylight outside, if that is what is arising, or the soft light of a northern winter—whatever is present right now in your field of vision. Appreciate the objects in front of you and around you.

Pause. Close your eyes. (If you're reading, then read this paragraph before you close your eyes.) Examine whether any images are present in your mind. We all have a kind of onboard video monitor in our minds, on which images can play. Take a look and see if any images are arising in your mind. We're not trying to see something, nor are we trying to have no images arise. We're just learning to be more aware of what is happening in our experience here and now, including images in the mind.

Now pause again, and this time listen for any talk in the mind. . . . Can you hear any words or speech in your mind? . . . Check for a little while. . . . Listen in carefully. . . .

Once again, we are not trying either to have speech be present in the mind or to have it not be present. We are simply seeking to be aware of whether talk in the mind is or is not arising, and be with whichever it is, without trying to change it.

Finally, let's check the internal volume of the trunk, and see if any emotions are present. Direct your attention down into your chest area. Can you detect any energies in the atmosphere around your heart? This is a bit like being a meteorologist and checking for weather systems. Can you sense any high pressure or low pressure, any winds or clouds stirring in the area around your heart?

Can you feel any heat or pressure? Any tightness, tension, contraction? Or is it hard to tell? It's fine if it is. Or perhaps you feel openness, spaciousness, calm, ease, or expansiveness? Perhaps it's just quiet in there right now.

Whatever you are sensing, or if you are finding it hard to be sure if you are sensing anything at all, it's all fine.

Let your experience be as it is. Trust that it doesn't need to be different.

Stay restful. Stay relaxed. Be like a caring mother holding her child. In the same spirit of caring, look kindly into your heart area once again, and let it be as it is. Be with it. Imagine you are holding your chest as if it were an infant, gently rocking it, soothing it, letting it be just the way it is, not needing it to be any different, loving it just as it is.

Just to be trying this at all is a good thing. It's good for your well-being, your self-understanding, and your self-acceptance. Over time, it will be good for the people in your life too, and good for the world. Just taking this time to take stock of how you are doing is a good thing.

Congratulate yourself. And thank yourself for trying this.

CHAPTER TWO

Loving Our Obstacles

Mountain Cloud Zen Center is an old adobe compound made of the earth on which it stands, in the foothills of the Sangre de Cristo Mountains on the edge of Santa Fe, New Mexico. During one of our classes one late summer evening a few years ago, twilight was filtering into the high-beamed meditation hall, making the old mud walls glow. An "insight dialogue" teacher, Nic Redfern, was leading a group of us through an old teaching from early Buddhism, in which there are five common "hindrances" that can make meditation challenging.

These obstacles, or hindrances, are a kind of checklist we can consult anytime we are finding meditation difficult. They are five emotional states that commonly make us unwilling to meditate or uncomfortable while trying to do it.

As Nic led us into the first meditation, on the hindrance of desire, or craving, she invited us all to explore the feeling of desire more closely than we might normally do. It was fascinating to find the ache hidden within it, and to discover that the feeling contained a subtle form of pain and unease deep inside. Essentially, the feeling seemed to be telling us that unless we got the object of our desire, whatever it might be, we would remain uncomfortable. Many of us were greatly helped by this discovery. To be able to sit with it, and be encouraged to stay with it in an attitude of deep acceptance, transformed not just our relationship to desire and craving but also to other kinds of emotions. The ancient guidance, articulated for today by our teacher Nic, gave us all a clear way to focus on an uncomfortable but hard-to-define sensation in the chest, encouraging us to allow our attention to rest with it, rather than trying to suppress it or ignore it.

For some, it transformed their experience of meditation. Seated in the warm glow of the old mud walls, in the dwindling evening light, they suddenly found a new way not only of being with themselves as they were, including with a difficult feeling, but also of releasing a gentle upwelling of self-love. It was as if by applying the old teaching to their immediate condition, a tide of gentle compassion was called forth that held and carried them.

This is another form of the benevolence that meditation can open up. All it took was a little guidance, and the ancient traditional advice came to life in ways we could experience as a real blessing in our current, twenty-first-century lives.

FIVE HINDRANCES

The philosophy of the "hindrances" is a helpful tool in our first inn of practice, Mindfulness. It dates back to some of the earliest Buddhist sutras that have survived, and offers a simple guide to mind states, or affective conditions, that if not recognized will hinder meditation.

Here is a quote from the *Avarana Sutra*, an early scripture from the Buddhist tradition:

> *Suppose there were a river, flowing down from the mountains—going far, its current swift, carrying everything with it—and a man would open channels leading away from it on both sides, so that the current in the middle of the river would be dispersed, diffused, & dissipated; it wouldn't go far, its current wouldn't be swift, and it wouldn't carry everything with it.*

(TRANSLATION BY THANISSARO BHIKKHU)

The river here is a metaphor, and the channels leading away from it are being likened to the common obstacles to meditation known as the "hindrances."

The river's current, weakened by runoffs, which dissipate its energy, is like the force of our practice being dissipated by these hindrances. There is a journey to be made, and if our flow is diverted and decreased, then the forward momentum on that journey dwindles.

By the same token, though, to be aware of the hindrances and practice with them—to harness their energy and flip it into a further impulse to practice—can in fact strengthen and motivate our practice.

ANYTIME WE ARE finding it challenging to sit, we can check in with the little list of hindrances and see if one or more are present. If a hindrance is present, then we recognize it and feel what it's like to have it be present. Primarily, we focus on the body, especially the chest and solar plexus area.

The solar plexus is an energy center in the middle front of the torso, between the abdominal area and the chest. Like the area around the heart, it is a center for sensations associated with emotions. We aim our awareness into these areas, and study what we can detect in the way of tension, contraction, discomfort in them. (This is one of the various effective, all-purpose ways of working with the five hindrances.)

The hindrances are as follows:

desire
aversion
dullness
restlessness
doubt

If it feels difficult to settle in meditation, then we can kindly inquire why, using this classic framework of five uneasy states as a guide.

So anytime we're not finding it easy to meditate, we can explore our experience in the moment, and check in with these possible conditions of mind and heart. Invite yourself right now to imagine you're having a hard time settling down during a sit, and enjoy the exploration that follows.

DESIRE

Is *desire* present? Is there something I'm wanting? Is there a condition of wanting? It could be as specific as wishing we had a cold drink or a slice of lemon drizzle cake, or as vague as a longing to be elsewhere, perhaps up on a high trail or beside the ocean or back in some former home. It could be a vague sexual desire. It could be a hankering for a project to go well. Or more generally, a wish for acknowledgment or acclaim or perhaps for greater income. Or even for more peace of mind. Any of these might be present.

If we sense that desire might be active, then we search for it as a body experience, as a sensation most likely somewhere in the torso. It can show up as a positive, hopeful condition, but more commonly it shows up as an ache, a weight, a contraction, or even a mild pain. Whichever it is, assume it is waiting to come under the beneficent lens of our all-welcoming attention. We find it and love it.

And how we love it is by locating the sensation and then softening around it, granting it its right to arise and be present. We allow it, unconditionally. As we do this, our orientation toward it pivots and swings, away from one of resistance, toward one of appreciation, even cherishing—even a gratitude that it is here with us, that we are able to experience it, and at that point we may find that we can open up even to loving it.

What a precious thing, this little ache—this tender longing or yearning. It's no problem at all. It's just that it can *seem* like a problem until it's recognized. Now that we see it, we welcome it into the heart of our meditation. Isn't it a miracle that our minds and hearts can conjure up this experience?

We can do likewise with the other hindrances.

AVERSION

Aversion is desire in reverse. It's like a mirror image of desire. It's wanting *the absence* of something that *is* present. Or else *not* wanting something to arise that is currently absent, but we have concern may come.

Again, if we aren't settling into a sit, then we can do a quick scan through the trunk and see if the sensations of aversion are present. Is something that feels unpleasant arising? Check it out. Scan the body and mind. Maybe we find discomfort in the heart area, and a painful thought in the mind—perhaps the memory of a difficult conversation we had forgotten or a situation we haven't dealt with. Notice unpleasant feelings and a natural aversion to them. Again, it could be aversion to something going on in our wider life—an issue with a colleague at work or a challenging dynamic in the family—or in our immediate sitting. We might have a repetitive loop of thoughts going on and a wish that they would cease. That would be aversion. We shift attention away from the annoying thought-loop and instead seek out the experience of our aversion to it. We don't bother about the thoughts themselves. Our interest is not in them but in the wishing that they weren't going on.

We zoom in on the wishing-them-gone. Once again, we search the chest and solar plexus for telltale signs of contraction or tension or wisps of energy that are uncomfortable. If we detect something, then we let it be there, whatever it is. We warmly welcome it.

This is the key step. Actually, each step is key, but this is the one of maximal help. First, we recognize that something is going on that is disturbing us. Next, we run through the hindrances until there's a sense we may have found the pertinent one. We're looking for a match. Then we check in with the internal space of the body, and see if we can find a sensation associated with that hindrance. And finally, we welcome the sensation.

At this point, which hindrance it is and what the sensation is like become less important. The reason is that as we welcome it—whatever it is—ever more warmly, so our awareness of the welcome grows stronger. Now the main thing is our welcome. Whatever it was, we allow it, love it, embrace it, and recognize that we are mortal, vulnerable, and sensitive mammals liable to suffering, who are trying their best, with the understanding and experience they have, to live well. We welcome ourselves as we are, including with this mental obstacle. And then our attention can actually shift to the sense of welcome itself, and we can become awash with that welcome, all through our awareness. We can bask in the lovingness that is a flavor of the welcome.

DULLNESS

The third hindrance—*dullness* or *lethargy* or *sleepiness*—is a spectrum that extends from simple physiological fatigue through shades of dullness, of blankness in the mind, and of finding it hard to pay clear attention to anything, all the way to lethargy, laziness, sloth, or reluctance.

Sleepiness can actually be an indicator of settling in our sitting. As we become more relaxed and attentive, and start to drop into meditation, our nervous system switches from the sympathetic side, which primes the pump for action, to the parasympathetic side, which promotes resting and digesting. As this side comes into gear, we start to settle and relax in our being. Stress starts to leave the system, and we begin to taste the simple ease of just *be*ing. At this point, if there is fatigue in the system, it will take advantage of this moment to show itself, and suggest, sometimes strongly, that we not only need rest but sleep.

If we're sitting alone, then we might try to sit through it for a while and see if it clears, and if it doesn't, then we might permit ourselves to "convert" the meditation into a nap. That might be the kindest thing to do, especially in the early days of establishing a practice. Otherwise, we might try letting ourselves nod off while staying in our seat. This can be surprisingly helpful. By sinking into the call of sleepiness, sometimes we do nod off, and almost immediately jolt awake again, as our body starts to slump or lean. This might happen several times. And we can find that after a few of these nods, we suddenly feel more awake, in a different kind of mental gear, as if we've slipped beneath the sleepiness into a new condition—smooth, clear, awake, deeply rested, and refreshed.

The artist Salvador Dali claimed that each afternoon in his studio he would have a brief siesta by falling asleep in his armchair while holding a spoon in one hand. Beneath the spoon he had a metal bowl positioned on the floor. When he fell fully asleep, his fingers would relax and release the spoon. As soon as it hit the dish, the clatter would wake him up. In that split second of true sleep, he claimed to get all the sleep he needed, and he'd emerge revivified for his afternoon's work.

A brief nap or a series of them can be a way to show love to ourselves, and to address the moment's most urgent need.

Another possibility is not to nod off, but instead fully allow ourselves to slump, both physically and cognitively, into a torpid state—just let ourselves be as sleepy as we are. This also can prove quite restful and restorative, as if we benefit from the sleepiness almost as much as if we had really been asleep.

There are various ways of trying to counteract sleepiness—splashing cold water on the face, opening the eyes wide, engaging in some brief vigorous exercise (doing push-ups or jumping jacks, going for a brisk walk, or jumping rope) can all sometimes help.

But perhaps the most effective method of all is to see what it would take simply to love ourselves here and now, just as we are, as sleepy mammals. We can slump and doze, or we can promise ourselves a luxurious slumber that night and get excited about an early bedtime. Or if our schedule permits, we can take a nap sooner, recognizing the value our meditation has already given us: namely, an opportunity to see how we are really doing. We can decide to tend to ourselves accordingly as soon as our timetable allows.

If the mind state is less about actual sleepiness, and more about dullness, we can try to find out if there is a reluctance to be practicing meditation at the moment. Reluctance translates to a form of aversion—of not wanting. If it's present, then we proceed as we would for any other kind of aversion. We find its sensation in the body and lovingly welcome it.

RESTLESSNESS

The fourth hindrance—"restlessness born of remorse or worry," as it's phrased in some early sutras—is interesting, in that it pairs phenomena we might think of as separate. Worry is surely akin to anxiety, which is probably the greatest everyday mental health challenge of the modern world. By some tallies, as many as one third of people commonly experience it. Anxiety is a primary symptom addressed by modern mindfulness. Its prevalence is likely even a key cause for the spread in popularity of mindfulness today. Mindfulness, after all, is widely marketed as a cure for stress and anxiety. In Mindfulness-Based Stress Reduction, one of the most popular mindfulness courses, created by Dr. Jon Kabat-Zinn in the 1970s, the emphasis is explicitly on "stress reduction," a large component of which could be called anxiety reduction.

Meanwhile, remorse would seem like a different problem. Whereas anxiety typically draws its unease from a putative future, remorse mines the past. But from the perspective of neurology, these are two functions of the same default mode network, which is part of the midline networks of the brain, which generate narratives about self. Whether it's a story of the past or the future, the default mode network always tends to generate narratives about *me*. These can make it hard to sit still. Restlessness makes us want to get up off our seats. Whether that's because of an urgency to address something current, to fix some problem from the past, or to preempt something feared in a possible future, we get uncomfortable in our skin at the thought of them and want to change our circumstances.

Here once again the method is to recognize that this is what we're experiencing, and ask ourselves what it's like to have restlessness in the body. What sensation, in what area, is telling us we're restless? Let's feel it. And what would it take to let it be there without minding it? With an attitude of patience?

The wisdom of allowing it to be there is that *allowing* doesn't seek to change it or transform it, or be rid of whatever experience we may be finding hard to accommodate. It doesn't say, *This feeling of desire or aversion or restlessness is incompatible with meditating*, and conclude, *I'm too restless to meditate right now*. Rather, it says, *How can I neither distract myself nor sit in ongoing distress, but find a way to* accommodate *this unpleasant experience?* The answer is to find out in what way we had *not* been allowing the distress and instead allow it. That way, it doesn't have to change. It doesn't have to vanish. Instead, what happens is that we grow. Our capacity to hold something difficult without reactivity expands. It's as if the practice demands of us that we find a way to grow just a little larger. The space we can offer to experience becomes broader. It's almost literally a form of growth, as if the spaciousness of our awareness expands.

When this happens, it feels pleasant and invigorating, and somehow purifying. Rather than contracting around an intention to be rid of something we don't want, or to get something we do want, instead we expand so that we can *love* and hold those very urges. Rather than giving in to them and obeying them—which would involve no growth—instead we grow, expand, and allow them to be in our field of awareness without following them. We love them and agree with them, but we don't obey their dictates. That's how growth happens.

By contrast, as long as we follow our urges, we stay, as it were, on the same level on which they occur. But once we allow them, and offer them a home, then we see that we don't actually need what they tell us we need. That's growth and it's a beautiful thing. It touches and opens our hearts when it occurs. And it affirms what Simone Weil meant when she said that by entering into our own experience, we will find that we already have what we most want.

TO RECAP, WHEN restlessness is active, try to find the feeling of restlessness in your body. There might be some kind of agitated energy in the heart area or solar plexus. See if you can detect even a subtle trace of discomfort in that region. If you can, then let it be there. Let your attention sit beside it, as if you were sitting on the banks of a river beside a swift current. Just let the current do what it does, and don't try to change it. Let it flow as it wants to. See if you can be patient with it.

What does it feel like to allow it to do its own thing?

DOUBT

The fifth hindrance, *doubt*, is considered different from the other four and harder to handle. We can't practice with doubt in quite the same way. To find doubt in the body is one possible path, it's true, but it may not be that effective in the long term. This is because *doubt* here refers primarily to doubt about practice itself: doubt that practice is worth it or has merit. Or we may accept that it has value but doubt the teacher or instructor. Perhaps we question their qualifications for leading practice, or have misgivings about the tradition or school the teacher is trained in. Or we doubt that this is the right moment or time for us.

Although it's good to be skeptical and have our wits about us, especially in the shifting sands of spiritual practice, where there can be sinkholes and unreliable guides, we can also acknowledge that there may be sabotaging voices within us that seek to hold back our growth.

The most common form of doubt is—undoubtedly— self-doubt. We doubt that we are capable of learning to meditate or getting anywhere with it.

Many of us easily doubt our own capacity for practice. *Am I up to it? If I find it hard, then does that mean I'm not cut out for it?*

Actually, doubt is natural and common, especially in the early stages of practice. After all, it's a new habit we are trying to instill, and like any new activity, there will be barriers to incorporating it into our life. Additionally, it seems quite counterintuitive to us that sitting still and basically doing nothing could in some way be very helpful and beneficial. Most of us are deeply conditioned to think that positive results can be expected only if we take action.

Yet practice seems to come with the reverse proposition: it is only by more or less doing nothing that good things will come. The famous, recently deceased Vietnamese Zen master Thich Nhat Hanh used to encourage students in their practice by telling them that most people think to themselves, when facing some problem, *Don't just sit there, do something*. Whereas he would say the reverse. A meditator thinks, *Don't just do something, sit there*.

The very sitting still is what can bring about deep, positive transformation, which will then change how we approach life.

But it's hard to buy this before we start to see some positive results, which generally only accrue gradually, as meditation becomes a more regular part of our life.

On top of that, it can be hard to enjoy meditation to begin with. It often seems a hopeless task to get our minds to quieten even a little bit, and to start to taste more settled and tranquil states in our hearts. But this is natural. We wouldn't start going to the gym and expect to do the hardest exercises and lift the heaviest weights right away. We build up the strength and fitness of our bodies gradually, over time. It's the same with the fitness and clarity of our minds. It takes time to train them.

If we add to all this the issue of self-doubt, or self-contempt, which is tragically common in the modern world, we can see how readily any of us might easily jump to the conclusion that we're just not cut out for meditation. We're not up to it. In some intrinsic way, we're not good enough for it.

The primary antidote for doubt is to press on and keep practicing. If we take doubt too seriously, then we'll talk ourselves out of practice. Better to think of doubt as a weather system: just because we've run into a storm or two doesn't mean the direction of our journey has been wrong. The project, the voyage, is well attested: there really is somewhere to reach. Practice *can* change our lives in valuable ways—so we just press on.

The forces of our own conditioning are strong. They are going to find ever new ways to throw up resistance. What doubt wants to do is engage our minds in mental wrestling around practice. So rather than pay it too much attention and get caught in ancient habits of argumentative discouragement—habits that prefer to maintain their own status quo—we treat these thoughts like any others: put them on the shelf and come back to our seat in the here and now.

Once again, we can remind ourselves that practice has a close relationship with self-love. Is our doubt trying to derail the project of self-care and nourishment? Is it seeking to undermine the growth we are committing to?

Try This

Come into a comfortable position. Relax, settle in, take a full inhalation, and then let it out slowly. Feel your whole body relaxing as the breath slowly leaves you. Do it again.

Listen for a moment. Slow down. Come into being here, just where you are, as you are, right now.

Now close your eyes and imagine some simple, tasty snack—a cookie, a piece of pie, or a scoop of ice cream. Or if a hot mug of Irish tea with cream is more appealing, then imagine that.

As you imagine this object that is appealing, feel what happens in your body, especially in the middle of your torso. Can you detect a little tightness in the middle of the body? A mild heat? A tension, or sense of contraction?

Keep exploring while imagining the object of mild desire. If no sensation is showing up, then you can escalate to a stronger object of desire—a holiday you'd love to go on, a kitchen you'd like to own, or a person you find enticing.

Now what can you detect in your belly or chest? Desire comes with a "signature" sensation in the body. See if you can feel it. And once you connect with it, you can drop the image of the object and rest your awareness on or around the sensation of desire in the body. Just let it be there. Don't push it away and don't turn away from it, but allow your awareness to settle with this sensation, even if it is a little uncomfortable.

Is desire pleasant to feel? Or unpleasant?

Does it bring peace? Or not?

Either way, whatever you're finding, just let it be present. Does the allowing of it somehow lessen it, make it less acute? Could your allowing it turn into a gentle appreciation? Even a kind of love for the little sensation of desire?

Now congratulate yourself for having given yourself this time of exploration and rest.

A BOWL OF WATER

Another traditional simile for the hindrances sheds further light on their operation. Here, the mind is likened to a bowl of water. Ideally, the water is still and clear. We can see down to the bottom of the bowl and catch glimpses of reflections on its surface.

The hindrances disturb the water in the bowl. In *desire*, the water is discolored by dye. In *aversion*, the water is boiling. In *dullness*, it's overgrown with algae. In *restlessness*, it's ruffled by a strong wind. And in *doubt*, the water is muddy, and in addition, it has been stored away in a darkened shed, so it's hard to see that there's a bowl of water there at all.

None of these sound good. But the metaphor of the water bowl gives us a way of working with the hindrances. Once we notice that the water is dyed, for example, or maybe boiling, infested with algae, ruffled by a breeze, or muddy and half-hidden in the dark, we are already recognizing the condition it is in, and are no longer so inclined to make unrealistic demands of it. We accept it as it is.

If it's dyed with desire, then we can start to examine what color has been added to it. We get to know the hue of desire. What is it really *like* to have desire active within us?

If it's boiling with aversion, how might we take it off whatever source of heat it's sitting on? What is heating it up? What would we need to cool it down?

And if it's clogged with algae, what does that feel like in the body? Can we separate the algae of dullness from the water itself?

If it's ruffled by the wind of restlessness, how might we move it to a sheltered place? Is there some way we could turn away from the wind and get into the protective shelter of some favored nook?

And if it's cloudy with the muddiness of doubt and hidden

in a darkened hut, can we shine the light of awareness on it and start to experience that muddiness within our very own attention?

Since in the analogy the water is not merely an object we observe, but is actually our own mind, our own awareness, once we recognize that the water is in the condition it's in, we can start to accept that that's just the way our mind is right now. And once we allow for that, once we accept it, then the state of acceptance also becomes part of the condition of the water. In a sweetly circular way, we have only to accept the state of mind we're in for that very same mind to start to taste the quality of acceptance, which immediately affects the condition of the water, our consciousness.

And because acceptance is always intrinsically clear and peaceful, as well as appreciative and loving, we start to find those qualities arising in us too.

No sooner do we allow the hindrance, whichever one it is, to be present, than the tender qualities of allowing also appear, bringing a little more clarity to the water. The bowl may start to clear, almost by itself.

LOVING THE HINDRANCES

What part does love play in all this?

Let's say we're learning to love the hindrances. Each time we love one as it's arising in our experience, it's the love that helps it to release. Or in terms of the water metaphor, love lets the bowl stand, so the pigmentation of the dye can settle like silt to the bottom of the bowl, leaving the water clear. Love is what takes the water off the boil and lets it cool. Love patiently sifts through the algae-infested water. Or it shelters the bowl from the breeze that's been ruffling its surface, until the wind is ready to ease up. Or it strains the mud out, so that once again the water of awareness shows itself, clear and at peace with itself.

But what part does love actually play in the process? And where does that love come from?

Love is like space in the sense that it gives space for things to be the way they are. It allows us to be in a troubled state. When we're no longer at war with the state we're in, our sense of identification can switch from being wrapped up in the trouble and relocate to the state of acceptance. So while the trouble is still there, our identity can migrate from the knot of trouble to the broader context that is accepting of that knot. It's the sense of love that pulls us there. Love is a magnetism. It's like gravity, except that rather than drawing us toward an object, it draws us into its spaciousness, which can comfortably hold the difficulty. Love *loves* what is difficult, which makes it no longer difficult.

Explore this for yourself and see if you agree.

But what is the source of this love? It's actually simple too. Once we are less narrowly focused, once we uncouple attention from what it has been contracting itself onto, we sense simply more of the *space* of awareness. Rather than being stuck in one little quadrant of awareness, we recognize more quadrants. Awareness itself is broader and more expansive than our knotted, narrowed mind, when it's caught by a hindrance, can allow us to recognize. But now we become more cognizant of the expanse of awareness as a context in which the hindrance had been arising. And—this is the main point—awareness is not separate from "original love."

One of the very features of original love is its unlimited awareness. At the deepest level, all forms of awareness are forms of *it*. It not only is aware of all, but also allows all experience to arise, and immediately and unconditionally meets it. It allows, it meets, it offers space to, and in fact it engenders all experience. This is the "activity" of original love. But even before we clearly see this for ourselves, once we are in a position to savor awareness, and to see whatever is arising as a thing *within* awareness, then rather than being tangled up in the *thing*, the object, we can start to recognize, however consciously or clearly or not, that our awareness of it may in fact have a flavor of love as part of its makeup.

ABSENCE OF HINDRANCES

I imagine there are infinite ways of working with difficult states, and I'll share one final beautiful way. It's to explore what it is like when they are absent.

Take restlessness, for example. We can note whether restlessness is present. If it is, then we proceed as already outlined. But if it is not present, then we focus on the fact that restlessness is absent. We explore how it feels for it to *not* be present.

How is it when no restlessness is present? What is it like to have no aversion arising? How does it feel when there is no desire asking for anything? What is it like when that part of the body where desire would register is instead open, spacious, free, and at peace?

And so on, with all the hindrances.

This can be a method for opening up to positive experience in our sitting practice. We may find a natural appreciation welling up when we notice more clearly that we are currently at peace. The ease we experience when no hindrance is present can become a cause for deep gratitude, which in turn makes us feel a love for life itself—for the bare fact of being alive. Then as this loving gratitude develops, we find that it, in its turn, starts to generate a wish that our own heart flourish and be well. This self-kindness naturally expands into well-wishing for the people we are fortunate to share our lives with, those close to us, as well as our wider circles of community. And it can also expand to include a wish that all beings be free from suffering and have their hearts met by a deep fulfillment. The love known as compassion, which seeks to relieve suffering, may awaken in us ever more keenly, and start to guide and orient how we act in the world, with the people around us and indeed with all the beings with whom we share this precious planet.

THE SENSORIUM

At this stage on our trail, as we are still getting to know the shelter and refuge at the inn of mindfulness, our awareness is growing clearer and more mature.

The path to awakening, to original love, can be summarized as follows. We start to settle down. We start to lessen the hold of the hindrances. The suffering many of us have lived with as a vague background condition—a sense of lack, of deficiency, or a hunger, a hankering after things not yet here—has come to the fore, and we are getting to know it more clearly. As a result of allowing it to be as it is, it is starting to dwindle and at times release itself.

As this happens, we begin to open up more to our actual experience in the here and now. We notice the whistle of the wind in the trees, the distant hum of traffic, and the sounds of a neighborhood. We relish the play of light and shadow, and we feel the magnificence of the weather, whether sunshine, cold mist, or crackling thunderheads. We remember how sublime clouds could sometimes seem when we were children. We are recovering a quiet enjoyment of the very fabric of our lives before we have even done anything we would normally think of as constructive or productive. We are returning to a natural appreciation for being, for the gift of living itself, without any need for accomplishment.

One way of looking at this is that we are starting to notice the "sensorium." The sensorium is the "box" of sense experiences in which we live. It consists of sounds, sights, sensations, smells, and tastes, and also of thoughts and emotions. This is a critical step on the path. The clearer we are about living in the sensorium, the more we can start to examine what the sensorium actually is. We can begin the process of "deconstructing" it—which is the direct path to awakening.

A TAPESTRY

One analogy for the power that our thoughts can hold over us works as follows.

Imagine a tapestry, woven of many threads. The threads are thoughts. Together, they weave a rich brocade, and we sit entranced by it. We often get caught by thinking of life as this tapestry of thoughts.

It has dark, troubling areas and sunny patches. And scary corners and scenes of rage. In time we are so familiar with it, so habituated to it, that we need only glimpse the glint of a single thread, and the whole tapestry is conjured up.

It can seem to become our whole life, what we see and respond to and live by.

When we meditate, we can start to see that the tapestry is actually made of individual threads. It's we who supply the implication of the whole. What actually happens, moment by moment, is that strands of thought arise. Because they have emotional tone, the emotions help to reinforce the sense of the whole tapestry appearing.

Sitting allows us to see the separate strands and to detach our gaze from the intricate weave. We start to realize that it is only a tapestry. It's not our actual life. Then we get glimpses that it isn't really even a tapestry. It just felt like it was. In fact, it's just individual threads. That's all. The *whole* that we impute to those single threads is a chimera, a mirage. We start to recognize that there is actually space between the threads, and then we start to abide in that space.

We start to find periods of being disentranced. A magical quiet settles over us. A powerful clarity, a new well-being, touches us. We are waking up from the tapestry's enchantment, coming home to this world, this moment, and our life. That's what *sati*—recollected awareness—means: returning to here and now, disenchanted, woken up from the spell of thinking.

The word *sati*—mindfulness—connotes this kind of "remembrance." There are traditional explanations for this, as already mentioned—remembering the categorizations of experience that the teachings on the four foundations of mindfulness offer and bringing them to bear on the elements of experience arising now; remembering the teachings on suffering and wholesomeness, also in the foundations of mindfulness; and remembering to be mindful at all. But there is another way of connecting with the tenor of "remembering" in mindfulness. It's to remember simply, *Yes, this is my life*. This is it, here and now. Am I appreciating it? Am I aware that it is temporary? If not, then what is stopping me from appreciation? From awareness? And whatever that hindrance is—if I can find it—can I somehow cherish it too? Once a sense of cherishing, even love, comes back into the equation, everything becomes easier.

Perhaps *sati* is also about remembering that we are loving creatures. It's about remembering to love. Somehow, love is our life. And this doesn't mean getting into a romantic situation. It's a different kind of love, bigger, more pervasive, and less conditional.

SET-ASIDE

Sometimes it seems hard to meditate in the midst of the stream of life's activities. I think of daily meditation as being like the multifaith chapels that many airports have.

Often, when I have time, I go out of my way to stop in at these chapels when changing planes. I love exploring spaces that have been set aside from normal daily activity.

"Set-aside" used to be a term in British agriculture. It referred to certain fields that a farmer had "set aside," which would not be farmed at all. These fields might be plowland or meadow, but they wouldn't be touched. They would lie fallow for years.

These little airport chapels are "set aside" as quiet havens midjourney, where you can interrupt the headlong rush to a new destination. You can say to yourself, *Yes, I have time*. Yes, rather than browsing for a snack, I will feed myself another way. I will give myself the sustenance of time set aside. Mid rush, lo and behold, I can do this.

I would find it a distinct pleasure to leave the glossy zones of the airport, full of commerce and haste, and suddenly be in a place of quiet. Sometimes I'd sit on a chair. At other times, if I had my inflatable meditation cushion with me, I'd pull it out of my bag, blow it up, and deposit myself on the floor in an out-of-the-way spot, with my shoes off, and meditate.

And that's how meditation typically will always be for many of us—right in the middle of the stream of life, we extract ourselves for twenty or thirty minutes, and sit quietly to one side of the stream. We allow the world to pursue its rush, such as the bustle of the airport just outside the chapel doors, while we rest in the great lake of quiet that was always here, set aside, just behind the world as we usually see it, waiting for us to notice it.

ORDINARY LIFE

It's all very well to seek boundless love on the meditation seat. But even once we start to taste it, is that a complete journey of awakening if we're not also grounded in love *away* from the seat, in the most ordinary moments of our lives? And how could it be if we are greatly dependent on transcendental experience for our tastes of love anyway? The humbler aims of basic mindfulness—of "ordinary" practice—are every bit as precious as the further reaches of the meditation journey.

We practice for happiness. And it can occur on different levels. We might meditate to regulate the nervous system, so we are less volatile, calmer, more contented. We might become less reactive in relationships and perform better at work. We might concentrate better, with greater clarity. The prefrontal cortex might be more active, less clouded by the alarm states of an overactive amygdala, which is the headquarters of the stress response, located in the oldest part of the brain, the brain stem. That's one level of well-being.

And we *can* go further. There are indeed levels of insight, of seeing impermanence, of selflessness, and of release from craving, which practice in the methods of the great traditions can bring us to, and which can lead all the way to an unconditional happiness, one that does not depend on anything. (Various schools have programs of remarkable insight and subtlety. But we don't need them in order to get the whole point of meditation. The simpler plan offered here, through the four inns of this book, touches the key points to orient a seeker who wants a clear overview of the whole sweep of the contemplative path.)

All the way through the different possible levels of practice, we're learning to be happier with less. We're becoming less focused on what we want, and learning to mind less when what we don't want *is* showing up. We're discovering an intrinsic happiness within, and so our concern with outer circumstances is gently tempered and lessened. We're developing a stability of character, we could say, independent of condition. And wherever we are on the path, when we taste that, we are well. We could have the least exalted meditation practice and still be fine. As soon as we taste any mindfulness, and the love it touches, nothing is missing. Life feels whole. Would anything then be missing? Undoubtedly not.

Yet the path goes on.

Up over the next steep slope, beyond the uppermost part of this valley, where our first inn stands, a new landscape is opening up. Over the ridge, nestled in another dale, off in the distance, we can just make out the roofs of another wayside inn. That's our next place of refuge, waiting for us to stop by.

Practice Tip

The key to learning to love meditation is to do it regularly but not try too hard. We hold ourselves accountable to doing it consistently, but we don't try to engineer certain kinds of experience in meditation. We take it easy. We let ourselves be as we are. It's more like "letting it all hang out" than practicing with a goal of perfection.

The more we learn to allow ourselves to be having the experience we are having when we meditate, paradoxically, the sooner we may start to find increased clarity in our sitting. By clarity, I mean being aware of what is going on in our experience, with a kind of awareness that is in itself intrinsically peaceful and fulfilling.

In other words, by not trying to make our experience a certain preconceived way, we can come into a deep clarity that is itself very pleasant. But we don't get there by trying to feel that way. We get there by letting things be as they are.

A critical tool here is learning to be with difficult emotions. Any of the hindrances will affect our meditation. If we ignore them, then they can make our practice challenging. But on the other hand, if we resist them and fight them, then we will end up getting frustrated. They tend to grow stronger the more we resist them.

But there is another way: once we learn to allow them, they cease to "hinder" our meditation and can even become a kind of fuel that takes us deeper into clear, peaceful awareness. To allow our emotions to be present, to rest kind and loving attention on them, and to welcome them, can release a broader self-love, a self-compassion that starts to deepen our experience of being alive.

GUIDED MEDITATION

Sitting with Restlessness

Settle into your posture. Become aware of the sounds all around you, enveloping you like a kind of bubble.

Be aware of sight, of seeing—if your eyes are closed, then see the grayscale before your eyes. If your eyes are open, then see the color, the shades of light and dark, and the shapes of objects before you.

Feel your body. Feel your posture. Half see, half sense your whole body in its current position.

Rest a moment with a kind of global awareness of your outward experience here and now: feeling body sensations, seeing the field of vision, and hearing the sounds of the world. Rest gently with them all.

Now let's check in with ourselves. In your mind, with a gentle voice, ask yourself, *How am I doing?*

Now try saying to yourself, *How are you doing?*

Notice what comes up. You might encounter a slight sense of unease of some vague kind. You might feel restless or antsy. Or you might experience a faint trace of anxiety. All these feelings are very common in our world. When we stop to meditate, we are more likely to notice them if they are arising. In addition, it's not uncommon to feel a certain kind of "performance anxiety" when we start to meditate. There is no need to try to get rid of this. Instead, we welcome any feelings we find, giving them a warm embrace.

Or it could be that you find a sense of well-being, perhaps a positive anticipation of entering into this new experience of being quiet and still, or perhaps a sense of gratitude for being able to give yourself this time of quiet.

Either way, in this meditation we are going to focus more on a difficult feeling—restlessness. We are going to learn to be okay with it.

Imagine you are feeling restless. Or perhaps you actually are feeling restless. Check in with your body, especially the chest area or just below the chest. What does restlessness actually feel like for you? It might be some kind of energy: a heat, a warmth, a density, or a tightness. Could you say what it looks like? Do any images arise in association with it?

Can you locate it in your body? Is it more to the left side or the right side? More to the front or the back of the body? Is it higher up or lower down?

This may seem counterintuitive. Sometimes the last thing we want to do is feel a difficult feeling. Often we will do anything to get rid of it, to turn away from it and avoid it. And we might believe that meditation is supposed to be about something other than being with difficult feelings. But actually, meditation is about just coming home to our actual experience and allowing it to be as it is.

So whatever you are finding—or not finding—in your body, in your being, simply let yourself be present with how it is. Allow yourself simply to be with whatever you are finding.

Imagine your shoulders and the sides of your torso softening like warm wax. Imagine that they are holding the part of you that has an uncomfortable sensation with a warm welcome and loving support.

Imagine you are wrapping your chest area in a velvet blanket. Feel its softness. Feel how it can be okay to give your attention to the part in yourself that is sore or uncomfortable or even hurting. Be with it. All it really needs is your attention. Like the parent of a child in distress, turn to it with a soft and loving embrace. Give it your love.

And paradoxically, meditation is not some magical state different from where we already are. Instead, it's turning to where we are with a warm welcome, with love. And in time, that same uncomfortable feeling may turn into something quite magical.

THE SECOND INN:

Support

◆

Soul Love

CHAPTER THREE

Not Alone

It's easy to think of meditation as a solo pursuit, analogous to working out at the gym. We put in the time on our seat, we keep doing it day by day, and gradually we will start to accrue the benefits of our effort. We will get "fitter" in mind. We will become more "toned" neurologically. Although there is some truth to this view—and a little self-discipline is surely needed to develop the skills of meditation—that picture also leaves out a critical dimension of practice: support and connection. We really can't have access to the help, the treasures, and the discoveries waiting for us along the path of meditation without support, without guidance, without connectedness.

In our second inn of practice, *Support*, we learn to open up, even if reluctantly, to our vulnerability, so we can reach out for and receive support. We explore how to recognize forms of support that are already with us and to develop more trust in them. This in turn opens up more trust in our connectedness, and in life itself.

"Oh no, love, you're not alone," David Bowie sings in "Rock 'n' Roll Suicide."

To awaken to support is to recognize that our life is an intricately woven web of dependences. As the Zen master Thich Nhat Hanh used to observe, the sheet of paper these words are printed on comes from a woodland of trees. The trees don't grow without rain, and there's no rain without clouds, nor clouds without rivers and oceans. All the labor that went into creating this very page was done by workers who felled the trees, milled them, transported them, and pulped them. The workers in their turn needed the farmers who supplied the food that sustained them— vegetables, fruits, grains, and proteins—all of which had to be grown and tended, as well as nourished by soil, sun, and water. Likewise, without air to breathe, food, or warmth, there'd be no *you* at all to even be reading these words.

Once we look, we see that what we think of as *our* life is in fact dependent on many things that are not us, yet without which we can't exist. To recognize our infinite dependence is to awaken to the support and interconnection we are necessarily part of. This can lighten our load, shift our sense that we are solely responsible for our life and our well-being. It can even awaken a sense of being loved by all creation.

If our meditation practice is like the hull of a boat in which we're traveling, it can be helpful to have "outriggers," which support our journey. We will be exploring some of the common ones in this second inn of practice.

THE FOX

There are beautiful hills surrounding the Zen center in the Black Forest where I sometimes go to lead retreats. Throughout the years, I've gotten to know the network of paths in the vicinity quite well, and one morning after breakfast, I decided to try departing from a familiar nearby trail, and instead head out among the trees.

There seemed to be a small vestige of a trail to follow, maybe only a deer path, and I trudged up through the leaves of the forest floor, following it. It soon disappeared, but I wasn't bothered about finding my way. I had a map of the local terrain in my mind from many walks over the years.

I knew, for example, that if I followed the slope upward, in maybe half a mile I would reach a saddle between two hills. Sure enough, I did. From there, if I headed straight, I would start to descend, and in a while would drop down onto another bona fide path, which would lead me westward toward the valley where the little village of Schönenbuchen lay.

I felt just a shadow of doubt about the topography. There were times I had hiked here, intending to drop down into the main local town of Schönau, and somehow managed to overshoot it or enter it by a different path than I'd expected. Sometimes the trails had seemed steeper and far longer than made sense, according to the topography as I understood it, but as long as I stuck to the trails, I always ended up figuring out where I was.

This morning, I was confident in my knowledge of the

hills. In my mind, I was crossing a hill like a long headland, going from one side of it to the other.

Things started to get weird on the descent through the forest on the far side. First, there was a lot of tangled shrubbery to get through. Then the ground steepened far more abruptly than I'd expected. I found myself climbing down through a thicket of saplings growing up among boulders.

Soon enough, a trail appeared below me, and in a final scramble I managed to drop down onto it.

Great. The only trouble was, it was not the trail I'd anticipated.

This was more of a dirt road, wider and firmer than the trail I knew. It was disconcerting. But what did it really matter? The hill was still the same hill. All I had to do was turn left, and this unfamiliar road basically had no choice but to wrap around the end of that peninsula (in my mind), and lead me back toward the other side, the one from which I had originally set out. Confidence firm, I marched off accordingly.

Within ten minutes, as I came around a bend, I saw a church steeple down in a valley ahead. As far as I knew, there was only one church it could be. But that should have been way back behind me. I stopped. For a moment, I was utterly bewildered. The map in my mind had to be wrong. But if it was, then where was I?

I had absolutely no idea. It was as if I'd walked over that saddle in the forest and dropped clean out of the world I knew. For a moment, I simply didn't know which way to go.

It was a damp August day. Right in front of me, a bush familiar from my English childhood drew my eye. Blackberries nestled among its leaves, huge, plump, and glossy

German blackberries. I reached in and started plucking them off. They were perfect, ready to come away with the slightest encouragement, and big enough to have just a little weight to them. Their juice was exquisite, with a faint tang of tartness still alive in the sweetness.

I devoured a couple of hungry handfuls in rapture. Then I set off the only way that made sense—back the way I'd come. I would simply retrace my steps.

At this point, I realized it would have been smart to have noted a landmark where I had dropped down out of the forest onto the track. But I was sure I would recognize something when I got there, and know where to start ascending again. But after twenty minutes of walking, not one slope seemed right. Then I came around a farther bend and saw a mountain ahead through the trees. That was totally unfamiliar. I had definitely missed my exit point.

None of this would have mattered except that I had to give a talk at the retreat later that morning. There was a bit of pressure growing. Forty-eight people were expecting me to be a good Zen person and show up on time to deliver a talk on koan practice.

It was kind of ironic. Here I was right in the middle of a koan that the gods of the woods had conjured up, and I was unable to resolve it.

I was pretty sure that now I was going the wrong way. So with a little more speed in my pace, I again turned back the opposite way.

At my brisk pace, I soon passed the point where that damnably placed church steeple came into view. And soon after that, I came to a fork in the road. The main track carried on at the same level, and another, muddier track branched off up into the woods to the left. Because that would assuredly be heading back up closer toward the upper edge of the steep slope of the long hill I still thought I must be on the far side of, I headed out that way. It had to be leading back up over the hill to the other side, where the center stood.

Fine, I thought. *Soon enough I'll crest the hill and then make my way down by hook or by crook, back onto the original path I started from.*

Alas, the new track started to weave this way and that, and also became muddier and more deeply rutted. Soon I was sloshing through long puddles. It was all getting weirder with every bend. But at least I was going uphill, which had to be right—except that finally the track stopped entirely, and I found myself standing among shrubs with no path at all to follow.

I didn't know what else to do, so I forced my way through the undergrowth, up onto flatter ground. At that point I thought I needed to follow the top of this hill, and in a while I'd scoot back down what I still took to be its far side. But all of a sudden I found myself facing a long, steep downward slope when by rights I ought to have been still on the ridge at the top.

It was then that I glimpsed the fox. It was a dirty yellowish fox. It appeared about thirty feet away from me. It had a wide face and stared at me for a moment. Then it trotted along a few steps and disappeared.

A fox! In Japan, folk legend holds that "fox spirits" mislead people so they lose their way. Here it was—the very fox that had been playing tricks on me.

I plunged on down through the thickets, now with no idea at all where I was, or how I'd gotten so confused. In the midst of my stumbling down the slope of bushes, I burst out onto yet another track. What? This really didn't belong on the map in my mind. I couldn't understand its being here at all.

I randomly chose a direction and pounded off, now resigned to being late for my own talk.

Soon enough, I saw a man with a silver beard pacing up toward me with hiking poles. I almost walked right past him and then suddenly realized that help might be at hand.

In my faltering German, I asked if he knew the way to the village where the retreat center was. He seemed surprised and didn't answer at first. He frowned at me in puzzlement and repeated the village's name back to me as a question.

"*Genau*," I said. "Right."

"But it's just there," he said. "You're almost in it."

I smiled and thanked him and turned around yet again. And within a few yards, I realized that I recognized certain trees and a stack of sawed logs up ahead. I knew exactly where I was—less than a half mile from the center.

But I couldn't for the life of me understand how I came to be there. The only thing I began to understand, as I doubled my pace, and in fact made it back just as the bell was ringing for the start of the talk, was that—foxes aside—the thing that had misled me must have been the map in my mind. I had been so sure I knew the lay of the land. Had I not had that map in my mind, I might not have gotten lost.

Be that as it may, what had righted my course was a word

from a fellow traveler. As soon as I met someone and asked for guidance, I found my way.

SOMETIMES LIFE IS too pressing and challenging. All we can do is lurch from one problem to the next. Sometimes our inner life is in turmoil. Anxiety or depression rise up and overwhelm us. And we have to do inner work to heal our psyches, bring things back into balance. At other times the waves recede, life becomes smoother, and the deeper questions may float up. *What is this all for? Why am I alive? What is this life? Who really am I? How should I spend my finite time on earth?*

Sometimes out of the blue we are hit with a sense of a merciful presence within things. Somehow this life is blessed, though it's hard to say exactly how or why. For the religiously inclined, they may feel there is a God, or gods, or angels, or whatever supernatural entities they believe in and sense. There is a power of benevolence hidden behind things.

Sometimes this benevolence may seem to want to teach us, to help us grow, and may appear in a guise that does not at first seem friendly but turns out to be. We sense greater powers at work.

How had I gotten so turned around that morning? Clearly, that long ridge I had been so sure of couldn't have been the straight hill I'd thought. The fact that it was covered in forest had not only concealed its true shape but had allowed me to construct a shape for it in my mind that was wrong.

There was something to be learned here. It's better to have no map than a false map, perhaps?

Then I quickly jumped to my past. I'd been unhappy for

years as a youth. That had changed quite consistently a long time ago as a result of meditation training. Perhaps in the years of unhappiness, I had been entranced by a false map too.

I'd never quite thought of it that way. But it made sense. It was consistent, in fact, with the "Four Ennobling Truths" of Buddhism:

1. There is suffering.
2. Suffering is generated by craving.
3. Craving can cease.
4. There is a path of practice that leads to the end of craving.

The fourth truth, the path of practice, is the prescription for living in a way that leads to less suffering. And the first of its directives is to have a clear understanding of suffering and its causes, and of well-being and its causes. This means you have to have a reliable map.

That morning, various levels of ignorance had been at work. I made an assumption and trusted it. I thought I knew something but didn't subject this knowledge to scrutiny. And it had not been my own knowledge, but another's knowledge, that guided me back.

That's one point of this little escapade. But there's another, lurking in the story: the fox in the undergrowth. I had ventured into more-than-human territory, without respect. And this territory showed me it had a kind of animacy of its own. I'd been no match for the fox.

Who's in charge? We like to think that basically we are. What if we're wrong?

TRUST

The broad theme we explore in our second inn of practice is *support*. And for support to really reach us, as we'll see, we also have to open up to trust.

In our individualistic Westernized world, we are inclined to think that everything is up to *me*. Career, family, friendships, exercise, and diet—I'm responsible for making all the elements in my life flourish. And now that mindfulness is being widely touted as a tool for well-being, on apps and podcasts, in office culture and elsewhere, I'd better take that on too.

For my physical fitness, I may get a session with a trainer who gives me a routine to follow, but thereafter it's up to me to do the reps and sets. So with meditation, I have to deposit my solitary self on the seat day after day and do my breath reps.

But that's a lonely picture. It's really only half the picture. Or less than half.

Actually, meditation—like life—is not, and in the end cannot be, a lonely pursuit. For sure, discipline is required for habit formation, and we must put time into our practice as we would into learning any new skill or developing anything of value in life. It's necessary but it's not the real point. If it were, how bleak this would all be.

This second inn is about why meditation is far from bleak or lonely or solitary. In some views, all it really is, is an uncovering of ever-broader support, ever-deeper connection.

In fact, if we start exploring how support is operating in

our life already, then we discover more and more ways that our life is dependent on things that are not us. There can come to seem no end to the kinds of support that make our life possible. Our DNA, our ancestors and families, the cultures in which we are reared—not to mention every breath we've taken of Earth's atmosphere, every meal we've eaten, every glass of water we've drunk, and every stitch of clothing we've worn—we might start to ask how much our life is really our own at all, and to what extent it is more like a constellation of a million dependences.

In this inn, what interests us most are the kinds of support that further our journey of meditative exploration—that is to say, the kinds of support that help us break down our pattern of seeing ourselves as isolated, fixed, and separate from all else. Each time we recognize our dependence on some form of support we hadn't noticed or had forgotten, it can precipitate a step on that journey. It may help us feel that in some unexpected way we had overlooked, we are loved. Support after all is a form of love. And to recognize that is to soften our often-barricaded sense of self. It helps to break down our separateness, our sense of having to do everything alone and by ourselves, including the practice of meditation.

But a first step to uncovering this kind of loving support, for many of us, is learning to trust it. In the end, we can't taste support without trust. But trust requires us to be vulnerable, and that's not always easy.

How can we develop trust if it's hard for us? And trust in what and in whom anyway?

"SELF-POWER" AND "OTHER-POWER"

In Zen, there are said to be two kinds of power: *jiriki* and *tariki*. *Jiriki* is "self-power," meaning the power that we have to help ourselves along the path of practice. *Tariki* is "other-power," meaning forces at work around us that help us on the path of growth through meditation. These other forces can be of many kinds, from the tangible—such as fellow practitioners or organizations geared to support practice and ease of access to teachings—to the intangible, which we'll also be exploring in this section.

If the first inn we sought refuge in, Mindfulness, is primarily about *jiriki*—what we ourselves can do to develop our meditation practice—this second inn is about *tariki*—ways we can open up to receiving help and support in our practice. It's about getting connected. It's about being vulnerable. It's about finding parts in ourselves that ache to be met, seen, loved, and supported.

For modern Western meditators, living in our individualistic culture, it seems quite natural to assume that meditation is mostly about solitary practice. It's a skill set we practice and master alone. The more we do it, the better we get, and the more benefit we gain. To see it this way is to view it as a matter of *jiriki*—self-power.

But this would be to overlook vital ingredients that propel the journey of practice.

There is a traditional formulation known as the Three Treasures, whereby no practice can flourish unless it includes three things: meditation, guidance, and community. The old terms for these are *Buddha*, *dharma*, and *sangha*.

We do need to do our sitting, following the example of the Buddha, who made the journey to awakening through the path of meditation.

But our practice can flourish more fully through ongoing guidance from the teachings he left behind, to which successive generations of practitioners have added. That is the basic meaning of the word *dharma*—the teachings that can guide us.

The teachings come in two forms:

1. **General**, meaning talks, audio recordings, books, videos, instructions, apps, and so on.
2. **Personal**, meaning individual instruction from a flesh-and-blood meditator with more experience than we have. In some traditions these more seasoned practitioners are known as *kalyana mitra*, or "spiritual friends"; in others, by various terms denoting "teacher."

Further, we need a *sangha*, that is to say, a community of fellow practitioners. How much we join them may vary from daily to rarely, but a community with which we feel affiliated is a helpful ingredient.

If we open up to all three treasures (which are also sometimes known as the Three Refuges), our practice becomes a "safe harbor," as some sutras put it. We are turning aside from the high seas of greed and ill will, from the pursuit of "name and gain," in which we chase after goals that offer us a lesser happiness but are a powerful entrancement, and instead entering a safe anchorage or port, where deeper well-being awaits.

The three treasures are forms of *tariki*—"other-power." We are relying on things other than ourselves to help ourselves, whether it's the example of the historical Buddha, teachings and instructions, or the fellowship of other meditators.

The *treasures* also involve trust. We allow ourselves to trust in the practice of meditation, in the guidance about it that we encounter, and in the support of other meditators. The more we settle into the practice of daily meditation, the more we may come to feel that we can trust in the meditation going on around the world at any moment, generating more peace and kindness in the world. Some say other life-forms are practicing too: trees are masters of stillness, fortitude, and graceful acceptance, and whales move through the seas suspended in oceanic awareness, communicating with one another across vast distances. Even smaller creatures move through their lives with the focus and intention of master meditators: ants tirelessly follow the call of their nature, and mice, moths, and patient cattle all practice and implicitly trust the life they are given.

Again, as meditators, what do we trust in? In the practice itself: we learn to feel confident that to practice will help us live wisely. We trust in the moment at hand, as it is: the way things are right now is how they must be, for now. There's a natural law of cause and effect at work, making this moment the way it is. As a concomitant of that, the way we think and act now will also bear fruit in time to come. A kind act or a thoughtful word will yield a little more peace in the world somewhere down the road. And if we sit still and settle down, then that too will have an effect on lives that we touch.

Trust can develop in other ways too: we start to trust our very existence. To be alive and aware, to be having the experience we call human life, is something we can come to trust.

Trust is an interesting condition to explore. It's a positive affect, composed of patience, hope, a sense of promise, and perhaps gratitude, and it breeds confidence in ourselves. And that last, vital aspect may come from the other side of the equation: learning to receive support.

It's one thing to be supported and not recognize it. It's another thing to recognize it. And it's still a further thing to open ourselves to the vulnerability of seeing how much we might need it.

Practice, in the end, is not just nourished by connection and community. Over time, we may get inklings that we are nourished by actually being part of a larger whole. The kinds of support we are most concerned with on the journey of this book are those that nudge us toward a less entrenched sense of self—away from a self that feels as if it exists in isolation, toward a more connected, dependent, and inter-relational self. Even from early on in practice, we may feel intimations of a wider, deeper support that is already here, yet is still somehow hidden to us. These are hints and glimmerings of the original love we are slowly uncovering as we follow the path. More and more, we learn to trust this love.

Somehow, it's good to feel we may not have all the answers yet. A little humility helps. A sense that there is a mystery, something we don't yet and can't yet know, toward which we are moving, helps. Without yielding to reckless or blind faith, trust in some kind of unseen wholeness, which many meditators throughout the millennia have found—to hold that in our hearts as a possibility, to practice as if we feel it may really be so, even before we are fully convinced it is, will help us along the path. And it takes trust.

ON LOAN

What do I—this body-heart-mind complex—need in order to exist? Right off the bat, there are the elements.

Air: Without breath, I survive a few minutes.

Heat: Without sufficient warmth, whether from sun, clothing, shelter, or fire, I die within hours.

Water: Without water to drink, the body has about seven days, depending on the environment, before it dies. In the desert, maybe two or three days.

Earth: Without the organic matter that the earth brings forth as food, the body survives for a few weeks at most.

All of these are needed on a constant, ongoing basis. Day by day, hour by hour, minute by minute, our lives depend on them. This may seem obvious, but how often do we take it in? Without any one of them, we simply don't last.

Some Tibetan systems also include space as a fifth element: the body needs the fact of space (the three dimensions) to exist at all.

If any one of the "five elements" (according to those systems) is removed, then we cease to exist. Our existence depends on things other than us, through and through, breath by breath. I'm not in charge of my existence. I receive it as a loan of many other things.

We can tune our awareness to our dependences as we sit in meditation. Every breath becomes a sustaining force, an element of goodness, a kind of lovingness sharing its existence with mine. Without that inflow and outflow, I don't continue. As the Zen master Sasaki Roshi apparently sometimes said to his students: "When I breathe in, the universe breathes out; when I breathe out, the universe breathes in." There's a constant, moment-by-moment give and take between the atmosphere and me.

And more than just the air is involved. I'm sitting as a warm body. The heat of the sun, which drives the dynamism of this whole planet and converts all the proteins and chemicals into living forms, is the energy source driving all my life. It sustains and feeds the plant-forms, which nourish me and which clothe me. I am utterly indebted to plants, as they in turn are to that great source of warmth, the "eye of heaven," as Shakespeare calls the sun.

Let me notice this and appreciate it. May I recognize my dependence on air and warmth and plants, which grow from the earth.

Then there's water—my body is a sack of fluids. It's a skin-bag with its architecture of bone, sinew, muscle, and its organs, which are like water balloons in which fluids exchange their chemistries. And let's not forget the electro-chemical jelly in my skull, which underpins my ability to be aware of all this as I sit meditating, and which allows me to choose to meditate. I am not an island, not an isolate. Just as I sit here, breathing, wearing clothes, with my heart beating and my system digesting nutrients, I am already infinitely dependent.

And consider the seat beneath me. It is a gift. Tirelessly, it holds me up. And the floor holds the seat. And the struts hold the floorboards, and the foundations hold the struts, and the earth is beneath them all—and beneath Earth's mantle is the magma, and then the core, and then the other deeper layers, and somewhere way down, the mile-wide spinning sphere of graphite like a vast ball bearing that some say whirs at the heart of the planet. All of this supports all things up here on the surface. We are not *in* a web of support: we are nodes that make up that very web.

And more than all that, my body and my awareness both occupy space—beautiful space expands around me, and clear space is present all through me. My body, my being, is an expansion into space.

Though in a lifetime of meditation we may come to recognize ever more kinds of support that sustain us, and much of it in tangible form, we will never enumerate them all. But there are also more immaterial kinds of support to be explored.

How come I am here at all? Our families, our parents, our ancestors—they made us. We are the fruit, the expression, of their genetic material. It's not ours. We are not "ours"— not of our own making. We owe our existence to just about everything *but* ourselves.

We are not indebted—we are nothing *but* a debt. According to Stephen Jenkinson, in his book *Die Wise*, we are a loan, to be paid on, perhaps, but certainly to be acknowledged, from our forebears, as much as to the soil, worms, microbes, and fungi. We are indebted to the elements and chemistry of this planet. We are indebted to our great mother—whether the earth or cosmos.

That's what this second inn is about: recognizing the powers that generate us, that hold sway over us, and that rule our deeper lives—not forgetting the ancestors, the forebears, and the ancient traumas we have inherited too, including the traumas experienced in the prehistory of our own lives, our earliest years, before memories formed. These are the most indelible impressions of all, which we can never quite call to mind, because they shaped our very minds. These are impressions we don't consciously know, but by means of which we know. Those dinosaurs that stomped through our earliest hours and years, and the powers that drove them—our very self has been shaped by them like wet clay.

And all the relationships we've known to date. They too shaped us. So many people. And maybe some beloved animals too. Each person's life is an interactive web of beings.

Just consider the impact that even an unfamiliar creature can sometimes have. Here is a poem of mine, "Heron," in which I encounter a bird on a day that happened to be the first anniversary of a death close to me.

The young heron
pauses mid-weir
to stare at me,
and waits so long
there on its single stilt,
mid-step—one
webbed foot held aloft,
a ribbon of froth fluttering

from the other that's planted
in the pour of the channel,
not a feather stirring,
just the long neck adjusting
like a snake for balance,
and the hazel target of its eye
locked on mine—
that there's time
for the damp day to turn bright,
for the elms to sigh
in a wind not made of air,
for the path under my feet
to soften like skin,
and the sound of the river
to press its cool hands
on my ears.
What is this pressure
holding my head?
Why am I remembering
all of a sudden
that today marks a year
since you died,
and wondering
where you've gone,
one year on,
or whether you've gone at all?
Who is this bird
fixing me with its eye?
Stately as an Egyptian prince,
as if wearing time

like a pair of wings
it has only to open
to bring back
all the years of your life,
at last it lowers its foot
and moves on.

Let's be humble. Let's be open to awe. Let's notice that we're privileged to be part of a great web of life. "Only connect!" as the novelist E. M. Forster wrote in *Howard's End*.

A CROWDED AIRPORT

I used to be sent on many writing assignments in remote and less developed areas of Latin America. Often I flew through Miami, and I remember one particular time arriving back in Miami at what must have been an unfortunate confluence of circumstances. Perhaps several jumbo jets had arrived at around the same time, or there was an unforeseen shortage of immigration staff.

Whatever it was, the place was jammed. Hundreds upon hundreds of people were filing in toward the immigration hall. Even the corridor leading into it was maybe twelve wide with people, and hardly moving at all.

At first I had a customary reaction. *Oh boy, this is going to take hours.* Standing upright, packed among so many people, all of us trying to get into the hall, where our queuing and waiting would really begin . . . *Ugh, this is awful*, I started to think.

It could easily have turned into something excruciating. But luckily, I had my practice. I took an inner step back. I became a mute observer. It all flipped. Instead of being a frustration, it became a wonder, a gift, a truly precious opportunity, to be among so many exquisite beings. It was a rare privilege—of course it was—to be pressed among this great gathering of these wonderful creatures, human beings, who all had plans and things they loved and loved ones in their lives, and who all had consciousness, and knew they were alive and knew how to love.

Suddenly, I felt blessed beyond measure to be among these upright, balanced, and exceptional creatures. Just to feel their physical warmth, their intentionality, and their innate kindness—it was a wondrous thing to be among that throng.

As I shuffled along in my place in the line, slowly creeping toward the immigration counters, I almost didn't want it to ever end.

THE SOUL

If our first inn, Mindfulness, is about our ordinary sense of self, then this second inn, Support, is more the territory of our "soul." But what is the soul?

The Greek word *psyche* is more or less antecedent to our concept of soul. *Psych*-iatry heals the soul, and *psych*-ology studies it. But the soul is not just the mind.

The ancient Greeks distinguished between two kinds of knowing—*logos*, which was logical, rational, linear, and the province of the thinking mind, and *mythos*, which was intuitive, mysterious, modulated by feeling, and the province of the *psyche*, or soul.

Experts on the soul, such as the Jungian psychologists James Hillman and Robert Johnson, emphasize that the soul is elusive. It's not a thing. It's certainly not, in their view, some immortal nugget within us that goes on into an afterlife. Rather, it's a process, an intuition, something sensed rather than seen, which can be felt and known but not examined. *Logos* and science seek to know through hypothesis, experiment, and evidence. Their straight gaze will never know the soul. *Mythos*, which is the soul's territory, knows through glimpses and refracted glances out of the corner of its eye. It is attuned to hints and hunches, yet what it knows, it knows deeply.

In his book *The Soul's Code*, James Hillman expounds his "acorn theory," in which he suggests that just as an acorn contains the impulse within itself to grow into an oak tree, so the soul knows it needs to grow, in order to become more amply itself. It has inklings about its pattern and direction of growth but can't directly tell us what they are. It can only indirectly nudge us, through intuitions, loves, impulses, enthusiasms, and bodily responses. Nor can we directly know it, or what it's aiming for, though after the fact we can track its path of growth.

One of the greatest works on "soul growing" is the poet William Wordsworth's long poetic masterpiece *The Prelude*, in which he chronicles his soul's development, fostered and nourished by the hills and rivers among which he grew up, as well as by poetry, friendships, and travels.

The poet John Keats called the world "this vale of soul-making." Souls exist in the making, not as products or entities. Suffering, from the perspective of the soul, is not all bad. It is grief, loss, and disappointment that forge and temper the soul, though it also needs nourishment, encouragement, and support to come into its own.

Mostly its growth isn't overt or explicit. Becoming an economist, a scientist, a teacher, a lawyer, or an accountant may touch part of the soul's wished-for trajectory, but its real growth is more hidden and mysterious. Yet it's central to the well-being of the personality.

If the self is a broad category, within it are defensive portions and also self-promotional parts, which crave the admiration of others. But there are also less distinct but deeper parts, which grow in ways less visible but nevertheless tangible. We can sense when they are alive and active. We know the soul by what it loves: art, beauty, and awe-inspiring landscapes. It recognizes something in a grand vista that it resonates with. It too is sublime, and in a sense closer to the infinite, perhaps. Wordsworth felt his soul was taught and shaped by the hills among which he lived during his childhood, and which he came to love more consciously in his adulthood.

And the soul loves the quest for original love.

Perhaps we can make a distinction between our ordinary, everyday mind and a somewhat different area of self, which has different priorities, ones that feel more precious to us. This other zone of self cares more about a bigger picture. Its concern is more with fulfillment. It's less linear in its ways of experiencing, and it's more expansive and connective in its ways of feeling.

Philosopher and psychiatrist Iain McGilchrist approaches the soul when describing his experience of studying poetry at Oxford University as a young man. He came to feel that a great poem offers an embodied experience (the flesh tingles and the heart rate changes). A poem's meaning is implicit, and each is unique, with its own way of being a poem. But in the seminars he attended, students were encouraged to take a poem as a disembodied experience, to make its meaning explicit, and to generalize and categorize poems. In other words, all its most important ways of being a poem— embodied, implicit, and unique—were directly misconstrued.

Through his work in neurology, McGilchrist came to see this kind of mismatch between the approach taken and the object studied as a symptom of brain lateralization. It is a case of a mismatch of right-brain and left-brain understandings. Poems, in this view, are essentially products of the right brain, whose ways of knowing are embodied, implicit, and appreciative of the uniqueness of things. In contrast, the ways of knowing by which the students were encouraged to study a poem were those of the left brain: disembodied, explicit, and category-making.

Poems pertain to *mythos*, in the classical Greek terminology, and to approach them by means of *logos* does them a disservice.

So perhaps the soul is what it feels like when the right hemisphere of the brain is more active in consciousness. The right hemisphere is holistic, connected, and thus it knows a natural abiding in a field of support. This would explain why this kind of support is commonly opaque to our ordinary left-brain view.

Life is much richer when we're in the zone of the soul. We know it when we are. We know ourselves more deeply, and we know how to appreciate being alive and feel grateful to be ourselves. Love is in the mix. And we have a sense of purpose, of how we want to live and grow.

Much of the study of mindfulness today has been taken over by neuroscience—and fruitfully so. What happens when we engage in mindfulness can be constructively viewed through the lens of brain activity. Early phases of meditation are about taming a restless mind and tending to a dysregulated nervous system. But even then, in the early stages of practice, we may sense a wholesome kind of growth that is asking to happen, one that is neither perfectly expressed nor met by an algorithmic, linear approach. As practice deepens, it engages not just the mind but the soul too.

This is important for various reasons. We need to have deeper parts of ourselves getting on board with the greater project of meditation. Our soul—the very principle of growth within us—will surely help the project to prosper, if allowed in. Whether the soul is in fact just the self in a more expansive mood, or merely the right-brain hemisphere coming more alive, doesn't actually matter. The fact is, it feels more whole, and more connected with our body's experience, and has a broader perspective, than the contracted, narrower view of our logical self. And more than that, the soul not only has hope but also courage.

And courage, as we will see, becomes more important as we proceed on the path. It takes courage to release ourselves into original love.

LITERARY FIGURES AND STORIES

If we think of long-term meditation as a canoe that ferries a practitioner across the wide river of suffering, as an old, traditional metaphor puts it, then sometimes it helps for the craft to have an outrigger. The main hull is our regular daily sitting practice, but at times we need additional support to make consistent, sustained progress. Common "outriggers" that can assist the voyage might be art, literature, time in nature, psychotherapy, bodywork, somatic therapy, dream work, dance, movement, and sports.

In the rest of this chapter we'll explore a few tastes of some modalities that can serve as adjuncts to meditation, offering a significant capacity to help us along in it.

AS EAGER TEENAGE poets, my friend Sam and I quickly got the point of a book of poems. The point wasn't to read it. It was to plunder it, ransack it for treasures. The book should end up dog-eared, as floppy as a flannel shirt. You wanted the light, the illumination, and it shone only out of certain pages. You had to find which ones.

We were hungry for inspiration. We tracked the contemporary poets we loved and then tracked the thread back to the poets *they* had loved: to Ezra Pound, Hilda Doolittle, and the Imagist poets of London just before the First World War. From them, we followed their provenance back to Wordsworth and Shakespeare, but also to ancient China, to the Tang dynasty poets they had loved and translated—to Hanshan, the "Cold Mountain" poet, and Tu Fu, Li Po, and Wang Wei, who had wandered the ravines and cloud-wrapped peaks of the Middle Kingdom, stalked by vagabonds and monks who had given up on urban life and taken to the hills. There, entranced by lakes and streams, gazing at waterfalls, drifting deep into the forests or high into the mountains, they wrote their clearest poetry. They drank wine and shed tears for lost friends. They also sat still in meditation, losing themselves, dissolving their minds into the peaks, becoming part of the land itself.

Those old poets were important figures for us. They loomed large in our psyches. They became forms of support or guidance that we imbued with soulful energy. They beckoned to us, and we followed their call, donning backpacks as teenagers and sleeping rough in the valleys near our home, trying to imitate them. We met in coffee shops in our hometown of Oxford, sharing our scraps of would-be poems while puffing on scruffy roll-your-owns.

Those same semi-legendary figures later drew us to the Beats and to Gary Snyder, and the practice that lay behind their poetry: Zen.

Zen: that little word, which meant "meditation"—but also meant so much more. It meant a wild, nonmaterial freedom. It meant fullhearted living. It meant trusting that there was more to you than met the eye. Or perhaps less, depending on how you looked at it. But either way, that one day, if you practiced in accordance with Zen, you would come to learn what that was. It would burst forth and astonish you.

Later, when I came to Zen training in earnest, I was drawn to sitting with koans, the inscrutable sayings left behind by the old Tang dynasty masters, their trail of breadcrumbs leading to whatever it was they had found. The old sages and adepts in the koans could fill the meditator's awareness until gradually, or suddenly, they might shove you into a glimpse of their world. You might then tentatively try to share this with your teacher—who, in my case, in her own way, then acquired another shade of spiritual force in my life, one of the greatest blessings I have known.

But literary characters might exert great force on us too. There's the cathartic power of watching tragic characters destroyed by their own insistent impulses, as famously explored in Aristotle's *Ars Poetica*. The heightening of fear and sympathy through tragic drama "cleanses" us of those emotions. Meanwhile, recent research into the origins of the oral epic narrative suggests that a primary source for these narratives was the "soul-journeying" enacted and narrated by shamans during their séances. The twentieth-century scholar Arthur Hatto, in particular, came to this conclusion in his work on oral epics of Siberia and northern India.

The implications are broader than we might think, once we consider the foundational place of the oral epic in the Western tradition. The classical education of Athens and Rome in their heydays was based on the epic poems of Homer, which had their roots in oral verse. If these two great poems, *The Iliad* and *The Odyssey*, contain distilled records of shamanic voyages, with their purpose and function reaching back to quasi-medical shamanic ceremonies of the late Paleolithic era, then perhaps even great narrative fiction today still owes some of its force to its origins in animistic mythological journeys made by shamans long ago. This would explain how we come to be (sometimes) so powerfully moved by characters in literature that they change the course of our lives. Their stories still have one foot in the mythic realm in which their ilk was born, and they stir an immemorial openness in our hearts. When they do, when they touch and move us, they may nudge us into new ways of living.

THERAPY

The first therapist I went to, back in my twenties, once told a story in his therapy group about a former client who had wanted to become a nun. They soon got to the bottom of that in her therapy. She didn't really want to be a nun; really, she was afraid of sex and intimacy. The therapy went well and after a few months she left. A year later, she got back in touch with the therapist to thank him for their work together, and to let him know she was doing great, better than ever, and that she had realized after all that she really *did* want to be a nun, and was writing from the convent she had recently joined.

The therapist was a remarkable man called Harvey Karman, who settled in London after a brilliant, checkered career in California. As well as being a psychologist, he was a pioneer for abortion rights and invented a cannula credited with making safe abortions available to millions of women around the world (a device he never patented). He traveled extensively, leading mobile abortion clinics into war zones soon after frontline fighting had ceased, where victims of rape, among them many underage women, could find treatment. (He also spent a short time in a California prison for practicing medicine without a license.)

Harvey was devoted to the liberating benefits of therapy. He held up the story of this client-turned-nun as a cautionary tale. This can happen in therapy, he explained: you're getting somewhere in your work, and then the old programming kicks back in with a vengeance, and you don't have the resources yet to counteract it, and it ends up winning. You avoid your real problems. It takes courage and time to get to the bottom of things and do the real work.

Had the phrase been in current parlance at the time, he might have called the nun's story a case of "spiritual bypassing." Meaning, to use spirituality—in her case, joining a convent—as a way of avoiding psychological and interpersonal issues it would be better to face and work through.

As a devoted groupie of his, I doubtless nodded knowingly when he offered his diagnosis of his former client's behavior, wholeheartedly agreeing. How pernicious the forces of denial can be, we groupies sagely told one another on a regular basis.

I don't see it that way now. First, perhaps no one has the right to question another's desires or aspirations, so long as they don't cause harm. But second, it may be a case of different "levels" or "zones" of human growth, of healing and wisdom, intruding upon one another. The former client's interest in spiritual growth may have been more than a mere avoidance of intimacy issues. Perhaps she was in pursuit of the mystical. Perhaps she wanted to lead a contemplative life. And maybe she did also have intimacy issues. But there's a place for acknowledging the different kinds of growth we may be seeking.

Among these different kinds of growth, one may be contemplative experience, which is a matter neither of distraction nor denial. Not only do some people seek it and taste it, but it's real. Yet it has basically little place in the majority of psychotherapies. Therapies tend to work with the separate sense of self, and rightly so. They are about personal and interpersonal well-being. There are few significant schools of modern psychology that deal with what is truly beyond the self. For that, arguably, you have to turn to the meditation manuals of Buddhism and other contemplative traditions.

There's nothing wrong with any of this, except when boundaries are crossed and territories are encroached upon that aren't part of the worldview of one kind of practice. It may be unhelpful for a dedicated meditator to be told to just meditate more, for example, when they're in distress about a lack of communication with their partner. And it may be equally unhelpful for a psychologist to tell them to quit the cushion and instead go to couples therapy. It might be best for them to keep sitting *and* get some therapy. The two practices operate in different "terrains" of well-being. Therapy is usually about significant distress and dysfunction; contemplative practice is undertaken in a different frame.

There can be a confusion of levels going on here, one born of a lack of recognition: hence, again, the four inns of growth that this book lays down as cornerstones of a healthy spiritual practice. Or, from the perspective of meditation, we could say that we seek to keep the main "hull" of our practice moving through the waters yet attach different outriggers to it, as needed.

LESSONS FROM NATURE

One early morning I was wandering up a thickly forested hillside in the Sangre de Cristo Mountains of northern New Mexico, aiming for a ridge I knew was up at the top. I was idly reflecting on how every one of us comes from a family. It may be a family we never knew, but at least three people are implicated in our existence if we include ourselves in the count—a mother, a father, and us—and three makes a family, no matter whether broken or whole. All creatures come from some kind of family—even the solitary octopus cradling the seabed, jet-propelling itself with a cloud of ink like smoke in water, is from a family. Even these trees I was walking among. Come to think of it—weren't they members of the very family they stood among? What is a forest if not a family or a host of families?

Then I came upon a veritable boneyard of dead trees, a charnel ground, where heap after heap of blackened aspen trunks lay jumbled among one another. It was like stumbling into some spillage of old telegraph poles, all black and higgledy-piggledy. It made for extraordinarily difficult going, sometimes having to stoop under a log while stepping over a fallen trunk, and finding only a small, triangular well in which to lower my boot, where three other trunks met. It was like a 3D maze.

What added to the treacherousness was that a new family—a flock of scrub oaks—had delightedly occupied the homeland of the fallen family, which by now I realized was a great stand of aspen, which had seemingly come down at once, likely in a fire, and was remarkable not only for the prodigality of its collapse, but also for the contrast between the shimmering silver vellum of the living trunks and the fuzzy old creosote look of their blackness in death. But among this boneyard, the young dwarf oaks had burst forth everywhere. And everything was damp from the night's dew. So the barkless fallen logs were slippery, and the oaks gave me a thorough drenching every time I pushed through them.

It wasn't night anymore—it was in fact midmorning—but the sun didn't get to work on this hillside until the afternoon, and I was starting to get chilled as well as wet and tired.

In spite of the prodigious obstacle of the log yard, and the utter soaking the oak bushes were giving me, I knew that I only had to keep going, and at some point I would have to reach that elusive crest, which I had to be making my way toward, and which, once I got there, would offer clearer walking.

So I plunged on, comforting myself by thinking of some kung fu trainees I had once seen in a movie, who had been forced to pick their way through a three-dimensional maze comparable to this one, except that in their case, all the elements were in motion, swinging, slicing, and chopping to and fro.

Again and again, I'd reach some taut nexus of fallen

trunks and just not see a way through—except, possibly, if I could just squeeze through that horizontal gap and plant a step on that next log—and find that yes, somehow it could actually work. So I kept going. I realized at some point that it was better not to look ahead. If I looked ahead, then it seemed basically impossible. Yet this next conundrum, the one immediately facing me now, could be solved, with some thought and application. And sure enough, slow, blinkered persistence paid off. I eventually caught a glimpse of gravelly ground through the foliage up ahead, and it really did betoken the more open stretches among the large ponderosa pines higher up that I had been hoping for.

Looking back, I realized that very soon in the painstaking journey through the three-dimensional charnel, I had reached a point where I didn't know whether it would be worth it to stay the course. The distance I had covered already might be greater than the distance left to go. But I couldn't be sure that I was making the right decision. In fact, it was only in the last yards, two hours later, that I knew for sure that pressing ahead was indeed the right course. But I'd kept on regardless, from quite early in the maze.

Life is like this. We arrive free and full of enthusiasm to live. Soon we find ourselves ensnared in the bones of our families, in our lineages of hurt and blame, in our inheritances of difficulty, trauma, challenge, and triumph too perhaps—and those of our friends and companions. The world is not an open field after all.

Yet it can be. On a deeper level, it not only can be, it can't *not* be. That's why life is not just a tangle—but rather a maze, a labyrinth, an apparent jumble that does in fact have a kind of secret order underlying it. And part of our purpose in living is to discover that hidden order, learn to live by it, and be freed by it.

On the path of practice, we never have the luxury of knowing when we'll get free of the briars that sometimes entangle our psyches. Often we have to just press on regardless. It can be hard to sit with our suffering, not knowing how long it will go on, while we are bereft of the distractions and flimsy mechanisms we normally use to avoid and evade our distress. How long will this particular challenging phase continue? We just don't know. Often we don't even know where it comes from. We undergo painful conditioning at birth and in our earliest years, which shape our malleable minds. We inherit traumatic experiences from our parents, as they did from theirs. None of us is ever a tabula rasa—we don't come into life a blank slate. We come in with the tangled lines of human history—of oppression, atrocity, cruelty, war, famine, and injustice—scribbled on us, which scar us whether our forebears were on the receiving end or the perpetrating end of the violence. It is hard to release this ancient material. But it is possible.

That's the promise of practice. If we trust the practice, keep going, and open ourselves to wise guidance and kind support, then sooner or later the tangled vines (in an ancient Zen phrase) will start to clear, and fall away, and a wider spaciousness will appear. Suddenly, there's a taste of peace, there's light, we're through something, we find an ease at last, and we can breathe more easily.

The wall in front of my meditation seat shows itself to me once again. How is it I failed even to register the wall's existence for these past minutes, hours, or days? Or the floor gleaming in the lovely sunlight, or the sounds of morning traffic outside, soft and familiar, or the songs and calls of birds? These were all lost to me, yet here they have been all along, patiently waiting for me to come back to the here and now, waiting for me to appreciate them.

In the dead forest, I finally made it to the upper edge of the steep slope, and found open ground and a trail I knew. The only downside was a sore back later on, from so much stooping and twisting.

And all along, I had been weaving through families, living and dead. The family of the aspen, the family of the scrub oak, and others too.

Families are hard to get through, says John Cleese, of Monty Python fame, in his book *Families and How to Survive Them*. In it, he speaks of the childhood miseries that pushed him to a life in comedy.

But there's no avoiding families. They create us and possibly rear us and live in us. We are of them. We owe them everything, however we may feel about them.

The trees I'd just clambered through in the forest were black as evidence of what had slain them, the entire family, at a single stroke. Namely, a forest fire.

Just one more reminder that though practice may seem to go on for a long time, it is, in a sense, never long enough. Our time for practice will surely come to an end. Our opportunity is very large but also finite.

Wherever we look, we are being offered lessons in patience, fortitude, determination, love, and death.

"The whole earth is medicine," says an old Zen teaching. The whole world—all of nature, perhaps—can be our help, guide, teacher. And it is our support, we might add.

Try This

Let's pause here. Take a couple of conscious, slow breaths—in and out . . . in and out. . . . Now let the breath come and go in its own natural rhythm.

Think of someone who has been a guide to you, who has helped you along the journey of life. It might be an elder, a friend, a teacher or mentor, or a family member. Or even an author, or a character from a book or movie. Someone who has inspired you and helped you find your way in life.

Give yourself a moment to take in what this person has done for you. Let yourself notice that they have truly helped you. Feel the good feeling of having been helped. Take it in.

And notice also that it takes some vulnerability both to recognize that we do need help and also to receive help. Neither of these is easy. To bare our souls even a little takes a particular kind of courage—the courage of being vulnerable.

Thank yourself for having been willing to be vulnerable. It's the foundation for all our deeper connectedness. Congratulate yourself for whatever openness you have been able to find, which allows you to receive help.

GUIDED MEDITATION

The Four Elements

Settle into a comfortable seated position. Or if you prefer, you could also do this meditation lying down.

We are going to notice and appreciate four key building blocks of our life, all of which are here right now, sustaining our very existence.

Take in a full breath, hold it for a moment, and let it out slowly. Keep repeating this for several breaths. As you breathe in, say to yourself, *Thank you, air.*

As you release the breath, say silently, *I release this air for others.*

Let yourself feel the gift that each breath is. Let your heart feel warm, grateful for the breath that flows in and out.

Now let's feel the warmth on our skin and on our flesh. We have clothing and shelter, or perhaps we're in a warm car or on a heated train. Whatever it is right now keeping you warm and dry, give thanks to it. Feel the warmth and notice that being warm feels good, in and of itself. Let yourself soak in the good feeling of having enough warmth right now.

After a moment, let's bring our attention to the fact that we are able to drink water when we need it. Our bodies are in part like sponges that need moisture to function. Right now, you have basically enough moisture in your system. Our bodies have a kind of built-in irrigation system, without which we would not survive. The organs within function through their moisture, as their fluids move through us. Our whole circulatory system requires enough fluid for the blood to flow. Notice that you have approximately the right amount of fluid on board right now, and that it is allowing your life to continue. Say thank you to this water, this moisture, which sustains you. Feel whatever gratitude comes up for you that you are "well irrigated," like a fertile field.

Lastly, feel the firmness of the seat that is supporting you, and of the floor beneath you, and of the earth beneath that. Sense the massive, silent solidity of the earth under us. And recognize that our bodies—our bones, flesh, sinews, and muscles—also share in the solidity of the earth.

We are in part solid too. And we are sustained and nourished by solid things—by the food we eat, by the clothes we wear, and by the houses that shelter us.

Breathe in. Feel the flesh and the ribs that move around the breath as you inhale and exhale. Take a moment to appreciate the solid matter that makes up your body. Try saying in your mind, *Thank you, my body. Thank you, my bones. Thank you, my flesh.*

Again, feel the flesh moving as you breathe. Be aware of your very own flesh as a gift to you, which allows you to have your life. Feel that flesh, sense it. Let yourself be grateful to it.

Thank you, body. Thank you, life.

CHAPTER FOUR

Unseen Powers

Along with more tangible, material forms of support, there are also immaterial, less tangible forms, unseen yet real for those who experience them. For some, this is what traditional religion is about: supplicating "imaginal" powers, invoking deities for guidance and support. For others, a similar territory of "archetypal" figures and entities may be encountered in "depth psychology," through practices such as dream work, shamanic ceremony, and plant medicine.

The psychologist Carl Jung believed we can all tap into less familiar registers of our minds, including what he called the "collective unconscious," which some scholars today call the "imaginal realm"—not a supernatural notion but rather parts of our consciousness to which we normally have little or no access, yet which can offer deep guidance and support if approached in certain ways. On this level, we can become more closely connected with all manner of entities, whether from nature, folklore, myth, dream, or religion, or from a shared archeology deeper in our consciousness. Whether by working with dreams, or engaging with figures from religion, or recognizing the great mystery of existing at all, we can come to feel the sway of greater powers active in this world.

We might think of this chapter as the upper story (or in some cases, the attic) of the inn of support, where we explore more exotic and unseen forms of connectedness. I offer personal accounts of some approaches I have experienced myself.

ANIMISTIC NATURE

Back in my early thirties, while wrestling with a bout of dysthymia, I attended a shamanic circle. A dozen of us would gather in the shaman's home on the edge of the genteel English city of Cheltenham, where we would lie on our backs in her living room while she gently pounded a drum in the background. Behind our closed eyes she would guide us through an imagined tunnel, from which we would emerge at the far end into another realm.

The first time I did this, I seemed to pop out into a brilliant green land, a hyperreal version of the English countryside I knew well, with its hills and meadows crisscrossed by thick summer hedgerows.

Almost at once, a deer came up to me. I greeted it as we had been instructed, by introducing myself and asking who the deer was. It immediately answered, "I am the deer you didn't kill."

I realized I had completely forgotten an incident from a year before. A US magazine had sent me to the Scottish Highlands on a writing assignment. In search of local experience, early one morning I had gone out deerstalking with a gillie, or guide. I had no intention of shooting a deer. I just wanted to experience walking the hills at dawn in search of large fauna.

After a couple of hours stalking the big, heather-covered slopes, which turned a deep blue, and then pink, in the early light, under a dawn sky striped with red striations, which seemed to give the sky a rib cage, like a vast human chest, suddenly we came over a steep slope, and there, 150 yards away, stood a doe, grazing with her head down.

We froze. The gillie silently motioned me to lean on his shoulder and take a shot. I set up the rifle and peered through the telescopic sights, inwardly berating myself for not having clarified right from the start that I didn't want to shoot any animals. I had assumed that the chances of actually coming across a deer within shooting range were low. But now that it had happened, I felt the full current of the exchange I was in—hiring this man to do what he did, take people hunting. And before I'd had time to gather my thoughts, here I was all of a sudden, leaning on this Highlander's shoulder, lining up a shot.

There the deer was—a perfect shot in the sights.

I paused, my heart pounding. Then I deliberately cleared my throat, with a light cough.

It was enough. The deer lifted her head, stood stock still, and then bounded away across the hill, dipping and leaping like a dolphin through the heather.

"Ach," said the gillie. "Nae bother." And we resumed our walk.

I had completely forgotten this incident. Yet no sooner had I traveled through the shamanic tunnel on my first "journey," than there that deer was, thanking me for not having killed her.

What does this mean? Not that an actual deer came and spoke to me a year later, of course. But perhaps the psyche has deeper registers than the ordinary mind knows, where connections and associations operate, in a manner similar to those forged in rapid eye movement (REM) sleep, when we dream, where different priorities apply.

A MODERN VIEW of this kind of experience can be found in depth psychology, where we go beyond personal psychology and venture into the realm of the collective unconscious. Sometimes through dream work, or "active imagination," or shamanic practice, we encounter archetypal entities who dwell in the unconscious and offer guidance.

In his research into Sufi tales, the French scholar Henri Corbin came up with the term *mundus imaginalis* to indicate a realm in which the Sufi folklore he studied took place. In his work *Mundus Imaginalis, or the Imaginary and the Imaginal*, he explains that this world is "imaginal" rather than "imaginary" to indicate that it is not merely "made up" in an individual's private imagination, but is rather a kind of shared and collective zone of the mind, immaterial but not personal, and contacted through a communal imaginative act, with laws and properties of its own. We can venture into it through the doorway of mythology, through shamanic trance, or through dreams, and find ourselves within reach of forces and entities that inhabit it. If we bow under the lintel at its threshold—often experienced as a tunnel—and surrender to the laws of this "land," and interact according to prescribed customs with the figures there, then we can meet with them in ways that offer transformative experiences for our personal psychology.

These archetypal figures, whether mythological or natural, acquire their power to reach us when we step through a membrane into the imaginal realm, where they can teach us about our responsibilities and potentials in the ordinary world.

(This is not to be confused with awakening. There are "awakened" people who never taste this realm, and "unawakened" people who do. When devotees of gurus, for example, relate tales of their teacher's powers of telepathy or teleportation, or when practitioners talk of visits from deceased masters or old masters reborn as contemporary figures, they are invoking this realm. Even though it's not a flesh-and-blood world, it isn't about awakening, because it's still a dualistic realm, in which a separate self in some way negotiates with other entities. And yet to ignore this kind of succor may be to disregard a treasury of support.)

Another shamanic journey led me to an old dolmen, a prehistoric monument, on a barren moor. In an underground chamber beneath the great stones, a figure in a hooded cloak sat with its back to me. According to the protocol I'd been taught, I approached and introduced myself. Full of trepidation, dreading what I'd see under the cloak, I watched it slowly turn round.

Sure enough, when I could finally see under its hood, it turned out to be the skeleton I had feared it might be. But I stuck to the script, introduced myself, and asked the bare, white skull who it was.

It replied, "I'm your skeleton."

After a shock of surprise, I felt a warm wave of gratitude welling up. For all these years, my own skeleton had been offering itself, unstintingly supporting me, yet never noticed by me. Its support was pivotal to my very existence, but I blithely overlooked it. Even when I had broken my arm as a youth, the injury had been nothing but an inconvenience, when it might instead have been an opportunity to recognize how much I depended on these very bones. Instead, I remained heedless of them.

To see my skeleton as an entity unto itself, dressed in a cloak, as not really "mine," but rather as offering itself to me, sobered me into recognizing how much I owed it. At once I felt the selfless love it apparently held for me. I also felt gratitude to the figures who had brought me to meet it—a crow and a horse—so I might recognize a support I had been blind to.

There was some kind of ethical guidance at work here. It struck me that although the delivery of these lessons might seem outlandish, the messages themselves were down to earth. Be grateful. Be kind. Recognize the relationships you're in. The obvious thing would be to call these "journeys" mere imagination. Yet the structures of these ceremonial encounters lent them a therapeutic potency a daydream seldom would have. These lessons, delivered with an other-

worldly authority that commands attention, can bring recognitions about our lives.

WORKING WITH SYMBOLS

What exactly is this otherworldly authority? Where does
it come from? And how does it operate? There are many
ways of approaching these questions, which range from
the philosophical and cultural, to the more religious and
supernatural.

One could think of the realm of the *mundus imaginalis*
as metaphorical. It is both personal and collective, and can
lead the soul through a journey of challenge and healing
that serves as a metaphor for events in the ordinary world.
Yet it can have powerful effects on the ordinary-world
psyche of a participant as well.

For the French anthropologist Claude Lévi-Strauss, who
spent his life studying Indigenous wisdom, the primary approach was cultural. As a young scholar he wrote a groundbreaking essay, "The Efficacy of Symbols," in which he
explored how it was that a symbolic journey could have a
potent, real-life "efficacy." The essay explains how among
the Cuna Indians of Panama, when a pregnant woman entered labor, a shaman would relate a myth to her as she lay
in a hammock. The shaman would recount the adventures
of a mythological hero fighting their way down to an underworld (shaman-style), interacting with various figures
as they went, retrieving something that had been lost, and

then coming all the way back to this world, to the very hut in which the expectant mother lay. By the time the shaman's story was over, the journey complete, the woman invariably would have given birth, according to the ethnography Lévi-Strauss consulted. The journey the shaman went on, the mythical ventures they passed through in the archetypal realm, somehow had an effect in this world. They would calm the mother in her labor, and help her find her way through the vast process she was undergoing as she gave birth. The structuralist theory that Lévi-Strauss went on to develop throughout the rest of his career was in some ways one long attempt to understand how it could be that a "mere" story could create such a tangible effect in another person, carrying them through a very real experience.

Many traditions that acknowledge non-dual awakening as a possibility also have more overtly religious practices, typically involving the supplication of diverse archetypal figures. Although this may be so, they don't confuse this kind of practice with awakening. The fully enlightened are free to practice on a more religious or archetypal level should they want, invoking the appropriate divinities as needed; but the traditions also see the open vastness of these figures too. The imaginal realms are, after all, as boundless as the material world is. Both realms, material and immaterial, are equally portals to a great openness—which is none other than the open embrace of original love itself.

For many, feeling closer to symbolic figures from the archetypal world, be they gods, divinities, animals, or other kinds of power entities, is a key gateway to opening up an experience of a greater love. As Zen puts it, sometimes the "original face" appears as a person, sometimes as a fox, a buffalo, a mountain, or a god. And all are equally the original love of the universe.

DREAM POWER

The archetypal realm has great subtlety and power. Another example of it at work, and of the support it offers from outside our own agency, can be found in working with dreams. In dream work, it is remarkable how the dreams anticipate our reactions and responses, how they show us again and again what we don't see—and need to see. They are a brilliant, ever-adapting zone of "shadow work." The "shadow" is whatever we don't see in our life or psychology. Again and again, our dreams can present new doorways of growth. They lead us through old trauma, and help us grow in resilience, clarity, and benevolence, encouraging us to let our lives unfold in new ways.

Whatever their function in our neurology, dreams offer themselves as a remarkable domain of love, growth, challenge, and healing. If we choose to let them, then they can lead us deeper into wisdom about our blocks, patterns, wounds, and potential healing. My Zen teacher Joan Rieck Roshi had done some intense dream work in her younger days, and she inspired me to try some. For several years, I trained in a form of dream work derived from the work of James Hillman, and reengineered by Marc Bregman, a maverick philosophy MA turned mail carrier turned psychologist, who developed his own powerful iteration of dream work. Rather than seeking to interpret the symbols in dreams, he had a unique way of using the dream figures and scenarios to cut to a person's deep emotional life, zeroing in on the healing invitations their dreams were bringing.

My dreams kept forcing me to engage with male figures I would rather have avoided. They came in menacing guise. A black limousine full of gangsters chased me through the streets of central London. Every time I thought I'd eluded them, racing down a side street or alley on foot, there they would be, at the end of it, waiting for me. When a dream finally came in which I stopped running away, they opened the car door and invited me in, and it turned out they were friendly, lighthearted guys, happy to see me. They were much less fearsome than I'd imagined. My fear had been born of a wider distrust of men.

I couldn't quite believe it or trust it, and the work I had to pursue was just that: to learn to trust the male figures who kept approaching me in dreams.

Gradually, in waking life, my distrust of men in general began to thaw also. In one dream, my own father rowed me across a Scottish loch to an island topped by a castle, where a banquet was being prepared. The laird of the castle sent me a wry smile across the hall, as I joined various workers in helping to set out tables and chairs. Then I found myself kneeling before the laird of the castle, in his high seat, and resting my head in his lap as he welcomed me.

The dreams were doing a kind of therapy on me. I was opening up to old wounds, especially around my father and his absence from my childhood, and being offered a safe context in which to grieve and release them. After working with that dream, I felt a kind of *penthos*—the sorrowful joy of repentance, according to the Orthodox Church—spreading through my life.

This wasn't just "personal" psychology. The figures I met in the dreams were "transpersonal"—that's to say, they seemed to emerge from a realm of consciousness beyond that of the everyday sense of self. Although the healing they sought to catalyze included biographical wounds and challenges, it also aimed at a broader, more spiritual homecoming. The child I sometimes became in the dreams ushered in a new childlike wonder, returning me to daily life in a fresh way, with a renewed sense of gratitude and humility. It also accelerated the Zen training I was undergoing at the time. An obscure distrust had held me back from fully committing to the yoke of training being proffered by my teachers. Now I released the last strands of an unacknowledged resistance. I learned to trust as never before.

As far as I can tell, this dream work was the closest I came to religion in the ordinary sense of the word. The dream figures took on an archetypal significance and power in my psyche. After that meeting with the laird in the loch, I felt like the prodigal son come home, as if to a universal parent, a deeply benevolent figure who somehow knew me inside and out, and who had emerged from a wound deep in my psyche. When I met them, my only right posture was one of humility.

My "grief-heart" opened, as some psychologists would put it. The sorrows of my childhood were subsumed in a broader, more ancient, and less personal wound. I lived in the *herath*—a Welsh word for the "old hurt," as grief counselor and author Stephen Jenkinson calls it in his book

Die Wise—an immemorial wound of humanity. I had a soul and at last it had been restored. It was healed in a tide of tears.

BEYOND OUR ORDINARY personal healing, which may lead to greater tenderness toward self and others, to more patience with ourselves and others, to healthier habits, to more acceptance of our lot, along with the motivation to change and grow and improve our world as best we can, there is the transpersonal, archetypal realm, of entities who are not merely imaginary—or who although imaginary are nevertheless imbued with an authority and a power that come from their communal recognition deep in the unconscious. To engage with them can be profoundly helpful.

Meditation teacher, shaman, and writer Spring Washam was "visited" in a long series of dreams, and occasionally in waking life too, by an archetypal or imaginal form of the great abolitionist and social activist Harriet Tubman. Tubman brought messages and teaching to Washam, inspiring courage and a new direction in her work. Washam's chronicling of these visits turned into her book, *The Spirit of Harriet Tubman,* a powerful account of an entity from the imaginal realm—in this case, the long deceased Harriet Tubman—bringing wisdom that inspired action in this world.

Although there are of course many material forms of support, these denizens of the unconscious offer another kind of support and guidance that can be critical and transformative, if we decide to trust it.

All of this can be seen as love in action. The archetypal

realm may challenge us, but its purpose is to help us heal and grow. In the course of the dream work I followed, sometimes it seemed as though every night I was taken into some ingenious virtual Hogwarts castle of the psyche, which could adapt and shape itself as needed to meet whatever particular wounds or negative patterns I might still be caught in, and instantly develop vivid simulations that could help me release them. The archetypal realm can open us up to help and support we've been unconsciously closed to, nudge us to feel whatever pain it reveals, and find the love hidden within it.

This is by no means always easy. The scariest dreams often seem like something we would most want to avoid and forget, shaking them off as quickly as we can when we awaken. Yet even in them, when approached with the support of an experienced dream worker, I began to find there would always be an invitation to witness and hear a message that in its essence was a call to healing—to surrendering a defense, beneath which would lie not only an old woundedness but also a love just waiting for me to recognize it.

How this comes about, how dreams if received in a certain way can match our psychic needs, our personal and communal growth, seems at times quite uncanny.

RELIGIOUS ARCHETYPES

What about religions? Clearly, religion is a primary field of support for many. Estimates vary, but around two thirds of the world's population subscribe to a religion. Religions offer community, the comfort of shared rites and practices, an intergenerational continuity of worldview, practical philosophy, moral guidance, and much more. All this, meditation can offer too.

Here we're exploring a full spectrum of spiritual experience without consulting with religion specifically. The kind of examination of conscious experience that meditation offers can lead to thoroughly freeing and supportive discoveries about the nature of our reality. Even the term "original love," which will come increasingly to the fore as we proceed, connotes an all-pervasive love that may be intrinsic to consciousness itself, resting in the very nature of experience. If seen clearly, it implies no need for any belief in the supernatural. Although the deeper contemplative paths of religions may well lead to something like this, for now we'll keep our gaze on the more supplicatory practices of religion, and the kinds of immaterial support that they invoke.

Surely, the many archetypal figures of religion can also meet their adherents with an accuracy of supportive understanding that can seem astonishing. People of different religious backgrounds often speak of how "personal" a deity can feel, how thoroughly this deity knows them, and how the deity seems to know the help they need even before they do.

The great Hindu mystic Mirabai said this in the sixteenth century:

Friends, let those whose Beloved is absent write letters—
Mine dwells in the heart, and neither enters nor leaves.

(TRANSLATION BY JANE HIRSHFIELD)

Religions clearly have archetypal figures—entities who are said to inhabit an immaterial world, and come forth into intimate consciousness to guide and support their followers. That realm may be thought of as a supernatural place, a "heaven," where holy beings dwell, for example, but can also be construed as finding its home within a zone of the human unconscious that is both personal and transpersonal.

The word *Buddha*, for example, applies both to a historical figure who taught in northern India twenty-four hundred years ago, and also, especially in traditional Asian contexts, to a figure who dwells in an intermediate *imaginal* realm, real to its devotees but not flesh and blood, ready to be invoked as an agent of succor at any time or place. In Christianity, there is not only Christ but also Mary, and many saints besides, who occupy a zone equivalent to the *mundus imaginalis*. The very notion of a "heaven," where the saints, angels, and other divinities dwell, might be another term for the imaginal zone of consciousness.

Once in Frankfurt, on my way south to the Black Forest for a Zen retreat, while walking off a long flight beside the River Main, I happened upon the Ikonenmuseum Frankfurt. The exhibit inside was of old Russian icons, religious paintings venerated as holy artifacts. Some of the pictures were full of theological symbolism that went over my head, but I spotted a little stone staircase in a corner of the museum's old stone hall and thought, *That looks interesting*. Upstairs, I happened upon something that made me glad I had come.

In a glass case along one wall, three simple portraits formed a triptych of three figures side by side: Mary, the Mother of God; Jesus; and John the Baptist. Each stared downward and to one side, with a gaze full of care, of suffering and forbearance, and of forgiveness—and also a certain sternness, as if admonishing the viewer, *Don't mess around; get on with the real task. Spread the love. Help.*

To my mind, these were figures staring clean out of the archetypal realm—appearing out of scripture, dream, myth, the unconscious, the unknown, wherever it might be—come to help our soul, our deeper sense of self, to nudge us along, to encourage, spur, and fortify us. They were intermediaries, a delegation from that realm, meeting us halfway. We could either supplicate or worship them, and leave it at that, or else surrender to their call, their encouragement, and let them inhabit us as a hand occupies a glove, putting our lives at their disposal, so they could use us as they willed.

One of the most moving portraits in literature of a religious denizen of this liminal zone is Fyodor Dostoevsky's Father Zosima in *The Brothers Karamazov*. Father Zosima is a humble, simple, loving man, a *starets*, an "elder," a church figure who took on the role of personal guidance for his followers, and operated partly outside the conventional hierarchies of the Orthodox Church. (Zosima is likely modeled on Saint Seraphim of Sarov, a real-life *starets* who lived from 1754 to 1833.)

When Zosima has just died, his devoted follower Alyosha Karamazov is heartbroken. While Scriptures are being read over the laid-out corpse of Zosima during an all-night vigil, Alyosha falls into a fitful sleep, in which he has a vision of Zosima sitting up in his coffin and joining the scene of the Bible story that, as it happens, is being read out loud by a monk at the same time—the story of the wedding at Cana,

in which Jesus turns water into wine. The wedding and
the deceased but now "risen" Zosima become intermin-
gled in Alyosha's mind. He encounters his beloved elder
alive and well, and he is inviting Alyosha to join the wedding feast too.

> *"Yes, my dear, I am called, too, called and bidden,"*
> *[Alyosha] heard a soft voice saying over him. . . . "You*
> *come and join us too."*
>
> *It was his voice, the voice of Father Zosima. And it*
> *must be he, since he called him!*
>
> *The elder raised Alyosha by the hand and he rose*
> *from his knees.*
>
> *"We are rejoicing," the thin, little old man went on.*
> *"We are drinking the new wine, the wine of new, great*
> *gladness. . . ."*
>
> *Something glowed in Alyosha's heart, something*
> *filled it till it ached, tears of rapture rose from his*
> *soul. . . . He stretched out his hands, uttered a cry and*
> *waked up.*

After Alyosha awakens from this dream or vision, he stum-
bles outside into the night, half broken with mourning, half
rapturous, and falls to the ground in a profound epiphany.

> *The vault of heaven, full of soft, shining stars, stretched*
> *vast and fathomless above him. The Milky Way ran*
> *in two pale streams from the zenith to the horizon. The*
> *fresh, motionless, still night enfolded the earth. . . .*
> *Alyosha stood, gazed, and suddenly threw himself*

down on the earth. . . . He kissed it weeping, sobbing
and watering it with his tears, and vowed passionately
to love it, to love it forever and ever. . . .
And never, never, all his life long, could Alyosha
forget that moment.
"Someone visited my soul in that hour," he used to
say afterwards, with implicit faith in his words.

(TRANSLATION BY CONSTANCE GARNETT)

Albeit an example from a work of fiction, this demonstrates beautifully how archetypal figures can function in spiritual growth. The deceased Zosima, appearing as an archetypal figure in Alyosha's dream, inspires him toward a profound change of heart.

GREAT MOTHER

Sometimes we can taste shivers of the presence of other powers in our waking life too. Once I took some ashes of a deceased friend to Big Sur, where I was teaching a course, and in between classes one lunchtime, I climbed down over boulders to the ocean, and scattered the ashes into the surging waters of the Pacific.

A little later on, I was standing on the cliffs up above, gazing over the ocean, when out of the blue I felt something like a ripple move through the world, almost like an earthquake. It trembled through my body too and cracked my heart open to a sudden sense of a love beyond place and time. It was as if my old friend had become one with some kind of universal love, and warped my sense of the world, and swept in to let me know that she was well. All was well.

I couldn't help but feel that some "great mother" had touched me. Even though I didn't have a belief system for comprehending this kind of experience, it moved me and stayed with me as a source of sustenance. Was this "great mother," as she showed herself then, operating in the archetypal channel? However we might understand or explain a subjective experience such as this, for many people, religion is *the* zone above all, where they find their deepest support. In religion, followers can find community, shared rites and practices, and life guidance of many kinds, which can help them live with more peace, fortitude, and kindness, even in the face of grievous losses. And there is also the *mundus imaginalis* in which religious adherents can meet their deities and divinities face-to-face.

But there is more too. Some schools of Buddhism teach that all things are born from a great womb, *Prajna Paramita*, which means "primordial wisdom." This great wisdom is "mother of all Buddhas"—or simply, mother of all.

This earth, the goddess Gaia for the ancient Greeks, Pachamama for the Quechuas, and "great mother" in many Indigenous traditions, source and womb of all creation—what if we can meet "great mother" in a visceral, experiential way, not just conceptually, and in doing so be touched at the most intimate level of our being, where we find we are part of a larger belonging, by virtue of being part of her? Great mother's love touches us exactly as another face of "original love," a wider love than we could ever earn or deserve, an unconditional love woven through the earth and all its creatures, including us.

GOD AS ALL

Long ago I was fortunate enough to join a group visiting Mount Athos, a peninsula in northern Greece dedicated to the monastic life of the Orthodox Church.

Our little party was led by a devout icon painter, Aidan Hart, at that time a novice monk, who was a beautiful man to be around. For years his practice had been the continuous recitation of the Jesus Prayer, beloved of Russian Orthodoxy, and some combination of this practice and his general faith had made him radiant, as if he brought a clear, refreshing daylight into any room he was in. His own primary spiritual guide was an abbot in one of the monasteries on Athos, someone he revered as his spiritual father, and he was delighted when it turned out that we would all be granted an audience with this august figure.

The old abbot had a long silver beard, and there was a stillness about him, a deep quiet. Apart from his long hair and beard, and the gold ornaments that adorned his black robes, he reminded me of some Zen masters I had met— the dark, shining clarity of his eyes and his calm, capacious presence.

We met in a large room overlooking the Aegean Sea. The monastery had been built into a cliff some fourteen hundred years earlier in its oldest parts. This ancient, raftered room had been resting here, high above the sea, filled with holy practice ever since. It was a lovely place, not austere, because although plain, it shone with the gold frames of icons on the walls, and the air was rich with candle wax and incense.

The abbot spoke to us in his excellent, careful French. At one point our guide, Aidan, encouraged me to share something about Zen and meditation, hoping to get a conversation going about parallel paths of spiritual cultivation. After all, here were two traditions—Orthodox monasticism and Zen—that believed in training the human mind in order to discover something like a loving reality at its core.

Awed by the man's presence, I found myself tongue-tied, able to offer only a few garbled, meager sentences about Zen.

The abbot listened and paused. Then he said that Zen was too foreign. It was like a long, narrow bridge—when a shock came, the bridge would fall.

I was quite young in practice then, and felt both shy and offended. I kept quiet and didn't tell him what I thought, which was that far from being a long bridge, Zen was the shortest distance to my own heart. There was no more direct shortcut to human nature than Zen. For me, it had none of the elaborate bridgework of Christianity, with its fantastical rites and stories. Zen by contrast simply brought us back to who we were, as we were, again and again, warts and all.

I felt rattled and chagrined by the abbot's riposte, in a particular way that perhaps only a young person distrustful of authority can be. Yet paradoxically, in the way of Zen, throughout the next year it was the abbot's rebuttal that made me determined to rededicate myself to my then-flagging Zen training, and drove me to find my first true

Zen teacher. And that came about because of what he talked about next.

Under our guide's prompting, he told us about a time some decades back when he had been coming home to Athos on the local ferry. It was the end of the afternoon, and the late light before sunset was turning the mountain of Athos, on which the monastery stands, into a glowing eminence. He gazed at it from the rail of the boat, fascinated, and before his eyes it dissolved into golden light, like a loaf of bread crumbling into dust. At the same time, everything else crumbled too, and became the same light. That was when he saw the face of God, he said. It was as if all this world had been the very bread of God, and broke apart to reveal the "Godhead" itself.

From then on, he hadn't doubted that God is in all things. It was only our fallen nature that prevented our seeing this. Therefore we trained, in order to recognize that face everywhere.

I was astonished to hear this. Remove the name God, and it sounded like Zen awakening. His story encouraged me. If these Orthodox monks could discover something so similar, who cared what we called it? God, Emptiness, Buddha Nature—what did it really matter? In all cases, it allowed us to see what we and this world really are—an original nature without space or time, and intrinsically loving. Against the reality of that, who cared what name it was given? Any name was chaff in the wind.

But there was more. It wasn't just about names. There was something way better going on: across cultures and epochs, people had been stumbling upon this great discovery of our deepest nature. It was wonderful that a devout Orthodox patriarch could find the marvel of unitary emptiness pervading all things—the dissolution of the fabric of our world, a dissolution that implicates us entirely, and shows us our inseparability from the whole experience we call "the world." It was wonderful that this dimension of our reality had been showing itself in India, China, Japan, America, the Rhineland, East Anglia, Castile—and Greece, over the centuries and millennia.

What a gift that we humans could make this discovery. That was way more important than the names we may have applied to it.

Since then, I have gotten to know a number of Christian contemplatives, for whom that very kind of experience is the heart of what they consider God to be. Indeed, perhaps we ought to divide God belief into at least two forms. As Yuval Harari puts it, there is God as "rule-maker in the sky" and God as "mystery of being."

For a thoroughly religious person like this abbot, the heart of his experience was seeing God. If others can come to see and experience the world in similar ways, then does that mean they are seeing God too? Or does it mean that the abbot was in fact "awakening" to the godless "original nature" that Buddhism speaks of? Are they indeed one and the same? The abbot might or might not think so. But how could we ever know?

We will explore this further in the section on awakening. For now, maybe it is better not to seek answers too soon but simply to rest in the *magnum mysterium* itself.

Practice Tip

Get into a comfortable position. Relax. Listen to the sounds around you. Hit the pause button on your day.

Read through this brief exercise. Then close your eyes and do what it suggests in any way that feels right for you.

Imagine that right now the presence of something great, and peaceful, is with you. Imagine that you can sense a great peace all around you. Imagine that just beneath, just behind, everything you are experiencing, there is a vast silence, which has a kind of immaculate, gentle power. Imagine this power to be an immensely peaceful force that is holding all your experience of this moment, holding everything around you, the whole "scene" in which you find yourself—a room or a car or a garden or a park or some kind of building.

Let yourself be held by this greater, unseen presence. Feel its goodwill toward you. Feel something almost like a mysterious love holding you in this moment—a love you might never fully understand or know, but can sense somehow as a deep built-in ingredient of this world.

Thank you for trying this. Feel free to come back to this little exercise anytime.

RELIGION AND AWAKENING

It has been said that the deep spiritual narrative of the West is that we are flawed, erring creatures, whose hope lies only in redemption—in being "redeemed" back to wholeness by an outside power. By contrast, the deep narrative of the East is that we are intrinsically whole and pure already. The problem is that debris and defilements have built up over that original perfection, obscuring it. Our task is "purification"—to chip and scrub away at the encrustations until the luminous jewel at the core once more shines through, reorienting our lives toward loving service.

Is it possible that these two views could be reconciled? That yes, we may somehow be originally perfect, and yes, our hearts are filled with distortions and delusions that must be cleared away, but at the same time, that original perfection within us is also a dynamic force, rather than merely inert, and is therefore something like a redemptive power too? Is it possible to be nontheistic and yet experience a power of love at work in things, which it is our task to uncover and then learn to live by? Could we come to experience things in such a way yet remain atheist? Or could we reach some intrinsic spiritual condition in which it no longer makes sense to distinguish between theism and atheism? Could it be that to "wake up," to find the "non-dual reality" this book leads to, is one way to obliterate that distinction? Could there be some kind of spirituality that lies behind our religions and philosophies, which even now is gaining credence from some of the latest understandings of the mind and consciousness emerging from new science? Could we be on the verge of understanding human wisdom in clearer ways than ever before?

One point we can offer about religion today is this: sometime in the early first millennium BCE, some twenty-seven hundred years ago, in both Asia and the Greek world, human cosmological thought began to move away from being zoo-morphic or anthropomorphic and toward the abstract. That is to say, most cosmology and philosophy back then was mythological. It consisted of animallike and humanlike deities and powers, who made and ruled the world. But around the seventh or eighth century BCE, in both Asia and the Eastern Mediterranean, people started to think of the universe and our human place in it in ways that didn't depend on mythol-ogy, or figures from religion. Instead, they started to think nonmythologically, abstractly, without extraneous elements being brought in. By the sixth and seventh centuries BCE, in both the Upanishads and in Greek pre-Socratic thought, it had become possible to think about the nature of the cosmos without reference to supernal beings from mythology.

Today, global spirituality is making an analogous step—away from "deities" and "divinities," toward the experiential reality of emptiness, unity, and boundlessness, as a kind of substrate to our lives. This is perhaps what the more mystical reaches of religion were in any case disguised expressions of, in the first place. It has become easier today than ever before to discuss deep spiritual experience without religious or theo-logical talk necessarily coopting the discourse.

That's all on one side of the picture, as spirituality moves away from Iron Age dogmas. Meanwhile, on another side, are there in fact things to be cherished in the old beliefs, even for humanists?

From the perspective of some Buddhist sutras, there is and can be no "other" reality than this moment as it is. Thus belief in anything like a "higher power" is itself just another phenomenon, in this case a thought or set of thoughts, with accompanying affective responses, arising in a mind here and now. But is it possible to sense a benevolent backdrop to life, even without explicit theism? Might some forms of theism in fact be renderings of a benevolence that is intrinsic to life anyway, regardless of belief? Is there a rational place for a religious-like surrender in life, for example, a trusting to powers beyond ourselves, without an explicit belief in gods?

Stoicism has been declaring for more than two thousand years that there is. There is only so much we can control. In fact, in the outward circumstances of our life, we can't reliably control all that much. Those we love will fall ill or die, or may make harmful choices of their own. Our projects may thrive and flourish for a time or may, through no fault of our own, decline and collapse.

On the other hand, there is much we can control of our inner life. We can develop and grow our character, our capacity to be steady in the face of setbacks and not be unduly exhilarated by successes. One piece of that inner turnaround and maturing is a deeper trust in ourselves, and in what life throws at us.

More than that, for a meditator, we can learn to trust more thoroughly in the present moment. In the sheer fact that this multifarious, infinitely various experience called "now" is arising at all. In the fact that the universe is producing the experience of this very moment, as you read these lines, including your awareness of this moment, and even your awareness that you are aware of it. The universe is blooming not just as the stars and galaxies but also as the trillion life-forms of this planet—including as your very own experience, and all our experiences, arising in consciousness right here and now.

Somehow, to experientially recognize the gift that this moment is, with all our awareness of it, requires a kind of trust in it. It needs to be let in, to be received, as a kind of support, even as a form of love.

If life is challenging, then it will change. If it's richly rewarding, then it will change. In either case, there is the raw wonder of its arising at all. That it is, and that we are part of it, and are capable not merely of participating in it but of being *aware* of it—all this is a kind of infinite generosity. An infinite love.

What is the source of that generosity? Presumably, it traces back to the big bang: without that, none of this.

Why is all this arising and being experienced by us? Perhaps we'll know someday. Until then, can we receive it as a gift, a sourceless generosity, an act of love even?

That's the flavor I hope the term "original love" will come to convey more vividly as we proceed.

HOLY TRIAD

Imagine if there were three states that could reliably bring you back to a sense of love, love for life, for yourself, for your close companions, and for this world. Actually, there is a kind of "holy triad" of affective states that can do this.

Anytime we taste gratitude, notice how it opens up a warmth in the heart that is automatically quite happy. To sense a grateful joy naturally kindles love. We can't help but feel it—love toward this existence and those we share it with.

If gratitude isn't accessible, then pivot and see if it's possible to feel a certain kind of humility. Recognize how all that you have in life may, in some areas, be a result of your own efforts, but so much more exists by virtue of forces far outside your control. Your life depends on a trillion contingencies. Yet it's happening. And not just through your own efforts.

Humility is a natural response. It's a close cousin of gratitude; it too connects us to an underground mainline to love. The more we recognize our smallness, the more we take a step back and silently admire this world and all it contains, the more we surrender ourselves and yield in quiet submission, the more the largeness of the world touches our hearts.

It may not be popular, but humility is an attitude that makes total sense. The fact that we get to experience anything at all is a wonder. When we recognize this it inspires humility, and humility breeds awe. Which once again reconnects us to a humble kind of love, one that opens us up to this very moment with fresh tenderness.

Then there's compassion—love in action. A loving act can bring forth the love. Just think of something, however small, you can do for someone else. Offer them a cup of coffee. Simply say hi. Ask how they're doing. Next time you're in a store, look the clerk in the eye and wish them well.

Every granule of love is a part of original love. Any grain of love makes life worthwhile.

GOD'S GARDEN

We humans have been ingenious in learning to recognize and find many kinds of support—many ways in which we can open up our lives and well-being to forces beyond our control, on which we depend. To remember them when we take on the self-developing practice of meditation is salutary. Yes, we can indeed help ourselves through practice. But its capacity to aid us is ramped up vastly the more we let ourselves open to different kinds of support and guidance that are often right here, just waiting to be noticed.

On one of my first writing assignments, soon after I left college, I found myself hitchhiking across the Algerian Sahara, and wound up in the oasis town of In Salah. It was on the main route south, in the heart of the desert, and we were detained there for a few days, waiting for a ride out. Some Egyptian doctors working in the town's hospital kindly put us up.

They were having a hard time. The medical contracts they had been given by the Algerian authorities offered good salaries. But only after they left their home country of Egypt, and arrived in In Salah, had they been informed that the salaries would be paid in Algerian dinars, a severely restricted currency that could not be converted into foreign money. They had been hoping to take home replenished coffers to their families at the end of their two-year stints, and it turned out that their salaries would be all but worthless.

Of the handful of these doctors, some were contemplating breaking the contracts and some seemed sunk in despondency. But one man shone. Each evening he changed into white robes, said his prayers, and wandered outside for a while. Then he came back to drink mint tea and join in the supper.

He smiled quietly and his skin seemed to glow. Not just his skin—his whole being had a sheen. It emerged that he was a devout man, and he regarded his time in the desert as a precious opportunity to be close to God. The desert was God's "private garden," he said, and it was a singular privilege to be here.

For him, this notion wasn't just a story—it was a lived experience. It gave him a calm and grace, a palpable joy that was infectious. I noticed that I felt good whenever he engaged me in conversation, and we had some beautiful evenings together, talking late into the night under the desert stars. Even though his belief in Allah was strong, it did not require him to make others believe too. He was truly at peace. Not once did he try to recruit me to his faith. But I could feel the vastly wider context in which he lived, the greater love that held him.

Somehow, just by being around him, I could almost feel as if I were touching the hem of the wondrous garment that cloaked his life, which he knew would keep him safe.

AND ONCE AGAIN our journey goes on, calling us deeper into the mountains, as we follow the trail of practice toward the shelter of our next inn.

GUIDED MEDITATION

Quiet Rest

Take a seat. As you breathe, allow your exhalations to become longer and slower. Don't rush. Give your breathing time. In a little while, after a few breaths, you will find it will become easy to let the exhalations slow down.

Let the out breaths become as if they have a little parachute attached to them, which slows down their lengthening descent.

Feel the calm, the quiet, which starts to show itself as we slow down. As we pause. As we allow ourselves a little space in our day.

Space just to be. To relax. To rest. To perhaps taste a little trust in the fact that we are alive here and now. Good.

Now listen closely. Open up your attention to the soundscape around you. As you listen in, can you notice that there is a kind of quiet, a calm, which shows itself when we listen? It doesn't even need to be a quiet place; wherever we are will do. When we let ourselves listen carefully, and allow sounds to show themselves more clearly—after a while a calm quiet simply starts to show itself.

See if you can sense this quiet. Let it descend on you like a soft shawl. Let it enwrap you and keep you safe. Let it furl itself around you.

Enjoy the sense of being safe. You are being given permission to rest. To simply be. Imagine that a wide, loving presence is here to help you, to grant you the rest and restoration that are exactly what you need.

Whatever in you needs to heal right now, this wide presence is bringing exactly the spaciousness and the restfulness you need for that healing to happen.

Rest and be still for as long as feels right, basking in the presence of a greater, silent power that is here to help you.

When you are ready, let yourself come out of this meditation. Give yourself a moment. Then thank yourself for being open to this, and for taking the time to try it. And continue with your day.

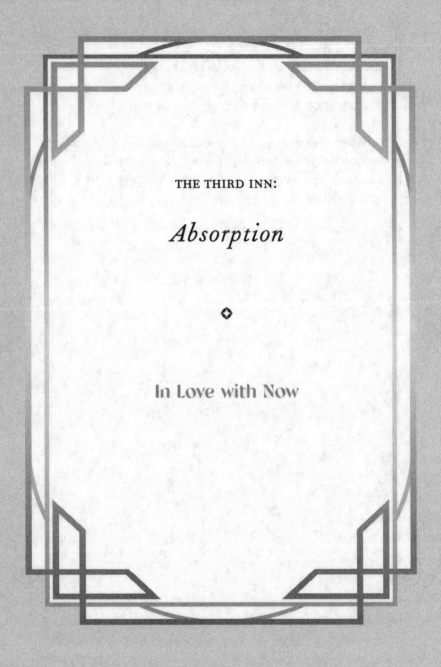

THE THIRD INN:

Absorption

◆

In Love with Now

CHAPTER FIVE

Flow

Welcome to our third inn. Here we explore how getting more settled in meditation can open up delightful, fulfilling states of mind, commonly known as *absorption*, or *samadhi*. These are akin to flow states, which can arise when we are engrossed in activities of many kinds. There is a special joy that can arise when we enter them in meditation, because we are then engaged in nothing but the wonder of our own being. It is here, as we become more absorbed in the here and now, that the distinction between ourselves and the world around us starts to blur and dissolve.

Even as novice meditators, we may suddenly find ourselves resting in a deep, wide sense of peace, as if a switch had flipped and meditation became easy and beautiful. This is what "absorption" can feel like.

We may not know what has happened or why. We might feel destabilized, or else become eager to get back to this blessed state of mind once it passes. One of the great "fruits of practice," as Zen calls them, is gaining access to deeper states of absorption and concentration in meditation, as well as increasingly in daily life. To call out and name these states, and to parse out ways in which they can be more deliberately developed, can be a great help.

BEAUTY IN A SICKROOM

In any moment, we can find what we need. All it takes is letting go—releasing our hold on our understanding of things. Letting go of what we think we know. Then we can become absorbed in what *is*.

I'm sick in bed. Outside the window, there's the dove-gray overcast sky. And the smoke-blue mountains in the distance. And the bushy trees stirring in a cool evening wind. In fact, it looks like there could be rain out there at any minute. And in this room the twilight is thickening.

All this—if I just forget the idea that I know what it is, then I can get much closer to it, and more awed by it. By *not* knowing it, I know it in a new way, a way that is hard to state—except to say that it is full of awe.

Even as I write these words, I see that outside the window, a shaft of late sun must have slipped under the cloud cover. Not rain, after all. The trees are suddenly brilliant in their stirring, like sunlight illuminating the movement of wind on the surface of a lake, making it glitter. So here, with the shimmering leaves, the crowns of the trees become a glittering dazzle, and their green turns wet and shiny, even though there is no hint of rain.

It was beautiful before the sun broke through, and it's beautiful now that it has.

We were made, we have evolved, to find this world beautiful. What is the evolutionary advantage of beauty? Beauty is an experience. It is a kind of love to find something beautiful. But what purpose does it serve, that there be creatures who experience beauty? Yes, if we find one another beautiful, then we might be more likely to reproduce. But mountains, trees, rivers, distant islands, sunsets, and dawns—is their beauty, as we see it, simply a misplaced target of our reproductively oriented appreciation of human beauty? (After all, some scholars even regard the landscape poetry of nineteenth-century England as sublimated eroticism.)

But what if beauty is an affective state without purpose? True appreciation of beauty doesn't drive us to do anything but feel it. Our hearts open. They recognize the wonder and generosity of being granted the experience of beauty. It makes us love the world, and life, and what we see or hear or sense.

When beauty is awake in us, even a simple breath can be a thing of astonishing loveliness.

The third inn of practice, which we are now setting foot in, is about becoming more adept at entering and merging with the moment as it is. Becoming part of it, with less separation from it. Merging with the here and now. A sense of beauty is often the fruit of such immersion. And conversely, feeling touched by beauty can be a gateway *to* this absorption.

It's as if once the human heart opens, the mind that feels itself to be separate becomes a little less dominant. And the moment opens itself a little and starts to absorb us.

This too is a kind of love. It's more like the love that draws two lovers into union. Perhaps it's what it's like to actually fall in love with this world. Perhaps we need the prior preparation—of learning to open to this world in different ways, as we start to acknowledge the infinite support it has been offering us—to love it as it deserves. The archetypal support, the readiness to be humble and to recognize our multiple dependences—these help to soften our hearts for the kind of heartbreaking beauty and the heartrending pain this world encompasses. Maybe we are being changed in ways we know, along with ways we will never know. And somehow our practice path "knows" what it needs to do with us, how it needs to open us and strengthen our capacity for love, long before we do. Beauty, pain, heartbreak, and tender support—as well as frustration, resistance, and disappointment—all these are needed in order that this path of growth function fully.

If our first inn was about the self—about managing, calming, and loving the self through practice—and the second inn was about the soul—about opening up to various kinds of support that nourish and sustain our deeper, broader sense of who we are—then this third inn is about unification, where our experience becomes whole, we find an ever-deeper belonging in the world, and we start to get inklings of not being separate from it.

It can indeed be like falling in love with another person. In romantic love, there are times when we feel fused with the other, as if a link has arisen that bypasses our ordinary sense of separateness. It's conditional on various factors—our desire to be close to one another, the mutual attraction, the circumstances of our lives, and so on—but the sense of connection we find feels as if it has bypassed ordinary conditionality. And in some ways, it has.

When something akin to this happens in practice, the difference is that it's even less conditional. It doesn't rest on the willingness of someone else to participate in the process. It rests only on our deepening practice. It's between us and the world, in a way that may seem to fulfill earlier intimations of it. It can feel as if this love affair of self and world has been around a long time, biding its time to come forth and occupy a more central position in our life.

To fall in love with the moment at hand is a blessed thing. Once it has happened, it can keep happening. It is pretty much the same as falling in love with life. The strangest thing here is the sense that the moment has been just waiting for us to notice it. *What took you so long?* it seems to ask. *I've been here waiting for you all this time. . . .*

SAMADHI

In this third inn on our trail, we explore absorption, or concentration. Both these words are attempts to translate the Sanskrit term *samadhi*.

Samadhi is a gold standard of meditation. Across traditions, it connotes deeply fulfilling states of mind, in which we become so absorbed in practice that we feel completely at peace, without need for anything more or need for anything to be in the smallest way different.

In this third inn we explore what samadhi is, and how it

relates to other, more familiar, states of mind, such as "flow" states, in which we taste effortless absorption in an activity. Samadhi also touches on beauty. This isn't something commonly examined in practice, but because samadhi states feel exceedingly beautiful, we may speculate that the experience of beauty is an affiliate of them.

After all, to be absorbed is to allow your experience to touch you more deeply. It is to open a channel of connection between something in your immediate awareness and yourself, such that "me" and that object, of whatever kind, become more intimate, to the point of being absorbed, or fused, in one another.

Something like this happens when the beauty of this world touches you. Because beauty is a part of meditative experience, and because beauty takes you out of yourself, I include it here as part of the world of absorption. And isn't this a description of love too? Isn't beauty a face of love?

FROM THIS POINT on in our journey, things become more rarefied and harder to tease apart. Some traditions consider some of the experiences we explore in this third inn to be "awakened," while others do not. There are different dimensions of awakening, for sure, and different depths too.

In one formulation of the path of meditation from early Buddhism, samadhi is a pivotal "factor of awakening." That's because it is a steady, abiding awareness, which we can either simply rest *in*, without directing it to any object, or else rest *on* a given object. In the latter case, the gaze is not merely fulfilling in itself but can become a tool, a laser-like lens that allows us to start "seeing through" our experience.

But samadhi is not merely a gaze. It's a "gathering to-gether" of our experience into "one-pointedness." We be-come "unified." The many streams that pull away from and detract from our focus and centeredness are now turned off, their sluices closed, their channels dammed. We become whole, complete, in and of ourselves.

In this state of samadhi, a practitioner may be able to sit in utter peace for extended periods of time. A Zen friend told me about her time in a Japanese monastery as a young woman, where every morning the monks sat in silence from 4:00 a.m. to 6:30 a.m. without moving at all. Accustomed as she was to meditation periods being interspersed with bouts of walking meditation, she found it desperately difficult to be still for so long. Then one morning she got to the Zendo to find that her sitting place had been moved, such that from her new spot she had a clear line of sight across the dark hall to where the abbot sat. Seeing the calm figure of the master there in the dawn twilight, exuding utter ease in her sitting, almost as if she were floating in the morning twilight, com-pletely at rest for those two and a half hours, seemingly light as a feather yet solid as a mountain, inspired my friend to find her own way to a deeper absorption within herself.

LAST GAS STATION

Some think of samadhi as the last step before the self-abandonment of awakening. It's like the last gas station before the freeway. It's the launch zone. This is where we wait, where we still get to be who we think we are. The fruit is still clinging to the old tree, but the juice within is sweetening and ripening, and one day, the fruit will be so full, so saturated, so mature, so ready, that it will drop from the branch by itself.

There are many images of transformation, of metamorphosis, in practice. The caterpillar stops moving, it becomes still, and its skin hardens into the chrysalis. It doesn't know what it is waiting for, what must happen to it, but it is compelled to be still. So at some point we have eaten enough of the fruits, the nourishments and pains of life, and are ready to be still. And we come to meditation, where our embodied stillness can produce further transformation.

What exactly that stillness may produce we don't know. We have inklings, but whatever they represent, however inspiring, they are likely to be somewhat wrong. It can't be like anything we imagine. Because we can only imagine with the "old" mind, not with the one to come.

In an old Chinese legend sometimes referenced in Zen, carp are driven to swim up a river. They finally reach a pool at the foot of an enormously high waterfall, consisting of a series of three vertiginous falls. These are the final barriers that the fish must swim up. Few manage it. But the ones that do, when they flip over the lip of the final cataract, turn into dragons, free to roam the sky.

Samadhi is something like the final pool before the last waterfall. It's like a waiting zone before the vast freedom of awakening. It is the place where we come to a profound inner stillness. Something can transform here. Can release. Can unbind. It's like that final stage of life in Hindu thought, in which a person relinquishes profession, family, and their role as a mentor, and goes into the forest to prepare to meet their maker. They settle under a tree and are still. The soul knows something can happen—that's all it knows. And the mind by now has been humbled by life, by sorrows, losses, and disappointments, and perhaps grown tired of its satisfactions too, and is less domineering. It has enough experience now to trust the soul. It agrees, it complies. We sit still. Gradually, in fits and starts, we lose ourselves in samadhi. Our leaks are stopped, our sluice gates closed, the current of the river of our being becomes whole, silent, and strong. We are on the ultimate journey. That's samadhi.

RECAP OF THE PATH SO FAR

Meditation rarely proceeds in a tidy way in practice. Only in retrospect does the road map we've been following appear clear. But with the ideal map, as we move from *sati* toward samadhi, from mindfulness into deeper unification of mind, we find ourselves in a fruitful place that can bring a lot of joy and healing. After broadening the basis of our practice through the exploration of support (in the second inn), in this third inn we now pick up the thread of mindfulness once again.

Here are a few examples of how practice might look when we're in the fertile zone where awareness of the here and now is developing from *sati* to samadhi, from noting and allowing, to becoming more absorbed and dissolved in the moment.

As we tend to and defuse the hindrances that we examined in the first inn, we are beginning to see the evolution of mindfulness into more beautiful experiences, which ripen in our meditation. We have become more adept at grounding ourselves in the here and now. If emotions come up, then we disentangle the threads of inner experience more deftly. Thoughts and feelings can be overwhelming when they come braided together, and especially when they "proliferate," as some sutras put it, weaving themselves into a virtual version of experience. Now it's easier to bring attention to body sensation, to contractions in the torso, and to sight and sound and breath, in order to return to the here and now, rather than being lost in stories or emotions.

To do this requires a lowering of defenses, a small but significant opening of the heart. This too we have learned to do more intuitively. Whereas previously we often would "close up" defensively when in emotional difficulty, in a way that we would fail to catch or notice, preferring to distract ourselves with long trains of thought rather than directly feel the discomfort in our body, now it is becoming second nature to turn kindly within and take a reading of the condition of our inner chest and midriff. Perhaps emotions used to scare us but do so less now. We're more adept at welcoming and soothing them.

We recognize now how commonly the thoughts we used to hope would distract us instead only exacerbated unwholesome mind states. We see now how if we let that go on for too long, then sometimes we came to dislike or even dread meditation. And as a response to that state of affairs, we might have thrown ourselves more determinedly into narrow-focus practice, striving to latch onto the breath, for example, desperately clinging to it as to a lifeline. Occasionally, this worked, but more often it just made things worse, as we slid off the breath again and again, and got frustrated.

We have been learning that to overlook emotional states may not work so well. Better to open ourselves to them, to feel them in the body. That way, the behaviors and conditions in our wider lives that may actually be causing distress in the first place are more likely to show themselves too. Our sitting may have revealed that some psychotherapy was in order. We find it easier to accept sitting as a barometer, as well as a healing agent, which can indicate if we need outside help. In some views, meditation is a complete cure—sure, but ancillary aid can often be wise too.

We have learned to sometimes alternate focused attention practice with open awareness. For example, we might have breath watching as our primary practice. But anytime we notice it is getting difficult to keep our attention on the breath, we switch to open awareness and check to see what is uppermost in consciousness.

We might then at once hear a voice talking in the mind, or realize that we have been watching an imaginary scene play out like an internal movie, accompanied by a running commentary—at which point we might also discover that an emotion has been active in our heart area, making the sense of being present in that scene more intensely real. So we note these phenomena. We wait until we have allowed them to be as they are, at which point they generally calm down and recede. Then we return to the breath.

Or again, if we're having a hard time staying with the breath, then we have learned to scan the body, letting ourselves feel each part of it in turn: foot, ankle, shin, calf, knee, and so on, left side and right side, working up to the cranium. Or we listen intently to the soundscape: first, inner ear sounds, and then sounds in the room, and then sounds in the building, and then sounds outside the building. We learn to "receive" sounds: hearing them without identifying them, just knowing their pitch, volume, and timbre. We know how intensely pleasant it can be just to listen.

Then once again, calmer and more centered, we return to the rise and fall of the breath.

We are starting to taste the state of "flow"—less self-conscious, more absorbed in the activity of sitting, and finding an ease, a grace, and a growing richness and effortlessness, simply in sitting still. And all this without being engaged in any outward task but just quietly being. We're not writing or sketching. We're not solving a calculus problem, riding a mountain bike, or playing a video game. We are just sitting still. Just being.

This is the beginning of discovering an intrinsic well-being. We are shifting from the efforts of early mindfulness practice toward the effortless states of unification known as samadhi.

FLOW STATES

The preceding is an ideal for the path of meditation. More commonly, the path is less linear, more higgledy-piggledy.

Many of us might already be more familiar with "flow states" than with samadhi. The concept of "flow" entered mainstream culture through the work of the psychologist

Mihaly Csikszentmihalyi, who coined the term in the 1970s
and wrote popular books on it in subsequent years (such as
Flow and *Finding Flow*). The term refers to states of deep,
fulfilling absorption in a task or activity. More recently,
commentators such as Steve Kotler have started using an
alternative term, "STER states," to refer to the same condition. This term is an acronym for the characteristics of the
state: selfless, timeless, effortless, and rich.

The same attributes could also be applied to samadhi in
meditation. The difference between typical STER states,
or flow states, on the one hand, and samadhi, on the other,
is that in the former, the person is engaged in an outward
activity. It could be a sport, making art, writing, intense habituated teamwork, or repetitive absorbing work. Somehow
in the course of the activity, the person's sense of self goes
quiet, so fully absorbed do they become in what they are
doing. Time seems either to stop or to become irrelevant
and unimportant, even meaningless. They may look at their
watch and find hours have flown by. There's a sense that the
activity, whatever it may be, is happening by itself, without volition or intention or effort on the part of the actor.
Yet the person is performing at an uncommonly high level
and feels uncommonly well. There may be a heightening
of sense experience, with light, color, shadow, texture, and
sound all becoming unusually rich, and body sensations
unusually pleasant or fascinating.

Csikszentmihalyi found that flow states are linked to more
general happiness, well-being, and satisfaction with life.
Those who more frequently taste them in their daily lives
are by and large happier. This is no surprise, considering

that flow states tend to be accompanied by a sense of fulfillment, a sense that *this* moment, *this* activity, is enough—in
fact, it's more than enough. It's giving us all we could need
or want.

To be clear, these states are not "awakening." The sense
of self may be reduced or in abeyance, but that isn't the same
as "seeing through" the self. The mountain biker comes
home three hours later, exhausted and happy from their time
on the hills and trails, feeling in love with their activity, even
with life. Then they have a shower, a beer, and a hot meal,
their sense of self intact. It just happens to be in a positive and
healthy condition.

The writer lays down their pen after an intense stint, having produced a thousand cogent words, and goes out for a
walk, marveling at the beauty of the trees, at the clouds, at
the sheen on the road from recent rain, and at the lovely
forms of the hills rising into the skyline in the distance, and
feeling that all is well with their world. But they are not
thereby thrown into a discovery that they *are* the world.

Nevertheless, these states are powerful bringers of well-
being and immensely valuable.

A TASTE OF SAMADHI

Up in the northern mountains of New Mexico, once again:
one morning I went out early and walked through the long
grass up the narrow valley as dawn was breaking.

No sun yet in the steep, dark vale at the very end of summer, just as it was turning to autumn. The valley was in rich

gloom at that hour. Very wet grass and plants. Cold too. No frost quite yet but frost was in the air. I came back with wet shoes and kind of wanted to pull on my boots and go out for a longer walk. But I was on a solo retreat, and I was here to sit.

I was staying in a remote "cave" hermitage in a high valley, at 9,400 feet.

I made tea in the big camping mug I had brought, and I set up for some meditation. I faced the wall in the dawn gloom, with the room still dark.

I spent the first few minutes sipping the tea. The thought of going out for a longer walk now, at this early hour, returned. Briefly, I wondered about doing that first and sitting later. There was a little pain at not doing it, at a momentary indecision, and then I got hit by something bigger—a bigger peace that made the thoughts irrelevant. Sweet meditation switched on, and I went off into a pervasive, creamy, and boundless peace for perhaps an hour and a half.

What seemed to precipitate it was that I had started noting sense experiences while sitting. One helpful aspect of "noting practice" is that it makes us attentive right off the bat. It requires us to attend to our actual experience. So I noticed that there were some images in my mind and some inner talk, and I labeled them: *Image* and *Talk*. Then I noticed a light contraction in the left side of my diaphragm and noted, *Feel*. And quickly, I then noticed the sensations of my lower legs and feet on the meditation mat and the quiet sighing of wind outside. So I labeled them all accordingly. And then the switch flipped.

I found myself in a glassy state I often enter in meditation, in which all sensations are present but none seem quite solid. Meanwhile, it was as if a smooth energy were flowing through everything. Except not exactly flowing, more drifting, pervasive, diaphanous as gauze, as if all things had become translucent.

It felt like a healing balm. Something I'd tasted many times before, but this time it was more intense, more inclusive and loving. I felt like this was exactly the balm I needed right now—to heal my heart, which was aching for a family member who had been having a hard time, and for injustices going on in this country. The samadhi seemed like a kind of amniotic fluid in which something new might be growing, and where healing and repair could happen.

The peace reminded me of my commitment to do what I can to serve and help this world and its beings—to heal the wounds of the world. Even though I may be able to help only a little, and even though all is manifestly not well, nevertheless I know I will do my bit. And in some mysterious way, all *is* well—which makes it easier to tend to all *not* being well. In other words, this "womb" of practice is not an isolating thing but connects us with the wider world, and contains a compassion, a love, implicit within it.

It was indeed like floating in an incomprehensible, vast love that knew no bounds and no conditions.

After two hours of blissful sitting, I got up and made oatmeal. I was going to make coffee, but decided I was tired and therefore only had the oatmeal, and then put on rice, which would take an hour to cook at this high altitude. While it was cooking, I had a nap. After that, I went out and breathed under the big ponderosa pines for a little while. Then I went back inside, turned off the rice, and settled in for more sitting.

It was then that I remembered something else that had precipitated the taste of heaven in the earlier sitting. It had intensified when I brought a koan into my meditation—an enigmatic nugget of Zen wisdom (about which, more later). It was a koan in which the ninth-century Chinese master Yunmen is asked what samadhi is, and he answers, "Rice in the bowl, water in the pail." Just those simple words. The statement of fact: *rice in the bowl, water in the pail*.

I had brought the phrase into the meditation. "What is samadhi? Rice in the bowl, water in the pail." It had been Yunmen's words that plunged me into the heavenly rest. All was still, all was peace, and that state seemed to spread wider and wider, all through the world.

That reminded me of the thirteenth-century Zen poet and teacher Dōgen, who said that meditation was the "gate of ease and joy." And somewhere in his voluminous poetic writings he also describes sitting as a "river of cream." I could relate to both.

What if every day we could taste life as a river of cream? And need only to sit still to find boundless ease and joy?

ANOTHER POINT ABOUT this third inn: it is where we may start to sense more clearly that all our practice has been a kind of womb in which we have been encouraged to develop new capacities for love, new chambers of the heart, new awareness that this life is to be tended, all of it. It can come to seem as if, while we have our linear paths and trajectories, at the same time all along there has been another, more hidden, path of growth, less concerned with our outward worldly "progress," more interested in our learning and growing as beings.

From this perspective, life is more like a series of lessons, cleverly curated as if by a benevolent universe that is seeking to bring us more into alignment with its truths, or its "implicit order"—in physicist David Bohm's phrase, the "order" by which it manifests and functions. We are coming to know this other order more intimately. And sometimes it feels as though it is happening because life loves us, and wants us to know it.

As the immortal lines from the musical *Scrooge* put it, "I like life / Life likes me / Life and I fairly fully agree." We can start to concur with this sentiment as practice develops.

Meanwhile, sometime during the morning of sitting, I heard the wind pick up outside and then the sound of rain starting to patter on the skylight overhead and ping on the window. Then thunder rolled through the sky for maybe an hour. After that, it moved farther away, still audible in the distance but faint.

Practice Tip

FINDING FLOW

For the next few days, be on the lookout for the experience of flow. Flow happens when we get absorbed in a task or activity.

There are different flavors of flow. Sometimes we simply realize that for a while we haven't been as aware of ourselves as we normally are. Instead, we have been engrossed in what we have been doing. Time has become irrelevant. Now that we are aware of it again, we are surprised when we glance at the clock and see how many minutes or hours have flown by.

But we haven't been lost in thought, rumination, or some kind of perseverative thinking. On the contrary, we have been absorbed in our activity.

Hallmarks of this state are a feeling of fulfillment, of being content and energized. Sometimes there can be a sense of purpose too, as if what we have been engaged in is aligned with a greater purpose we have in life.

Sometimes it's a little like a river's current has picked us up and carried us along in our endeavor.

See if you can note when this happens in the course of the next few days. Keep a log, either mental or written, of the circumstances and activities that seem to bring on the state of flow. They might be as mundane and ordinary as washing dishes, mowing a lawn, or sorting the recycling. They might also be a period of time during a run, when the running becomes effortless and curiously energized. Or flow might come on when we are at work at our desk. Or engaged in some creative activity, such as painting, singing in a choir, or journaling.

Note how it feels to have been in flow.

Conversely, if it seems as though you're not tasting much flow in your life, then try doing something that you might enjoy that you don't normally do. Go for a walk in a place where you would not ordinarily stroll. Linger in an art gallery for no particular reason. Explore your neighborhood, either on foot or on a bike, seeking out nooks and crannies, alleyways, and lanes you don't normally visit. Do something new. Go on a "date" with yourself, as Julia Cameron, author of *The Artist's Way*, recommends. Be by yourself for a couple of hours, and spend the time investigating something new—an activity you don't normally do, or a nearby place you don't ordinarily go to. Try putting on some music and dancing. Get out some crayons or watercolors and paint. Go for a walk in your neighborhood, looking for sights you have not noticed before. Randomly open a book of poems and slowly read whatever you land on.

See what happens.

INTRINSIC WELL-BEING

Whenever we experience samadhi, our practice is immediately rich and rewarding. We find fulfillment in the bare fact of being. We're tasting that it is enough just to exist. In fact, it can be more than enough. A sense of lovingness may well up at times, which in turn may make our love for life keener.

I first tasted meditative absorption in Transcendental Meditation (TM), which I learned in my early twenties and was my first experience of meditation. In the TM classes, they taught that experiences of what they called "transcending" could arise in meditation. These were states of uncommon ease, clarity, and steadiness, in which there was a broad sense of restful peace and no need to do anything. I found these did indeed come on from time to time. Sometimes there would be a soft roar in the inner ear, as of a distant ocean, accompanied by either a sense of vibrant stillness in the body or of dust sifting, floating, settling all through the body, like motes in a sunbeam. Or an abiding sense of rest that was acutely, peacefully, and pervasively clear, as if suffused with a quiet awareness.

This is perhaps the core and heart of the healing power of meditation.

When I moved to breath practice in the Zen tradition in my late twenties, absorption began to manifest in other ways: it was like slipping into the waters of a deep, dark lake, abiding in a calm so profound that all attention went quiet. In Zen, it's as if first we get engrossed by the breath, so the coming and going of the breath becomes larger, to the point where it seems to be the only thing, and fills our awareness. We may experience distortions of size and proportion. We can't tell if we are very small or hugely expanded. Breath gets so big in our awareness, it's almost as if we can see a fingerprint on each one, so fine-grained and magnified has the lens of our attention become. We can sit utterly engrossed by it while the quarter hours whir by.

In time, it can also be as if we get so absorbed in the breath that it disappears. We don't "see" the breath anymore. We are entranced, in a state of deep, clear awareness, but all has become a kind of transparent darkness, thoroughly beautiful and all but free of content.

These are exquisite states of mind. They are also auspicious. The quality of our concentration is getting more refined. Like a fine wine that has been laid down for a decade, the practice-awareness we have been gently allowing to grow is coming to fruition.

Who could want more from practice? We don't need any more. We are finding peace and fulfillment—therefore the very idea of "more" has become irrelevant. Our hearts are full—with love for life, with love for the world, and with compassion, which urges us to help and tend to the suffering

of this world. We commit to positive helpful action on behalf
of others.

And yet if we are on a path to awakening, then there is still
that matter of awakening itself, waiting for us down the road.

BEAUTY HEALS

I heard a graphic account of the healing force of samadhi
from a parent who had long been living with worry and grief
for their grown-up child, who had serious mental health and
addiction problems.

One evening she went alone to the beach near her home,
in search of respite from the torment in her mind. Standing
near the surf in the evening, somehow she became captivated by the sight of the waves. Each one left behind a sheen
on the bare, dark sand as it withdrew. (With her permission,
I'm paraphrasing what I remember of our conversation.)

Imagine the scene. She's sad. Her child has been unwell
for two years now, and her worry is near-constant. The sun
has gone down and it's almost night, but the sky is still pale.
And just now the sea catches her attention: the way each
wave slides up the beach like a lapping of paint spilled from a
pot. Up the slope it pours, pale as cream, and then turns into
a landslide of gray gravel in the dim light as it withdraws,
leaving behind a tile of sky-like sheen. Then all the shiny
tiles suddenly fade, their time of brightness brief, draining
down into darkness, drawn down into an underworld.

Then in comes the next wave, covering over the dark
place, and the process repeats.

She watches, entranced. What she is seeing is incomparably beautiful. And that beauty is being met by a long tone of sadness or longing or unease within her. Almost as if the beauty calls forth her pain, speaks to her pain.

Then it dawns on her that what she is seeing, the experience of this sight, requires her consciousness in order to be seen and known. The beauty is a double act: both the scene and she herself are needed for it to arise.

If this beauty couldn't exist without her, then was it the sea's beauty or her mind's beauty? Whose beauty was it? What, in the end, was this world, whose beauty could sometimes be seen? Where was the beauty? In the world or the mind? And where was the line that divided the mind from the world?

It was wonderful to be seeing it, and at the same time to be feeling the hum, the drone of emotion, ringing like a guitar string, within the same awareness in which the sight also arose. They spoke to each other, the sight and the sound responded to one another, and for a moment she felt that that recognition between them was in some way how the world was made, how the experience of this world came into being.

For a moment, there was nothing else. Just this magical sight and this hum of emotion in response, and the two things were all there was. They were like two magnets that almost touched one another, generating the magnetic field between and around them.

It was utterly beautiful—that was the most important thing. She felt she was touching life itself. To have experience—that was the great wonder. To be still enough to notice that we are having experience—that was where the true gold of life lay.

For a moment her pain wasn't pain, the troubles of her child were bearable, and her heart melted. She sensed that all the practices, the meditations, and the teachings she had allowed into her life—they were all there to help her find this beauty: the beauty of the simplest fact of all, that she was alive. And she knew she was loved.

SOUL, SAMADHI, AND KOANS

Another perspective on samadhi: perhaps it is what happens when the mind and soul start to agree on practice. The mind has been told that meditation is about thinking less and resting in the moment more. But the soul has recognized from early on that meditation can be a crucible for a deeper kind of growth. And it loves that. It certainly doesn't want to be left out of this process. But how is it to participate?

As Iain McGilchrist has observed, the soul resonates with a few things that are helpful here. Samadhi is a journey of release, especially of release of our hold on our bearings. We let go of our sense of direction, of knowing where to go next. We allow ourselves to be absorbed in the experience of the moment here and now, without rational, executive overview. This is a kind of "not knowing"—of wordless trust. And the soul chimes with this *not knowing*. It thrives on mystery.

The soul also thrives on *beauty*. It loves beauty and comes alive in beauty. Likewise, samadhi, as we've seen, is often beautiful. Among its qualities is a recognition of the beauty of being.

And the soul also vibrates and hums at the sense of the *infinite*. Of things not having boundaries. Of things having no fixed size. Of there being an order of experience without limit, an experience that spreads forever. And this too is a feature of some flavors of samadhi.

And when all—or any—of these are present in embodied experience, the soul is on board. So samadhi may be the pre-eminent experience in meditation in which mind and soul are in unison, in which they unite in practice. Samadhi emerges from a release of our hold on needing to know; and it blurs boundaries, both between things—for example, between our body and what is beyond it, and between our attention and what it rests on—and in the dissolving of limits. Absorption can feel like it goes on in all directions infinitely.

ALL OF THIS is helped by being given a conducive space in which to unfold. In the old days, much practice went on in cloistered monastic settings, where the austere atmosphere and the want of creature comforts threw practitioners back on themselves. They had to find intrinsic comfort and well-ness within, rather than from outside. To learn to be okay with less of what we want can be a salutary thing, a kind of "soul hygiene." As the waters of comfort withdraw, they lay bare the craggy rocks of our cravings more starkly. For people on the journey to freedom and "original love," that is a good thing. Once our cravings are clearly exposed, if we're not in a position to easily distract ourselves from them, then we have to call on deeper resources of patience and toler-ance within ourselves. This can lead us to finding an intrin-sic well-being not dependent on outward conditions.

But austere circumstances also serve another purpose: they can provide an external setting conducive to samadhi. They make it easier to develop samadhi, and also to sustain it once it has emerged.

But there are other spaces, of different kinds, that can also help. One highly portable "space," requiring no buildings or special locations—nothing except a seat for meditation—is "koan practice" in the Zen tradition.

A koan is a baffling phrase culled from the biographies of enlightened practitioners of Chinese and Indian Buddhism. *What is the sound of one hand? Put out the fire a thousand miles away. Make Mount Fuji take three steps.*

A Zen student sits with these imponderable, paradoxical, and apparently nonsensical utterances, and with luck, the wisdom hidden within them may suddenly break open in the student's heart and mind. But even without some radical shift in perspective occurring, koans can still bring a sense of shelter, of refuge. They can cast a kind of spell over us as we run them through our minds in meditation, which expands our sense of things and helps us settle into deeper samadhi.

Some Buddhist programs of practice have the virtue of making sense as maps. Mindfulness, for example, follows a kind of algorithmic approach. By contrast, the koan way has the virtue of being messy, as life is, and chaotic, as wild as the land of awakening itself is. Koans are far more elusive in their methods and results, more like chaos theory. They are unpredictable, capable of fostering massive enlightenment experiences—as well as unrelenting frustration. They are puzzles that refuse to be figured out or solved. In the end, all we can do is entrust ourselves to them.

As we sit with a koan, it may seem to refuse us entry and then suddenly offer a wild welcome. The one thing we can do is wait for the koan, and our state of samadhi, to meet. Only when we get absorbed in a koan do we start to feel why it is worth sitting with one.

There's a further point here. To enter the wildness, the not-knowing, the chaos-like core of reality that koans bring with them, is to forgo the order our minds cling to. This can be scary to the mind. Koans are an odd form of practice. But they come down to us intact, unadulterated from the time they were first created by enlightened practitioners long ago. They offer a kind of timeless support to our practice. The very masters who uttered them more than a millennium ago are still with us, as it were, when we meditate with a koan. And so are the millions of practitioners who sat with them before us, throughout the centuries. They offer support, in other words. They offer a kind of shelter. And this is critical.

Support matters, even with samadhi. It's helpful to us to be steered, guided, and inspired. But there's a more fundamental element, too, that support awakens in us. It gives us courage.

Courage is a vital ingredient in our most valuable kinds of growth. Just knowing that support is available, that it's out there, ready to touch us, can make all the difference. It may be the one crucial ingredient that brings the soul to life. And with the soul on board, we are primed for samadhi. It's easier to let go of our own efforts, and allow effortless practice to pick us up and carry us. With samadhi in full swing, we entrust ourselves to it more completely.

And that relinquishment of control can further prime us for another leap, one we can't imagine, and don't even know is waiting for us. One where we find what this entire project of meditation, of growth, of realizing our potential, has been all about. This is what we'll be coming to in our final, fourth inn of practice, Awakening. But meanwhile, before we move to it, there is more to explore in our third inn— much more.

GUIDED MEDITATION

Releasing into Samadhi

Come into a comfortable seated position. In this meditation we will explore doing less, and still less. Rather than trying to do anything, we let our experience simply be what it is.

What is it like to do less? What is it like to trust that it's okay to release all our plans for our meditation? What if we don't know what meditation should be or needs to be? What if our only intention could be to have no intention?

Let yourself feel your body. Notice that your body is here. Let it be warm, relaxed, and at ease.

Let yourself open up to the soundscape all around you. Let yourself be enveloped by the soundscape. Imagine you are sitting in the middle of a snow globe, enclosed by a bubble of sensations. Sounds and body sensations are present, and you need do nothing at all. You can rest in the midst of all this gentle experience going on.

Feel your body relax. Feel your mind relax. Truly, it's okay to do less. It's okay to do nothing. Just rest. Just be. Just allow yourself to be exactly as you are.

Maybe your breath becomes softer. Perhaps breaths start to come and go as smoothly as silk. Listen to how quiet your breath becomes. Feel how smooth and light it can be.

Again, just rest. Give yourself this time of doing nothing. Allow yourself this space, where for a little while, time doesn't matter. What if just now there really is no time? What if the clock were quite imaginary? What if, truly, there is only now? No effort. No time. Nothing to prove, nothing to attain. Just now. Just this.

CHAPTER SIX

Deep Absorption

SCALE AND PERSPECTIVE

Much of this book has been written in a cabin under the Brazos Cliffs, in the mountains of northern New Mexico. I was hoping I wouldn't have to write about the cliffs. Because as crazy and fanciful as it might sound, sometimes I thought I could feel these pages coming out of their 1.8 billion-year-old rock. At least, it was helpful to imagine they'd been presiding over this project.

Today I woke feeling dull-headed, my mind temporarily sterile. When I glanced out between the curtains, the cliffs, as if mirroring my mood, looked moody and reluctant, standing there under the seeping clouds like apartment blocks in West London under a gray sky, blank and faceless, offering nothing. I dozed for a while, feeling uninspired. Then I walked down to the river and plunged into the frigid waters and was revived by the shock of cold. I remembered the cliffs up above, and slowly relearned how to be patient like them and allow the mind to be sluggish.

This place is beyond stunning. For example, when I go down for a swim—usually in the evening—it's half an hour of walking, first across the clearing where the big ponderosas spread out, a branch's length from one another; then on down a mossy, stony track; then across a slope padded thick with decades of pine needles; and then off over the edge, down into the final ravine beside the river.

Here, faces of blue rock catch a late gleam of light. The rocks underfoot as you descend have a kind of preternatural presence. But soon you are under the canopy of the pines, down in the dark world of their trunks. It's like an old temple down there—the bare pillars of the trunks, and the richness of the air down in the deep, soft dark of the trees.

It's only when you come out at the river, through the last willow wands and bushes, that you get to the light. A broad strip of sky is pale in the early daylight this time, and the gushing, frothing river also has quivering flats, which carry the sheen of the sky on their backs.

But that's not all—up above, when you come back out of the actual gulch, up onto the slopes and plateaus stepping upward in the higher valley, all the time you feel them—the craggy faces of the enormous cliffs. They're always there, presiding over this valley, even when you can't actually see them—great faces of granite, blue at dawn, gray in the afternoon, and gold in the evening.

They're almost half the age of the planet. They rise nearly half a mile high from the river. The forest scales their skirts, and then they rise up sheer, leaving behind the loose stones and the trees at their feet.

They put everything in a different scale, a different perspective. A book like this—perhaps it's a dot of pollen on a single stamen, in one flower, which itself is just one bloom among many, on a single stalk, in a meadow of a hundred thousand wildflowers, which in its turn is just one meadow among so many that lie open to the sky underneath the massive presence of those cliffs.

The same is true of our lives. Of us. A person is a dot in a valley, in a continental landmass, on a planet circling a great sun, which is a mere dot in the great meadow of our galaxy.

What a relief to see ourselves in a bigger, slower context, one that is not in fact optional, but real.

Absorption can show itself like this. As we become more and more absorbed in the moment, as we sit, we may lose all sense of size. Are we immensely tall? Or tiny, microscopically small? We can't tell and it no longer matters. We are neither. Our sense of comparison, or relativity, is gone, because all there is, is this sitting. Except we can no longer even call it sitting. It is one deep peace. One awareness.

We never knew we needed so little to be utterly happy.

JHANA

In the early maps of Buddhist meditation, the gold standard of meditative accomplishment for an adept was *jhana* (*dhyana* in Sanskrit). There are eight *jhana* states, a series of absorptions in which peace and joy arise not from outside input but merely from the state of being that practice opens up.

Often when the Buddha finishes teaching in the early Buddhist sutras, he is described as going off into the forest to practice *jhana*. A subtle point here is that although accomplishment *in* meditation is commonly recognized as *jhana* states in early Buddhism, the ultimate accomplishment *of* the path of meditation is the final insight into reality that radically and irrevocably liberates a person from craving and suffering—namely, *awakening* (to be visited later, in the fourth inn of this book).

WHEN I WAS a child, suffering from severe, chronic eczema, the affliction boiled and seethed in my skin and smoldered in my belly. It was a witch's brew of pain and itch: ten thousand mosquito bites, five hundred bee stings, an acre of stinging nettles, and a bed of grinning coals.

No one could reach me. Sometimes people became irrelevant. It didn't matter if they came or went. It was just me and the enemy. Me and the skin. Me and the furnace in the middle of me that made the skin boil. The affliction was a defining trauma of my early life.

It has taught me many things throughout the years. But as a child one thing I learned was that it offered one strange escape. Right in the middle of it all, there was a place to go. A place of great peace. It was weird, it was never expected, and I somehow learned early on that I couldn't get there by wanting to. The only way in was that you just found yourself in it. The door opened by itself. And then you noticed. You had escaped the disease and gone into a place of deep refuge.

First, the hands would become big, like giant mittens. Along with their prodigious size came a lovely numbness. But once you noticed that, then the numbness wasn't just in your hands. It was as though your whole body inflated. It became five times its normal size, ten times. And it wasn't really numb either. It was spacious and warm. And tingling all through. And glowing with a gold haze. And you felt locked in, safe and sound. You were snug as a bug in a rug because you had no size. It was so strange. Everything went quiet and peaceful, and it was as if the world had been pushed away. Even your skin was farther away than usual, and blurry like a cloud.

Except on the other hand, your skin and the world it touched—they were also incredibly close, and tender and lovely. They had become friends. There was nothing frightening about them now. They were sweet and intimate. They loved you. You loved them.

You could float here, with a rippling, warm current flowing through you. Sometimes a stillness fell, as if a spell had been cast. The whole world fell away and there was nothing but peace.

When it was like that, sometimes I'd feel as though I had become a barrage balloon. These were giant gray balloons, used to frustrate enemy air strikes, which hung above the hedgerows out by the old airfield where the paratroopers trained, at Weston-on-the-Green near our hometown of Oxford. We drove past them sometimes. There were several of them, looking like big gray gloves the size of houses, tethered with cables so they could be lowered or raised for parachute practice.

Sometimes alone at night I became a barrage balloon, far bigger than normal, floating in giant peace, feeling warm and safe.

Years later, when I took up daily meditation, sometimes I would pop back into that state. Once again, it would come on suddenly, as though a switch had flipped. There I would be, sitting on my chair or cushion, grinding through the minutes of silent sitting, when suddenly I would be floating in blessed ease. It was undoubtedly one of the reasons why I took to meditation. But it wasn't until well into my meditating years that I discovered meditation knew about this condition.

The very first time I was guided toward *jhana* practice by a *jhana* master—*boom*, suddenly there I was, in exactly the condition I knew so well, a warmth buzzing in my hands, and the whole body suddenly alight like a neon bulb, hovering in incandescent, buzzing peace.

Everything else switched off. All there was, was this glowing, humming buzz, which had suffused my experience.

What a surprise. This was exactly the state the teacher had described as "first *jhana*." This gorgeous, rippling, warm energy had a name: *piti*. The word can be translated as "rapture" or "glee" or "delight." And once it came on, all you had to do was—basically nothing. Rest in it. Let it become you. So I did.

After that, I could get sucked back into it most times I sat. Sometimes it was like glittering fountains, like a rain shower of golden particles. It was deeply pleasant. It was impossible not to have a smile on my face while it was happening. But there was more, much more, as I began to learn. There was not just one *jhana*, but eight, and they were progressively more and more refined. The "glee" could become quieter in second *jhana*. The joy could turn into peaceful, pervasive contentment (third), and that could become the stillness of profound equanimity (fourth). And beyond these four, there were four more, the "formless *jhanas*," in which space became infinite (fifth); in which consciousness spread in all directions, infinitely wide yet intimate too (sixth); and in which all phenomena disappeared (seventh). And finally, there was the eighth, in which a single sphere of experience was bereft of any knowing subject or experiencer.

There are more details to *jhana* practice. Each one has specific factors that must arise and be present. And there are visualizations known as *kasinas*, which can be taken up within each *jhana*. They intensify the experience and are said to purify the psyche.

The four "higher" *jhanas* necessarily involve non-dual experiences, at least in the *jhana* design of the Burmese master Pa Auk Sayadaw, in which I trained under one of his successors, Stephen Snyder, who had made the *jhanas* the heart of his practice. Jhanas are as near as we can get to awakening without quite touching the live circuitry of the universe, as we do in *kensho*, or awakening itself. They wear us as thin as we ever could be worn—into a threadbare veil through which the deeper reality of nonseparateness starts to shine. One breath of wind and any single thread may snap, and the whole veil fall open.

TO GO INTO any *jhana* is wonderful. And any one of them can take us deep into its chamber-like inner recesses. That is perhaps why some teachers recommend practitioners hang out in any one of them, rather than seek to rattle through them, as if hurrying up a ladder and back down again. When they intensify, whichever one it is, our agency dramatically diminishes. The deepening of a *jhana* seems to correlate with a surrender to it. We don't make it stronger. We hang out in it without doing anything—just steeping in its wonder and well-being. When *it* wants to, it ramps up, and we find ourselves being pulled in deeper.

Jhanas seem to have a mind of their own. If they decide to intensify, that's up to *jhana*, not us. And unless we let it be that way, perhaps we won't get to experience it. That may be part of why it is helpful as a practice that foreshadows awakening, and brings us a step closer to awakening. This dynamic of surrender and not-doing, the way the *jhanas* draw us in deeper through our readiness to allow them to, rather than any effort on our side, has a major resonance with awakening. Awakening too is something we can't bring about ourselves.

The poet John Keats talks of "negative capability" as a poet's defining capacity. Poets know how to *not-do*, how to be open and receptive, Keats says. There is a recessive quality that is the condition for great poetry. If a poet sets out to make a poem the way they think a poem should be made, then it is unlikely that a good one will appear. Comparably, with the *jhana* states, they develop and envelop us by our being patiently present to them, rather than from efforts by us.

They also weaken our sense of being a separate entity

in the midst of a world arising around us. So it's no wonder the *jhanas* have been viewed as a kind of stepladder to awakening.

THE HEALING POWER OF *JHANA*

For years, my psychology was polarized. After an early awakening experience, I found myself on a plateau, where I could be quite peaceful, with more positively organized priorities, yet could easily trip and fall from the plateau down into gulches of shame-based dysfunction. I'd get episodes of guilt, regret, despair, frustration, or envy. Either mix-and-match cocktails of those toxic spirits or straight shots. Sometimes it felt as though my psyche were polarized, like some country dance hall where the shy girls were all pressed up against one wall, and the timid boys were all up against the opposite wall. The dance floor itself was empty.

My psyche was like that. The middle was empty, and I was up against either one wall or the other—either well-being or shades of misery.

Different things helped to heal the gap. First, to understand the situation better, to see it more clearly, helped. To see that I was often either in a healthy, loving, and somewhat awake state, or else caught in trauma-based contraction—either tasting the first fruits of awakening, or stuck in a long shadow of trauma and retraumatization—was helpful.

It could seem pretty bald: When would I get over this stuff, be more whole, and stay consistently well? But then, granted my psychology and early trauma, I came to see that this was a necessary phase, and it was wholesome that I could see it operating. What needed to happen? The two sides of me had to start to look at one another, take a step away from their respective walls, move a little closer, meet in the middle, and take one another's hand. The awakening and the wound: they could realize that together they had the capacity to hold and heal this life. In some way, they needed each other. Then the two of them might start to dance together.

One key step was to stop demonizing the trauma, and to recognize that suffering had to be included in the healing. There could be no wholesomeness without recognition of the suffering and the heartbreak within it.

Another was the practice of absorption, or *jhana*, states. As they rekindled in my sitting, I started to find a middle zone, in which my troubled self could soak in the extraordinary well-being that the *jhanas* nourished. It was like basking in the richest balm, a healing solution of ease and subtle joy that knew exactly how to bring the polarized parts of my psyche together, and have them meet in some kind of chemical suspension of glorious, self-soothing, and soul-restoring peace.

I'd grown up traumatized by my skin. Life had been a scary place. But I had also had inklings of a place of freedom, peace, and love. At the age of nineteen, I'd leaped over a whole lot of middle ground and found my intrinsic awakened nature. But I had a lot of backfilling to do, and the *jhana* states helped with that.

Had I found some peace in *jhana* as a child because the misery and despair of severe eczema had driven me to search for inner relief? Somehow I had been approximately entering the first three *jhanas* as a boy, inexpertly and randomly. Had those experiences set me up for the awakening I underwent at the age of nineteen? Possibly. Yet at the same time, the wounds that eczema inflicted on the psyche remained unhealed, and therefore I'd had to revisit them through therapy of different kinds, and throughout the years I'd been backtracking through the middle ground.

Or were trauma and awakening connected? And they *wanted* to dance together? The wound and the cure. The imprisonment in dysfunction, and the liberation—were they as separate and contradictory as they seemed? Or did they somehow arise together? Were they part of one whole? Part of one greater love?

The repeated experience of *jhana* states started to offer trauma and awakening a place where they could be with one another, and indeed begin to uncover a love common to both, that in different ways lay hidden within each of them. In the trauma, that love had been bitterly thwarted; yet without the love, perhaps there would have been no trauma. And in the awakening, the unconditional, universal love that could pull every last sorrow to its breast burst forth.

ZEN BEAUTY

Another take on absorption, from a Zen perspective, is that the purpose of Zen is not *just* to train our minds. It doesn't *just* want us to learn to be more peaceful citizens, kinder neighbors, and better denizens of this earth, so that the world may flourish as a better home for all its beings. Zen wants us to know how gorgeous the world is.

It doesn't offer a teaching over *here*, about how human beings can be trained in positive ways, and meanwhile over *there*, there's a precious, troubled world. It wants us to be better humans *in* the beauty and heartbreak of the world.

Imagine the hazy breakers of a Pacific beach at the end of an afternoon. Long strands of hair seem to stream back from the waves as they plunge toward the shore, and the air is misty with spray, and that mist is suffused with light, a golden mist. Through the bronze haze comes a line of slow-flapping pelicans. The big birds beat their way up the shore, swerving to and fro, forming and re-forming their line, spreading wide and then closing in again into tight formation. Like a squadron of old warbirds—military airplanes—they swing into the face of a swell as it rises into a tall and glossy wall, and just as it's about to break, they lift clear, veering up and away, and rewrite themselves, like a group of words forming a thought, once again becoming a single sentence that beats up the coast. Then they swing toward another growing wave, dipping down so low that it seems their wing tips must touch the water, narrowing into a single short line as the angle of view changes.

Now they move across the blinding path where the lowering sun dazzles the water. They flicker through it, barely visible, as if no more than a flapping motion, without any ostensible solid thing creating the movement. On the far side of the broad highway of light, once again they become solid entities, steadfast in their beat over the water.

How can there be a sight of such grace and grandeur as this stretch of breaking waves with the great birds flying over them? The scene is of another order of scale than human life. The birds glide across epochs, commensurate in their powerful bodies with the scale of oceans and tides, yet moving with the grace of a calligrapher's brush.

What is this world that offers such beauty? And what is our vision, also made of this earth, that can appreciate it? Whatever it is, Zen is that. Zen is not us. Not our minds, to be examined and known more intimately. Zen is our minds knowing this beauty. Zen is the mind of beauty. When we know *that*, we know Zen.

Nor is this limited to nature.

One afternoon on a hot drive from California back to New Mexico, I stopped for the night in the far-flung town of Holbrook in Navajo County, Arizona. Strolling along the road after long hours of driving, I noticed a broad strip of cleared dirt near the road. It caught my eye and I scanned it up and down. Then a faded wind sock and cluster of low buildings gave it away: it was an airstrip. And not long after, by chance, I heard a distant, high-pitched moan, which made me look back just in time to see something white and fast disappear behind the buildings and then reappear: a twin propeller plane taking off.

Years before, I had worked at an airport, and my ear still knew the sound of a twin in takeoff. I watched the plane tip a little and then rise. I watched its nosewheel fold up, and then the wing wheels tuck up. I saw it climb and then bank, turning slowly in its ascent, before heading off, perhaps toward Phoenix, 150 miles away to the southwest. Soon the pitch of the engines dropped as it settled into straight and level flight.

Its path was beautiful.

"Freely I watch the flying bird, and sketch the track of its flight," wrote the wild Zen adept Ikkyū in the fourteenth century, expressing the freedom and beauty of the world after his awakening.

Freely we see the plane take off and settle into its evening flight home.

Somehow the moment was perfect. A middle-aged couple weary from hours on the road, and also from tending and supporting the lives of their newly grown-up sons. An afternoon entering its crystalline end, just before the sun set over the desert. A quiet motel in the dusty expanse of land. And a plane taking off from a remote airstrip made of dirt, heading back to a city somewhere, where its passengers probably had air-conditioned suburban homes waiting for them.

This was how it is. Just like this. Here was life.

To feel the intrinsic beauty of that scene was to be deeply absorbed in it. It was to stand in it, as part of it. The heart dissolved and opened in the face of such simple, powerful beauty, and the sense of being separate in any way vanished.

Try This

Either stand up or sit up, so you can see out your window. If there isn't a window nearby, then gaze across whatever space you are in, and let your gaze be soft. Either way, let your eyes absorb and receive what they are seeing. Become more aware of your peripheral vision—be aware of the sides of your field of vision, what you can't see directly but can sense to the left and right margins of your sight.

Be aware also of what you can hear. Let sounds be present to you.

See if you can, at the same time, be aware of the sounds around you and also aware of your field of vision. It's easier to do this if you soften your belly, allowing it to be loose and relaxed. Experiment.

Let yourself be at peace in the midst of sights and sounds. Can you taste a restful beauty simply in the fact of seeing and hearing? No special sights or sounds are needed. There is a place of receptivity in the middle of us, a place of calm, that has its own special beauty, and that senses the beauty inherent in our being present to the experiences of seeing and hearing. For a moment or longer, let yourself rest in the beauty of experiencing anything at all.

THE TRAIL GOES ON

The previous two inns of our journey, Mindfulness and Support, explore "dualistic" practice. In mindfulness, we uncouple from what ails us and learn to be a quiet, loving witness of our experience. In "soul work," we meet entities in the archetypal realms who support us with their wisdom and power; we open to other kinds of support too, in all of which we remain a self who receives the love of "other powers." Self and other are by no means transcended; instead, they are greatly helped.

Here too, in our third inn of practice, with its various forms of expanded or refined mind states, there is still some kind of observer or witness present—a self of some kind, ready to reclaim its ordinary seat once the state of mind passes. But that self is starting to merge with its experience. It is learning to fall in love with its experience and join with it.

In the end, in all three inns, the thing that matters is our heart, and how much it breaks open. It wouldn't be wrong to view the entirety of a life of growth through practice as an ever more breaking heart—a heart that can handle ever more heartbreak and still be at peace and know love.

On a related note, we could track the whole path of awakening through the lens of beauty. At first our experience is scattered, out of focus, random, and haphazard. We're gusted about by the winds of our hopes and fears, our likes and dislikes. Through mindfulness, the heart-mind starts to become more coherent and orderly. In that more harmonious sense of the moment, we start to detect beauty. And as we open to support, outside forces exert themselves on us, such that we feel them and are changed. They break up encrustations over our soul. As scars and crusts crack open, more beauty breaks through. And in absorption, we clearly see the beauty of this world, inherent in the experience of being. We see it and know it and start to merge with it.

At every step of the way, we are confronted by whatever we are still holding tightly, protecting ourselves. The challenge is to let the love in, which we can do only by releasing our grip on a defense. Every time, it's the same process: find the holding, the closing up. Let it be. Let it release. Let it go. Whereupon more love floods in.

All these different levels, or zones, are merely a measure of how deeply the love inundates us. Perhaps in the end it's possible for simply everything—self and the whole world—to disappear entirely, so the original love shows it-self in its wholeness. We find there is neither a self to hold back nor a world to occupy any space the love couldn't reach.

Like an incoming tide, it comes in, in successive waves. The tide of love covers ever more beach, it laps around the foot of a rock, it fills a tidal pool, and then it withdraws a little. Then in it comes again, swamping the first pool and smothering another, filling it to its frothing brim. In time, rock by rock, it swallows the landmarks, and finally all the beach is gone.

There was a beach we used to visit as kids during our annual family holiday in Cornwall, in the far southwest of England. That beach stood in a cliff-lined bay underneath the Logan Rock, a precarious-looking rock perched three hundred feet above. We had to time the visit to the beach with the tides, because at high tide the beach was completely hidden. Only once the waters withdrew was the golden sand revealed.

We loved that place—that secret, magic beach—in spite of having to lug all our beach gear over three fields and then down a long, snaking cliff path to get to it. In the late afternoon, we'd notice the broad expanse of sand being eaten up. Great sheets of glistening waves would glide on and on, getting closer to the final crescent of gold, where the last sand bulked up against the cliffs.

This is a clumsy analogy for a life opening up to awakening. But wave by wave, the great original love of the universe breaks over us, and swallows more and more of us. Our part, our remembrance, our "mindfulness," is to remember that we don't have all the answers, that we know so little, that our life is just a matchstick tossed on the waters, and that our role is to be humble enough to let that little matchstick allow in more moisture from the surrounding waters. We have to open the pores, allow the water in. And gradually, bit by bit, we become a little more waterlogged. Which eventually allows us to break the surface tension of the body of water. Our holding together of the world as we know it starts to release, and we open to a great relaxing, a not-knowing. We surrender into the possibility that we could be wrong, that the image we had wasn't the whole picture. There might be more. Or less. Either way, what we don't see touches us most intimately because it touches our heart.

So those breaking waves eating up the beach—they are waves that come from and go back to our true heart. They eat up all that isn't our true heart.

And the levels of practice—all they are, in fact, is levels of love. If this whole path of practice were not about love, then it wouldn't be worth it.

But at the same time, love itself has no levels. Once we taste the love, on no matter which level—mindfulness, support, or absorption—we are well. We are okay, we are home.

And yet we can abandon ourselves more and more to love. So in another sense, there really are levels.

But why love? Does that word indicate that this avowed "atheist" believes in some kind of universal love, also known as "God"?

On the contrary, the discovery of universal interconnectedness as an *experience*, not an idea, and of an all-inclusive dimension that makes us and all things one—this *is* some kind of ultimate love, without any "supreme being" needed. Unless our connection to this love *is* the supreme being itself.

Likewise, the discovery of a yet deeper reality, which is utterly without form and void, yet has the capacity to *be* all—that too is something like a heart-stopping love.

SO YES, DIFFERENT faces of love. All we have to do is keep opening to them. And a time can come when we cross some kind of hump, turn a corner, or go over a steep slope—something can happen where the center of gravity of our life tips from being located in the separate, anxious, lonely sense of *me*, to being more centered in the nameless love whose true face is always this moment just as it is. Coffee cup. Morning light. Yellow pad. Pen getting a little sluggish, just one shade fainter, just one micrometer thinner in its line, as its reservoir of ink gets a little closer to being used up.

This is it. If you want to meet ultimate reality, encounter the supreme being, here it is. Right here. Right now. Staring you in the face, flooding into your ears, nudging you on every side—table edge under your elbow, hard bench under your buttocks, warm barrel of pen in your fingers, and the whole spectrum of experience flooding in—and there is nowhere to flood in *from*, and nowhere to flood in *to*.

Instead, there is just *this*. Boundless. Perfect. Fully realized, fulfilled. Totally accomplished already. You. You yourself. Forever *this*.

If you don't feel the love, if you're not quite getting it yet, then no worries. All of us will. We surely will.

So without further ado, let's take the step into the ineffable, and see what *can*—in spite of its being ineffable—in fact be said of awakening.

GUIDED MEDITATION

Samadhi

The view in many schools of meditation is that samadhi, or meditative flow, is an attainment not so easy for the novice. But there is another view, wherein meditation is seen less as a series of successive accomplishments, and instead as a process of greater releasing, of letting things go. And from this perspective, in a sense there are no attainments, only a gradual expansion of our ability to try less, and to let things be, simply as they are, more and more thoroughly.

In this meditation, we are going to explore what it's like to drop any "efforting," and to let go of time.

Come into a comfortable position, likely but not necessarily seated. Let yourself be relaxed and balanced. Check that no effort is being expended in staying upright. Imagine letting yourself fall, but because you are balanced, you don't fall.

Allow your jaw to relax and sink a little. Let your chest relax and be warm. Let your shoulders settle and relax. Let your arms be slack and limp like old ropes. Now let your hips relax and spread a little. Let your legs also go limp, like old ropes.

Good. Nice. Body is totally relaxed.

Notice how good that feels. Perhaps your body has a comfortable warmth in it. Perhaps you can sense a subtle tingle in it. Perhaps it feels almost a little hollow and loose, somehow spacious within. However your body feels for you right now, let it be the way it is.

Now spend a little while simply listening to the sound-scape. Just listen.

When you feel ready, expand your listening to in-clude your breath. Can you hear the movement of the breath in your body? It may well be too quiet to hear. In this case just track it, sense it. Imagine you are lightly touching the movement of the breath with a fingertip. Let that finger feel the breaths gently coming and going. Continue with this for a little while. . . .

Now imagine that you have nothing at all to do. For this period of stillness just now, allow yourself to do noth-ing at all. Instead, let stillness itself hold you. Let stillness carry you. Imagine that a wider stillness is gently seep-ing into you, almost like a kind of presence, and that it knows just how to hold you and carry you. There is noth-ing you need to do. Let this wider stillness do everything for you. What if all that mediation really is, is you allowing stillness to do everything for you?

Stillness helps you listen. Notice that.

Stillness itself helps you sense the wondrous body that you are. Notice that too.

Stillness lets you just be.

Allow stillness simply to help you be you.

At the same time, everything that needs to happen, happens freely, all by itself. Whatever sounds are arising, they arise by themselves. Whatever sensations you can feel, they arise by themselves.

You're free to do nothing at all. Just be.

Now imagine that you can see a little clockface down in the corner of your awareness. Most of us, most of the time, carry a subtle sense of clock time through our waking hours.

Imagine this little clockface disappearing. It simply vanishes. For the duration of this meditation, time evaporates.

You are completely free of time. Imagine there just is no time. All there is, is now.

Complete rest. Complete peace.

Stay like this for as long as you like.

When you feel ready, come out of the meditation. Thank yourself for doing it. Well done. A pat on the back to you. Perhaps in time, all of us may come to feel that there is nothing more important than doing nothing, at least for a little while every day. Thank you again for being open to trying this.

Part Two

The Second Wheel-Rut

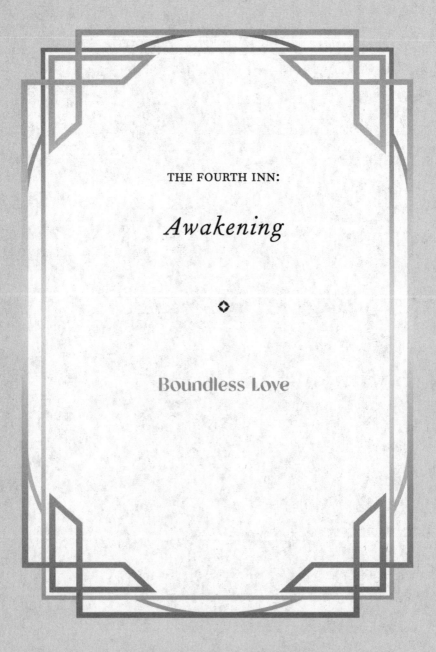

THE FOURTH INN:

Awakening

◆

Boundless Love

CHAPTER SEVEN

Not Two

ON THE ROAD

Meditation practice really got going in the West in the 1950s, when Japhy Ryder, hero of Jack Kerouac's novel *The Dharma Bums*, and his beatnik buddies got the juggernaut of the "dharma" to choke out a few chest-sundering roars of its prodigious engine and then set out to throb and hum down the highways of America, crisscrossing the mighty continent.

What got the practice started in the West was not modern mindfulness, invaluable though that is, but a deeper deal: the dharma. The one true *fact*. The discovery. Awakening. The inexplicable and unconveyable fact, which any and every human being can discover, with a bit of luck, some determination, some hope, and a nudge or two from a trusted guide.

The word has different meanings, but to Kerouac and his colleagues, *dharma* meant pretty much the experience of

awakening pointed to by the Zen practice they enthusiasti-
cally adopted.

The marvel, which is here, right now, hidden in every
moment, usually just out of sight. The reality that allows all
to be one, and each thing to be all things, and each thing to
stand alone in its perfection, with all else fallen away. The
dharma: totally empty, utterly full, free, boundless, and
"uncompromisingly one," as my teacher Joan Rieck Roshi
would sometimes say.

Anything less would not have been enough to get the juggernaut rolling. But awakening could do it.

To awaken from the torments of self and other, from the
intoxications of greed, clinging, grasping, and hankering,
and from disappointment, anxiety, and terror; to decontam-
inate from hate, ill will, malice, spite, and envy; to have this
moment come into an easy, heart-opening clarity; and to see
so differently and yet to see in a way that needs no justifica-
tion, so familiar is it, in spite of its utter novelty—this is the
reality of awakening. And it had the power to open the heart
of a generation.

No wonder. It feels not just familiar, but like love. It's a
strange property of awakening that you cannot get close to
it. You cannot see it from a middle distance or even from
up close. You can only know it when you discover that you
already are it and always have been. It's like coming home
to a fierce love.

The writer Barbara Ehrenreich says this about awakening
in her book *Living with a Wild God*, in which she reckons
with a random experience she stumbled into in her youth:

Like fire you can't get close to it without being consumed
by it. Whether you're a dry leaf or a gorgeous tapestry,
it will coopt you into its flaming reality.

Exactly. And yet it's a relief sweeter than any other. The
end of all woe. A sense of being infinitely beloved, and in
turn, of loving. A belonging that is beyond belonging, because you and the fabric of all things are single.

In the novel *The Color Purple*, Alice Walker puts it this way:

One day when I was sitting quiet and feeling like a
motherless child, which I was, it come to me: that feeling
of being part of everything, not separate at all. I knew
that if I cut a tree, my arm would bleed. And I laughed
and I cried and I run all around the house. I knew just
what it was. In fact, when it happen, you can't miss it.

This *oneness* mysteriously does not preclude each thing
being uniquely itself. As we deepen in experience and insight, we start to see each thing as entirety in itself. The
shadow of this little thumb falling on the table: it is *all*. Just
to see that, can melt the heart. It makes you fall in love with
the shadow, and with the thumb just above it. And with the
little vase of five daffodils standing nearby, and even with
the person who thought to put these daffodils in that jar.
What a wonder an ordinary moment can be.

Love, boundlessness, oneness—no wonder dharma practice took off down the highways of America. And the form
it set off in back then, in the 1960s and 1970s, was Zen.

Zen: a tiny word but packing such a punch. Capable of pushing through the walls of the house of self-and-other.

To tweak the metaphor, as an elder dharma brother of mine, Sato Migaku Roshi, once put it, "Zen is the express train. No local stops."

WHAT ACTUALLY IS AWAKENING?

But we've been making local stops, in our first three inns. On balance, it's wiser to do that for a while, before hopping aboard the Dharma Express.

A brief reminder: we're exploring four broad approaches to spiritual development, which human beings have devised or discovered. We visited the first two—Mindfulness and Support—and can see that they are necessarily dualistic. Their logic rests on our being a separate self, one who is getting trained, through practice, to become wiser, happier, and kinder, in the midst of a world in which it lives as an individual entity, separate from all else.

The third inn, Absorption, as we've seen, begins to blur the distinction between self and world. In states of absorption the sense of self is quieter. The boundaries of self become softer and begin to dissolve into the world around it. We and our surroundings start to feel like one whole—like a cloud, a mist, or a warm buzz, in which the human skin-bag becomes more permeable. Inside and outside are beginning to flow into one another.

This sense of things rests on certain conditions—for example, meditating deeply, perhaps in the context of a retreat, with some years of practice behind us.

Now we're approaching the fourth inn, in which we leap out of that skin-bag altogether. But here things start to get a little strange.

First, I want to touch back into a metaphor we encountered earlier.

THE CART TRACK REVISITED

An ancient Chinese Buddhist document from the sixth century CE likened the path of meditation to a cart track with two wheel-ruts. The first rut is the kind of practice we have so far explored, in our first three inns. The second rut, which we are now beginning to explore, pertains to our fourth inn, Awakening.

But here we meet a different way of thinking about the process of meditation. According to the cart track metaphor, the second wheel-rut, awakening, has been beside us all along. If the three inns so far visited are sequential, one following naturally from the previous one, then this fourth inn is a bit different. In some way, it has been present all along. It's just that we haven't noticed it until now. In fact, it has been with us throughout our lives, just unrecognized.

This points to another oddity about awakening—namely, that our experiencing it cannot be reliably induced, as to when, where, or how. Unlike our other three inns, in which if we follow the practices with reasonable diligence, we are likely to reap their benefits, in the inn of awakening, it's all a bit less certain or predictable.

So although it is possible to "leap out of the skin-bag"— and what that means we will come to shortly—it may not be possible to do so deliberately. We can't actually make it happen. The best we can do is set up conditions that make it more likely. As the Zen teacher Robert Aitken Roshi puts it, "Enlightenment is an accident, and practice makes us accident-prone." But that's all practice can do.

Nor can anyone package up awakening and hand it to someone else in such a way that they get it. No one can even give us a tidy conceptual framework for understanding it. Again, we can do that with the first three inns. But once we hit the fourth, even the image of an inn starts to break down.

This fourth inn is more like one of the tents in the Harry Potter series, which looks like a small, regular tent from the outside, but step inside, and you find yourself in a veritable casbah of chambers and rooms, filled with people, furniture, bustle, and busyness, more like a medieval city that might possibly go on endlessly. The view from outside, and the experience within, seem to have virtually nothing to do with each other.

Awakening is similar. It's not containable. It's not actually expressible. It's unspeakable. It's vast and all-encompassing. Yet it also has no size at all. As Sor Juana Ines de la Cruz, a seventeenth-century Mexican writer, says, "As love is union, it knows no extremes of distance."

It's smaller than the smallest muon or boson. Yet from the perspective of awakening, one tiny muon is also the entire vast cosmos.

It's so hard to find it. It's so hard to see it. Yet it's always right here. "Just because it's so obvious, it's all the harder to find," says Wumen, a thirteenth-century Chinese Zen master.

THIS IS YET one more reason why it's sensible to meditate in various other frames that support our greater well-being, as we did in the first three inns of our journey, and not just with the ideal of awakening in mind. If we ignore all the manifold benefits that can accrue from regular meditation, and focus exclusively on the elusive goal of awakening, then we may neglect to cultivate the very tangible benefits we could be gleaning from our practice in the first three inns. And on top of that, awakening seems almost to dislike being pursued. If we look too directly toward it, then it tends to hide. The Zen master Sister Elaine MacInnes says it's like a deer in a forest. If you turn toward it, then it will tend to run away. But if you stay quite still, then it may come closer.

Nevertheless, we can't pretend that awakening doesn't happen or doesn't matter. It does, both. It's just not directly caused by us or by our practice. Unlike virtually everything else we have looked at so far, we can't do a whole lot to create it or bring it about. Rather, we *discover* it. It "falls" on us, like grace. It's more like a revelation than a feat of inward engineering.

But what *is* it?

It's experiencing firsthand the reality of the "non-dual." It's what is revealed in "waking up" precisely *from* the sense of being a separate self—a "dualistic" self that divides all experience in two: "me" and "not me." Awakening overrides that distinction. It predates that distinction. We might say that awakening targets the sense of being differentiated—this person here and everything else there—and eradicates it.

THE EXCLUDED MIDDLE

Western logic holds to the "dilemma": there is X and there is not-X. By definition, X cannot be not-X.

Therefore the West has the law of the "excluded middle." There is no middle ground between X and not-X.

That would seem logical enough. Whatever X is, it can't be not-X.

By extension, there is *me* and there is *not me*. I am *me*, and everything else is what I am *not*. Nothing can be both *me* and *not me* at the same time.

But Eastern logic has the "tetralemma." It goes like this:

There is X; *there is* not-X. *There is both* X *and* not-X.
There is neither X *nor* not-X.

Phew. What does this mean? What it's saying is that there *can* be something that is both X and not-X, at one and the same time.

What that means about *me* is that there can be something that is both me and not-me. And something that is neither me nor not-me.

So in Eastern logic, the "excluded middle" is not excluded. It's included. It *can* exist. Something *can* exist that is both me *and* not-me.

This all sounds pretty abstract. So what does it mean for *us*? What would seem to be either me or not-me can actually be both. And it can be neither. I *can* be precisely that which I thought I was not. I am one with what I thought was not me. I am both. "I" include both me the person, and the world, which seems not to be me. That's because there is another level, or dimension, of reality, of experience, which is greater than either me or the world. Which includes both me and the world. And on *that* level, the world and I are one.

The great twentieth-century Hindu sage Sri Nisargadatta puts it this way:

> Love says, "I am everything."
> Wisdom says, "I am nothing."
> Between the two, my life flows.

His great two-volume collection of teachings is called *I Am That*.

There are different modes, methods, and ways that awakening is known and understood, but most teachings of it agree on two essential criteria:

- First, the sense of "me" as a separate agent in the world vanishes. The "I" is seen through.
- Second, there is a discovery of consciousness being all-inclusive. All that we experience is somehow a single fabric. With our separate identity gone, we find that we are part of that very fabric. We are not separate from anything.

Even to say we belong to everything is not quite strong enough. Awakening is an experience of not just belonging but of being inseparable from anything.

MOONLIGHT SWIM

Tonight I had my first nighttime swim of the year. Actually, it was very late dusk, and a three-quarter moon was up, so I had just enough light to see what I was doing. But still, the paths are different at night.

It's spring and much of the snow has gone now, although thick sheets of dirty snow-crust still cover stretches of the meadows. It's best even now to follow the old snowshoe trails, where the packed track will usually support your weight. Occasionally, the crust collapses and you find yourself up to your thighs in snow. As I'm dropping down toward the river on the trail that hugs the side of the ravine, close to the blue sheen the basalt rock gives off in the gloaming, and then dropping under the big pines, the scene gets pretty dark. I keep missing the good spine of the trail, where the crust is still strong, and find myself plunging into old, soft snow. My ankles soon get wet and cold.

I know the way even in the dark, and scramble over some fallen logs still encased in snowdrifts, and soon I arrive at the river.

So much snow has been melting up in the mountains that the river is three or four hands deeper than usual. Right here, a few weeks ago, before the big melt started, it was barely bathtub deep. Today it's much easier to get in and get a good soaking. Having carefully taken my clothes off, endeavoring not to stand on any sharp twigs or rocks, I find it's waist deep, so I can lie down just about anywhere to get immersed.

I float still for a moment, feeling the prodigious chill of the current. That same snowmelt is making it biting cold, and the flow accentuates the bite.

I half sit up, still submerged, and see a star in the sky over the ravine. Its double shimmers on the quivering current between my knees.

As I'm getting up, I see the moon behind me, and the water sparkling beneath it, a little upriver from where I am. I gaze at the star and then at the moon. Then as soon as I'm out, I get that wonderful warm feeling that comes after very cold water, and start to feel quite dry already. In no time, it seems, my skin is being evaporated by the dry, high-altitude air.

Then it's a slow business getting dressed, after a quick and nearly unnecessary rub with a small towel. On my way out, I step into a bar of moonlight. It looks yellow under the trees. Then back up the cliff path, stepping up on rocks and over roots that seem as though they were made for human beings to use as steps, just as good as a human-made staircase. At which point it occurs to me that their "fit" isn't so surprising. We were indeed made for them. These right here are the conditions for which our limbs evolved. We are actually made to walk and climb over these very rocks and logs, and sometimes to wash off in these brisk, cold rivers. This is not new, this is old, and feeling this way is an old human stirring.

Is it the same in meditation? A recovery of an old humanity hidden deep inside? Perhaps not from all our ancestors, but some? A few who learned to meet the world by being still and letting it seep into them, and dissolve them, so that they rediscovered their kinship with all things, and woke back up into an old dream-life in which they were separate from nothing, and could be all things?

I contemplate this as I continue my walk back to the cabin, under the lofty ponderosas, and for an instant I disappear. There is nothing but now, nothing but this ancient forest cradled in its valley, and the somber, dark-blue face of the cliffs ahead, showing between the great trunks, and all of it is smoky, insubstantial, as if made of one single gauzy fabric, and its very evanescence makes it indescribably beautiful. As if this whole existence is a single, momentary flash of beauty.

AN ILLUSION

So far in our journey, the first three inns have played along with a fundamental illusion, and have not challenged it, but rather worked with it—the illusion that what we really are is some kind of center of consciousness that lives in the middle of our cranium. Like a little homunculus that sits behind our eyes and between our ears, it receives sense impressions of the world outside, makes decisions about how to operate, and controls the body's actions.

We know this is a fallacy. Neuroscience has failed to find any locus in the brain that could correspond with such a fixed, stable entity. We know that we are not in charge of multitudes of processes in the body and mind. We also know that the idea that what we really are is some kind of incorporeal awareness—a "soul" in the biblical, Iron Age sense of the word—which gets installed at conception or birth, is a myth.

Rather, we are part of the organic web of life on this planet. We are more like a leaf that grows from the great tree of life. The fact that our nervous systems have developed to such a degree that they can be aware of their own existence, of their mortality, and even of their own awareness, is wondrous. But conscious awareness of the kind we have can be thought of as a kind of computer screen or desktop, a "user interface," as some cognitive researchers put it. In his book *The Case Against Reality*, the cognitive psychologist Donald Hoffman proposes that various systems of the body and mind compete for airtime. Consciousness is an enhanced processing system for making decisions among a multitude of complex systems. We know that it correlates with larger brains and more complex social systems. Our sense of self correlates with our capacity to sense that other people have intentions and feelings, as do we. Known as "theory of mind," the development of this awareness of the inner life of others emerges along with our own sense of self.

In other words, the sense of self appears to be contingent on brain size and on complex social systems, and is conditioned by interactions with others. It's not the independent entity it feels like it is. It's perhaps best thought of as one particular aspect of our conscious awareness, one that grows from it, as a bud grows from a branch. It can be engaged for certain uses at certain times. It is much more episodic than we realize—it is not active all the time, though we tend to feel that it is.

To "awaken" has much to do with this illusory sense of self. It is to see that the sense of "I, me, mine," has been an illusion. In other words, it is to discover—not intellectually but experientially—that what I have taken myself to be has, in fact, been a mirage, a phantom, an illusion. To break free of the enchantment of this illusion is a big deal. Most of us have lived in some kind of thrall to this "I" for much of our lives. It's an extraordinary liberation to realize that it has never really existed.

When we see this, we not only see through the illusion of self, but we also discover that all along there has been another dimension of our experience that we haven't noticed, in which all things are joined, as if belonging to a single fabric. It's as if just behind our ordinary experience, there is another level of consciousness in which all things are one thing. There is a panoramic union of all that is. And we are part of it. So when we experience it, we see that we too are that greater whole.

This does not mean that all things become an amorphous lump of plasma. Rather, it's like discovering that all things are parts of a single body. In his book *Zen: The Authentic Gate*, the twentieth-century Zen master Yamada Kōun (pronounced "Koh-uhn;" 1907–1989) uses a metaphor to explain this, inviting us to imagine a single hair from our head and one drop of our blood side by side on a table. The first is a long, thin black solid, and the second is a drop of red liquid. They seem quite different. Yet both are parts of one single life.

So too with our experience. There is a table, a chair, a tree outside, a cloud in the sky, and a person sitting over a sheet of paper. All seem distinct. Yet all are at the same time part of a single experience, held by a single awareness. To discover what holds all these disparate elements together is not to deny their nature as diverse entities. Rather it is to discover a level, a register, a dimension of experience in which they are not separate but all parts of one thing.

It's a little like being caught up in a dream, where there may be many distinct elements. A car, a bridge, a tree, two people, and so on. Yet once we wake up, the whole of the experience is seen to have been a single dream. All the elements in it are united by the dream consciousness that held them all.

To awaken from our sense of separateness is akin to that. It can indeed feel as if our whole life has been a kind of dream, and all its infinitely various elements are held together by the fabric of the dream. Or it can seem as if we have now tasted a single *mind*, in which all this created world is arising, and all things are inseparably part of that mind—including us. A great sense of love, of peace, of all being well, spontaneously wells up, because we have seen that all the apparently disparate things of this world belong together.

This is the famous "oneness" of awakening. It is a breathtaking and heart-stopping thing to encounter. It can transform a person's sense of who they are, and of this world, and of their place in it. It can transform priorities in a flash.

AWAKENING AND ORDINARY LIFE

But this doesn't mean we have to abandon our current lives and go off to a monastery or hermitage. If anything, it reconnects us more intimately with our life as it is, and with our beating heart, which is now more open to life and feels closer to others.

Here is an account from a music and tech entrepreneur,

founder and CEO of an agency, which she runs out of Los Angeles, who was struck by a random awakening experience, which left her radiant but feeling destabilized. Lindsay wrote to me a few days later, wondering if she was going mad, or else should give up her life and retreat to a mountaintop. (I told her neither. And I encouraged her to write down what had happened.) With her permission, this is her account:

> *I lay in bed getting ready to go to sleep. I felt myself starting to dissolve but it was almost like I was splitting open from the inside out and as I opened it was the strongest "remembering" sensation I'd ever felt (like when you forget something, and then it comes to you but × 10,000). Then once I opened/dissolved I was all that is. I was God. I was consciousness. . . . It was this deep knowing of truth and meaning of everything in nothing. It was beautiful, infinite, and I understood our imagined dream state completely. It was home. There was a loud, freeing sound of an absolute hum that I can still hear at times. The word that kept coming to me was* unity. *There is no word that can describe it though. It is so vast, so raw, so awesome, so real . . . literally nothing can describe it. It's a feeling beyond words or expression. As I write this, I feel like it does no justice to the experience. I just wish everyone could feel it. When I came back to this body I was so complete, quietly elated and assured.*

Today, a few years on from that experience, Lindsay still knows firsthand of another dimension to life, to her existence. But she continues her work in tech, and has branched out into angel investing in start-ups too. There was no need for her to dramatically change her life. Awakening doesn't contradict our life—it just opens up a much broader and intimate sense of it. It opens our hearts to a boundless, loving spaciousness that is already holding all of us. And the love is unconditional. It doesn't require us to leave our homes and become wandering mystics. One of the great gifts of the surge of interest in awakening today is that it is meeting and merging with contemporary science. No longer is awakening the exclusive province of religious orders and institutions, of sequestered and cloistered practitioners. Really, it never should have been in the first place. Awakening is an unconditional freedom and love—and who could claim any exclusive right to that?

The only cases in which awakening might lead to an upheaval in life is when something is seriously out of alignment with our values. If someone's livelihood is based on cruelty or oppression—working in armaments, or to promote addictive substances, or on behalf of oppressive institutions, for example—then they may suddenly realize the harm they have been causing, and feel it's no longer tenable. One old acquaintance of mine from school days, a gifted scientist, wound up working for a live-animal research facility in the United Kingdom. After a few years of meditating, when his practice suddenly deepened, it led to his quitting his job. He went to work in the field of animal welfare instead, becoming an advocate for greater legal protections for animals.

INTIMACY

The closer you get to something, the more it expands into several things, and then many things.

To see a mountain range at dawn, way off in the distance, with the sun behind it, is to see a single undifferentiated sheet, a silhouette as solid as iron. Get closer as the sun rises, and you start to see crevices and gullies, along with individual hills and mountains. Closer still, and each mountain begins to show its own shape and become something distinct.

"Awakening" is comparable to this. From afar, it's just one solid, impenetrable *thing*, of concern to perhaps a few people. But take up a meditation practice, and you may soon sense that your own consciousness is a territory waiting to be explored. It may occur to you that the plain on the far side of which rises the mountain range called "awakening" is contiguous with the land under your own feet. Your very own consciousness can lead you there; and your practice as a meditator may inevitably do so. Awakening is not actually remote. It has something to do with you yourself, intimately.

Sure enough, as you move closer, the mountain range of awakening starts to become more knowable and distinct. You suddenly find yourself standing in its foothills. You discover firsthand that whatever awakening may be, it's not after all far off. On the contrary, it implicates *you*. It's always been with you. It's not just part of you, it's you at your core.

So you've just reached a brow, and a new vista opens up—great! Now you see hills all around you, and you start to understand that the deeper territory of practice is not a single thing. The plain has vanished. Brow upon brow awaits you, inviting you further, into the discovery of ever-new perspectives.

To some, awakening might sound like a boring business, a dreary pursuit. Or that when found, it is a bland, uniform oneness. In fact, it is without doubt the most interesting thing a person can experience.

It changes nothing, in one sense. The contents of life are the same. But in another sense, it changes everything. It is a revolution in the heart, from which there is no going back. It changes our relationship to everything.

It's like solving the greatest problem ever posed, one so great that we can't even know its full dimensions until the solution appears. And then we can only gape in awe.

Yet awakening is the most natural thing in the world. It's clear, emphatic, and irrefutable when it happens.

LEAVING THE SELF BEHIND

One last caution, before we dive in deeper.

Sometimes Western psychology takes on Eastern spirituality and tries to show that it is aligned with it, and works on the human psyche in similar ways. It doesn't always "get" that awakening in a sense leaves the psyche behind, goes beyond it.

For sure, things can get weird here. Our normal understanding is of less use. It's like going from Newtonian physics to quantum mechanics. Standard intuitive logic and common sense are jettisoned.

In his inspiring book *Yoga and the Quest for the True Self*, for example, Stephen Cope suggests that the Western psychology he has trained in pursues the same liberation that "awakening" connotes in the Eastern traditions. The book, brilliant though it is, does seem to equate psychological wellness with the boundless unity discovered in awakening. But they are not the same. It's one thing for the self to become more whole and integrated, and something else for the "ocean of realization," as it's sometimes called, to overwhelm the dam of self, so that a human being finds they are nothing and all at one and at the same time.

To flatten the glorious living reality of all-surpassing oneness into a notion of psychological integration, to equate non-dual experience with a holding together of different parts of the psyche is not quite right, invaluable though those psychological conditions surely are. But non-dual oneness and psychological health are different "inns" of development. Once we taste "non-dual experience" for ourselves, we recognize what the dry-sounding words are actually pointing to. There's no figuring it out. There's no lassoing it with a rope of concepts and tying it up in a holding pen of understanding. It is always a leap *out of* understanding into the unknown, into an unapproachable kind of unknowing. It's a whole new way of experiencing everything. The very "skinbag" that seems to separate us from the rest of the world turns out not to have been any kind of barrier at all. We and the world belong together as a single reality.

In fact, as we enter this territory, ideally we'd have a 3D pop-up page right here. This text, this page, would stop being a flat, 2D phenomenon. Up would spring a lotus bloom, right from this very paper. As I fumble to try to describe the reality of it in words, you'd *find* yourself in it, here and now.

You'd realize that the 3D pop-up lotus emerging from the flat page is actually everything around you right now. The *real* lotus is the room you're in; it's the chair you're sitting on, the bed you're lying on, or the couch you're sprawled across; it's the window across the room, the walls, the trees outside, and the sunshine or moonlight outside; and it's you yourself—all of this *is* the very world of awakening, showing itself perfectly right here and now, wherever you are. Showing you that what is around you is actually *you*.

Try This

Beginner's Mind

"Beginner's mind" is free of preconceptions. We can all find it. We just need to notice our habit of naming and knowing what we're experiencing, and let it rest. Then we may taste a lovely, quiet peace, like turning over a page in a notebook to a fresh blank sheet.

Right now, sit comfortably, keep your eyes open, and let your mind relax. Allow your mind to take a break from telling you what things are. Let it rest. Let it go silent.

Instead, just see, feel, hear, and sense whatever is present right now. See the objects near you but don't name them. Let them show themselves to you. Don't attach any names to them. Simply let them be as they are, with no name added.

What is it like to be present but without needing to know what anything in particular is? See what it is like to be present without telling yourself what things are.

> What if everything is fine right now, just as it is, and you don't need to fix anything? Nothing needs fixing. Just for right now, imagine there is no problem to solve.
>
> What is it like when there is no problem to solve? When there is nothing you need to fix?
>
> What is left when there is nothing to know?
>
> Now sense the watcher within, in the center of awareness, who you identify as "you." Study that sense of "you." Is there really someone there? Or is it more like a space, a hollowness even, or perhaps a cluster of sensations or even a refreshing silence? What is it like to let go—just for a little while—of knowing who you are? What if we release our hold on who we think we are, just let it go? What then?

PRODIGAL CHILD

Something in us knows who we've really been all along. It knows that the anxious, craving being we may often feel we are is not the whole story.

The Lotus Sutra, a Mahayana Buddhist text from the first century BCE, tells the story of a "prodigal child," who comes from a wealthy home but drifts off into the country-side as a young adult, falling into bad company, squandering their inheritance, and wandering as a beggar in rags for many years, forgetting their true origin.

One day they return to their ancestral town but are terrified to approach the grand old house and ask for work. The old prince spots his child outside and recognizes them. Fearing he'll scare them off if he openly greets them, he sends out two laborers to offer them work shoveling out a refuse heap. Gradually, they are brought on as a regular worker on the estate. After twenty years of letting his child work their way up the ranks, finally the old man shares the management of his estate with them, and on his deathbed declares them to be his heir—the prodigal child who left home so long ago.

The revelation has to go step-by-step. The truth would have been overwhelming if it had landed on the child all at once. The wise parent knew from the start who the wanderer was, but let them work their way up the ladder in their own time.

It's an allegory for the spiritual life. Somewhere inside, we know our ordinary sense of who we are is incomplete. Perhaps we recognize quietly, so quietly that we hardly even hear it, that who we really are cannot be who we habitually think we are, that the person we present to the world, and to ourselves, is in part a masquerade. Sometimes we sense it but don't know whether we can trust the feeling.

At the same time, something in us *does* know. But it's hard for us to listen to that voice. So our discovery of our true self needs to take time. It's a process. It comes in stages, in fits and starts, in sudden recognitions, followed by years of those recognitions being absorbed and integrated. And sometimes it's simply forgotten or dismissed.

But if we keep at it, if we have a path of practice we're following, then the recognition will gradually deepen and stabilize. In time we'll accept the truth of who we are— unbounded, part of everything. And even with our foibles and shortcomings, we will come to cherish and treasure our experience of the world, and in our flawed ways will do what we can to make it as happy as possible for as many as possible—at our best, perhaps even a little like the patient prince in the tale.

TASTING THE LOVE AND LIVING THE LOVE

Most meditation traditions acknowledge awakening in two ways—as an experience, and also as a new, changed condition of life. Zen is useful on this subject, as it has a grounded understanding of awakening compatible with contemporary, science-based perspectives. In Zen, an awakening experience, a direct glimpse of non-dual reality, is known as *kensho*, which means "seeing your original nature."

These awakening experiences are of two kinds. The first opens and reveals an indescribable beauty that is utterly new yet tastes of a strange familiarity, and then it closes again, leaving an afterglow that fades in hours or days or weeks, becoming a memory. The second kind doesn't end. Its peak intensity ends, for sure, but it leaves a kind of space inside a person, a marvelous spaciousness, and something like a welling spring of sweet water that never ceases to bubble up. If we remain committed to practice, then we will feel this precious spring within us is being given exactly what it needs to grow stronger. Some traditions call this process after awakening "nourishing the sacred infant."

This treasure within may stay for the rest of our lives. Or it may morph into other things—as long as we keep practicing, it is ours. We have uncovered a source of loving awareness, which has been unblocked by digging up a root system of attachments. We have seen through the self that was identified with that knot of roots and have unplugged a boundless stream of love, which is free to flow naturally.

Original love has been undammed. But how does this happen? We discover that we and the world are one, and always have been.

A TAXONOMY OF AWAKENINGS

Aside from the suddenness or durability—from brief glimpses and glancing blows all the way to cataclysmic experiences, after which our suffering may never reconstitute itself in quite the same way again—there are also different faces of awakening. We'll explore four primary ones here.

1. ONENESS

The most common direct experience of original nature reveals that "all is one." Somehow, underneath this world of separate appearances, there is a level of reality in which every separate thing is part of a single fabric, ourselves included.

All of a sudden, the seat of self, the place of observation within, has not just gone quiet. It has been ejected, like the "ejector seat" in James Bond's old Aston Martin sports car, which could suddenly eject a passenger, leaving an empty seat. With the ordinary observer within gone, what takes its place is the discovery that all experience is one dream, one body, one mind.

Full moon in the Trades. The old hooker driving fourteen knots. I lay on the bowsprit, facing astern, with the water foaming into spume under me, the masts with every sail white in the moonlight, towering high above me. I became drunk with the beauty and singing rhythm of it, and for a moment I lost myself—actually lost my life. I was set free! I dissolved in the sea, became white sails and flying spray, became beauty and rhythm, became moonlight and the ship and the high dim-starred sky! I belonged, without past or future, within peace and unity and a wild joy, within something greater than my own life, or the life of Man, to Life itself!

This is the playwright Eugene O'Neill, speaking through the autobiographical character of Edmund, in the play *Long Day's Journey Into Night*. The preceding passage is in fact an account of an experience O'Neill himself had as a young man, while working on a sailing ship. The character continues:

Like a saint's vision of beatitude. Like the veil of things as they seem drawn back by an unseen hand. For a second you see—and seeing the secret, are the secret. For a second there is meaning! Then the hand lets the veil fall and you are alone, lost in the fog again, and you stumble on toward nowhere, for no good reason!

This states clearly the sense of not just seeing oneness but of being ineluctably part of it. Indeed, it can't be seen without our seeing *that* we are part of it. In O'Neill's case, as in most, the glimpse is temporary, the "veil" drops back into place. We discover the great oneness and then it's gone. It may leave an afterglow, but the vivid moment has passed.

One consequence of this "oneness" is that distance vanishes. Because it's all *one* fact, no object is more distant than any other. Even if we watch a car drive down a road, it's clear now that on another level, the car simply isn't going anywhere. It's like looking at, say, a depiction of a medieval rustic scene by the painter Jan Brueghel the Elder, with many figures in it. A cart is rolling down a track, a horse carrying a rider clops along a lane, and someone is digging in a field—yet all are part of one painting. It's as if we see that the world is a single show, or model, or dream, and its mirage-like quality unites all of it. On the level of the mirage, the mirage is one. It's one whole, we might say. And even though it functions with its apparently various parts, all parts are parts of the one mirage.

Another feature of awakening is that when *we* are freed from our constricted sense of self, we see that *all* things are also liberated. That's why in the Zen tradition it is said that there is no such thing as individual awakening. In a sense, the only thing that had been *un*awakened was *us*—that is to say, our ordinary sense of being contracted into a separate self. Once that has gone, all things are found to be already awakened. We awaken to a fully awakened world.

It's astonishing. And now that we taste the "wine of astonishment," referenced in the Psalms of King David, it's clear that the one thing that prevented our knowing it earlier was us. Our self. *We* were the cork in the bottle. Once we are gone, the wine flows freely.

My teacher Joan Rieck Roshi once explained that all

phenomena have two sides: "discriminating conscious-ness," which engenders individuation and separation; and "originating consciousness," which all things share. See the originating consciousness of a bar of soap, and it meets you in your own originating consciousness. You and the soap are separate on the level of discriminating consciousness. But in originating consciousness, you and the soap are one.

It can have a tremendous impact on our hearts to discover this. It can provoke an overwhelming sense of love—both of being loved and of loving. If we are still in the midst of an experience of oneness when the love wells up, then the love itself becomes one with all. The sense of an all-healing force naturally arises, wherein we become part of an all-encompassing love, which has the power to heal trauma and psychological wounds, and open up any heart, no matter how defended. New research suggests that this kind of experience, even when induced by psychoactive drugs, can help in the treatment of post-traumatic stress disorder (PTSD), becoming a kind of beneficent counterbalance to the experience of trauma.

Various contemporary trauma researchers, such as Gabor Maté and Bessel van der Kolk, have concluded that the heart of trauma is not only the horror of a moment or period of our lives in which intolerable events and emotions took over the nervous system, but also the sense of being alone and iso-lated in that horror. This sense of isolation can happen even if others are present, but are for whatever reason unable to meet us with comfort in the moment. Awakening, by con-trast, brings the exact opposite sense—namely, that we are indissolubly linked to the bottom of our being with everything else. We are utterly connected. We are bound together with all things by an infinite, preexisting, *original* love.

2. EMPTINESS

Of all the forms of original love, perhaps the deepest, and the hardest to grasp, is emptiness.

The term *emptiness* is easily misunderstood. First of all, Buddhist teachers and commentators who reckon with this difficult word often interpret it in different ways. For some, it means that things do not have the "thing-hood" that we attribute to them. A wooden chair, for example, is actually some pieces of wood that have been shaped in certain ways. The wood was originally parts of a tree growing in the forest, and that tree in turn was composed of the soil and rain and sunlight and air that allowed it to grow the way it did. All things are so interdependent on one another that the way we make distinct and discrete entities of them with our human minds gives them an individual thing-ness that they don't actually have. They are "empty" of it.

On the other hand, for other Buddhist thinkers, emptiness is about relativity. There are no absolute values. Put your foot in a pool on a hot day and the water feels cool. Put it in on a freezing winter's day after stepping off snow, and the same water will feel warm. Its temperature is "empty" of any absolute value. It is always relative.

Still others say that emptiness is much the same as "oneness"—it's the discovery of nonseparateness. No thing exists independently. All things are part of one co-arising flow. All are part of one fabric of forms arising. In that sense they are really all formless—or empty—because they belong to a single whole. Any sense of shape or individuality that we perceive is given to them by our interpretative perception.

And then there are others who go whole hog. For them, emptiness pretty much means what it says. All things are an appearance, a manifesting, without any solidity at all. One tweak in the angle of light, and you see clear through it all, to an all-pervading emptiness, or absence, which is always here, just behind the surface appearance of things.

The Tibetan master Chogyam Trungpa Rinpoche said that emptiness is like falling out of an airplane. The bad news is that you have no parachute. The good news is that there is no ground.

It's radical. Perhaps it's not for the faint of heart. But it just may be the greatest marvel of all.

Trungpa also said that one glimpse of emptiness is so horrifying that compassion naturally arises. Then he reflected for a moment, and added that one glimpse of it is so *marvelous* that compassion naturally arises.

In this sense, *emptiness* connotes an experiential shift, and the word is an attempt to describe it. Things aren't real in quite the way we'd thought. This apparently solid world is a *show*, a movie, a chimera, no more substantial than a reflection on a calm lake at dawn. You might see a forested hillside appearing on the lake's surface so clearly that it seems undeniably there. Yet if one pebble is thrown into the water, then the forested hillside vanishes. So it is with awakening but applied to the world. The apparently solid and real world before us is real as an appearance. But on the level of emptiness, it's *only* an appearance. The whole cosmos as we know it is an appearance.

So why is emptiness about love? It sounds more like the absence of anything at all, including love.

There are two possible answers here. The first is that our human response to finding this basic emptiness is an eruption of joy. It triggers a state of blessedness. It's like finding that all our life has ever been is an unconditional goodness. Somehow, stripped of all its show and disguises, bare existing itself is an unalloyed goodness.

As if the most basic reality of all, beneath and behind every other, is a total absence, and to touch or taste it is to find the ultimate relief from all suffering. It is to find a truth that can't be reduced or damaged or corrupted in any way. And it is to find that it is the ultimate core of our being. All else—all our life—is secondary.

That unassailable truth is an absolute love. It's perfect, it's untouchable, it's an absolute good.

Phew. That's a lot—but the critical point is this: what's behind any appearance is an all-loving, empty openness. An all-unifying spacelessness. An all-embracing wholeness without knowable size.

The second aspect of the love in emptiness is that emptiness is not inert. It's active. It's generative. It is continually giving, creating, flashing into being. Every moment is its activity. It's the source of all existence. All things are born of it. Some say it's what the big bang banged out of. And that the pre–big bang reality, whatever it was, is still here. The big bang in action is this very moment. And what it emerged from is right here too, as the origin of this moment. It is the ultimate source of all. Yet it's nothing. But it's also nothing but love.

That's the real meaning of emptiness.

AN ENCOUNTER WITH EMPTINESS

What is it actually like to experience emptiness? It's notoriously hard to convey, but here is an account by a young musician, Hobbs Magaret, of his experience meditating with a Zen koan. (The koan in question, mentioned in the account, is the single word *Mu*, considered an early "breakthrough koan." The report also mentions his mother, a yoga teacher and nurse, who had been practicing the same way and inspired him to start meditating with the koan.)

That afternoon, I had a lesson with my one guitar student. After we finished changing the strings and tuning up the guitar, I decided to put on some music. We listened to a recording of Son House singing "Don't You Mind Nobody Grinnin' in Your Face," one of the earliest recorded blues tunes.

I began to feel a familiar heaviness, as I become weepy at soulful music. As I heard Son House singing about not minding if people are talking about you, I had a realization. I turned to my student and said, "This song is about one man realizing that he is the world. When people are talking about you, they are not talking about you, they're talking about their conception of you.

You *have nothing to do with it. It's like they're shooting an arrow at nothing."*

As those words left my mouth, I saw in my mind's eye an arrow strike nothing. In that instant, it was true. A deep and curious and indescribable geyser of joy and light erupted through me, and I began laughing . . . then crying, at first subdued, but then rising to a level that was slightly alarming to my student.

The only words I could manage to get out were, "It's true! It's really nothing! Nothing at all!"

I continued to laugh and cry for another several minutes, even putting on another track to try to calm myself down so as not to alarm my student further, but there was no stopping what was happening. In a slight lull, I excused him and told him I would talk to him tomorrow. With this, I went upstairs, still in my stupor, to inform my partner that I would be going to my parents' house to talk to my mother, the only person I could talk to who could potentially understand.

As I got in the car and began driving to my parents, six miles away, the slight lull abruptly ended, and Mu came crashing over me in waves. Wave after wave, rising in a symphony of awareness. Awareness of nothingness. Crying and laughing, laughing and crying, looking at the mountains and the trees. I was the mountains and the trees! In more of a moan or wail than an exclamation, I was effusive: "Oh my god! It's true! There is nothing! I am nothing!"

I arrived at my parents' house, let the dog out of the car, and walked around to the back of the house. Looking

*out over their garden and pond into the mountains, I was
overwhelmed and awestruck by the beauty and magic of
it all.*

*Mom came out the back door, looking concerned,
greeting me. I returned her greeting with, "It's true!
It's true! It's nothing!" She quickly realized to some
degree what was happening. I cried, laughed, stomped
my feet, waved my arms, stood up, sat down, stood up
again, walked around, sat down again, and generally
felt as if my body was on fire. I saw eye to eye with
the Buddha. Everything was me. Everything flickered
back and forth with the blinding light of eternity.*

*After what must have been at least a half hour, the
experience eased enough that I could return home.*

*That night, I could not sleep. I tossed and turned all
night, finally getting a couple hours of rest.*

*The next morning, I awoke feeling a type of "hang-
over" or, as my mother later corrected me, "afterglow."
I sat in meditation that morning and wept the entire
time, laughing some, so overwhelmed with gratitude for
those who had come before me and discovered the gate
for me to walk through. Through their insane willpower
and insight, I was able to see the glory of my true nature.*

*Now, and since the experience, I feel profoundly
present, equanimous, and grounded: a peace beyond
description!*

Finding emptiness can be something like finding Platform 9¾ in the Harry Potter series. No one knows that the
magical platform in J. K. Rowling's version of King's Cross

Station in London exists until they suddenly burst through a wall and find it. You don't know emptiness is here until you find it for yourself. But because it *can* be found, and is not a freak experience, and because it can be so beneficial, attempts continue to be made to point to it.

This experience was a big surprise for Hobbs. But after a few days, he settled down again and resumed his ordinary life—playing gigs in bars, recording a new album in a friend's studio, and giving guitar lessons.

He continued his commitment to daily meditation, and in a few months he and his girlfriend got married. Later, they moved to a smallholding in Texas, where he had grown up, and he started a small cattle farm. There he deploys an innovative pasturing technique, which allows the cows to always have fresh grass and at the same time regenerates the soil. His wife works in digital marketing, he still plays music part-time, and they have two young children. He has also healed a difficult family relationship and enjoys the richness of his ordinary days.

Once we know the vast, loving peace of "emptiness," we feel more free to live in ways that make sense to us, to carve out a course that resonates with us. There are fewer internal obstacles to our leading a healthy and helpful life. We feel the peace that comes with knowing a boundless, unconditional love firsthand, and we have the practice of meditation to maintain our connection to it.

WHAT IS EMPTINESS?

In his book *Being You*, neuroscientist Anil Seth articulates a view current in consciousness science, which is that our experience of the world is a kind of "controlled hallucination" produced by our brains, and constantly updated by sensory input. The actual phenomena of our experience—colors, shapes, objects, sounds, and so on—are created by our neurology. The world as we experience it is a series of events in our brain. It's not that there is no world "out there," but rather that what we think of and experience as the world is, in fact, a best-guess simulation, designed to help us navigate the world. It is not the world itself.

In awakening to emptiness, we see through that "controlled hallucination." We recognize that it's just a simulation, contingent, evanescent, and transparent—and in that sense "empty."

To parse out emptiness further: on this level, we can see *either* that our sense of self is a self-conjured illusion *or* that the world through which we move is a kind of illusion—or both at once. The world is the complex of solids, gases, and liquids that we take it to be, yet at the same time, our actual experience of it is "gone," as some Buddhist texts put it.

What is left in its place is an absence, a gulf, a marvelous gap—but one filled with boundless benevolence and generosity. To touch it brings profound relief. It unplugs reservoirs of well-being, which inundate us. It can reorient us back into our lives with new tenderness and love, with a heart filled to the brim with sympathy, caring concern, and quiet joy.

To see the emptiness within things leaves us less entranced by our cravings and fears. We become less enthralled personally by the pleasures and pains of the world. A kind of bondage gets broken, a prison door unhinged. Now we see the beauty of the world more completely, the wonder that each moment arises as it does.

So emptiness is very far from being a recipe for harrowing nihilism, which we might easily fear it could be.

As it helps us soften and loosen our attachments, in their place a new loving joy wells up. When we are no longer so spellbound by our demands and cravings, we are freer to respond and care for this world, the way our broken-open hearts tell us to.

Awakening in this way is a kind of heartbreak. Our hearts open wider than we ever could have imagined possible. Sharon Salzberg has spoken of having "a heart as wide as the world" itself. And our hearts can't get that way without, in a sense, breaking out of their mold.

But at the same time, awakening opens up a spaciousness that can hold and carry all our heartbreak too. And sometimes people even come to awakening through heartbreak. When we face losses and griefs that seem too great to hold, it's not unknown for awakening to sweep in and reveal a breadth to the universe that had been silently embracing us all along. We sense a wider peace, which can come as a kind of radical answer to our pain.

Heartbreak and awakening are intimate with one another.

3. NO WAY BUT THROUGH

There's another kind of sudden experience that can happen.

What we've been looking at so far is something like this. Suddenly a crack is knocked through a wall, and now the light can't be kept out. A ray bursts in. This is the glimpse of *kensho*. Over time, more holes in the wall break open and more light floods in. What was beyond the wall, and previously kept out, starts to illuminate what was within more consistently. Finally, with repeated fractures, the wall loses its structural integrity and comes crashing down. Now, what was within the wall and what was outside become one.

In other words, the world of awakening and the world of ordinary experience are seen to have been one from the start. They can no longer be separated. The piece in us that was able to separate them has vanished.

This is a deeper kind of *kensho*, known in Zen as *daigo*, which can knock out something that never seems to come back. Access to the openness of things is stable now. We sense a beneficence in the heart of every moment. There is no going back. We have gone through a door. The flipping back and forth between a more "enlightened" perspective and the old-style "deluded" view ceases. It's not that there is no more training to undergo, but a crucial watershed has been crossed. We are freer than we ever believed possible.

The eighth-century Chinese meditation master Yaoshan said that before awakening, he felt like a mosquito trying to penetrate an iron ox. After it, he said, "the true body was revealed."

Here, there is no more witness to awakening. It's more like going *through* something. We don't *see* so much as we *lose* our sight, lose our senses, and even lose our awareness. We go through this experience, body, heart, and soul, all at once. It's like going through the eye of a needle. But we come out the other side. And what comes out is the same but different. Now all is intimately connected. Nothing is separate anymore. Separation has ended. Yet you get to be exactly who you uniquely are, and more thoroughly than ever before. You get to live your life among the people and things you love more vividly and intimately than ever before. It may sound like a kind of death, but it's much more like a new way of being alive.

None of this involves becoming unfit for ordinary life. Quite the reverse. The path of awakening is a way into a more beautiful, intimate, and love-filled life, in which we commit ourselves to the well-being of others more readily. We can be less self-centered, and more "allocentric," meaning concerned for others. We open ourselves to our loved ones, to our friends and colleagues, and to our wider family with a new tenderness. We turn to work, to our projects and jobs, with a fresh enthusiasm.

One of my meditation teachers, Yamada Ryōun Roshi, has had a successful career in business over several decades. Alongside his work, he has meditated daily for over sixty years, since the age of sixteen. He has also raised a family with his wife of many years. As he describes it, after years of practice his meditation practice and his worldly life are a single field. There is no distinction between them. Each informs the other. They go together like a hand in a glove. He still does all the things the chair of a large company needs to do: meeting with top management, meeting with the board, visiting international clients, and spending time with business partners in Japan and overseas. When not at work, he's at home with his wife, helping to prepare meals for guests or working on their English-style garden beside their home down an alley in an old district of Tokyo. Once or twice a month, he hosts a day of meditation at the Sanbo Zen school's main center in Kamakura, and once a year he leads a gathering of seventy-some international Zen teachers, either in Europe or North America. And every morning he sits for an hour at least.

A STORY FROM the annals of Chinese Buddhist practice:

> *Yaoshan (who lived 751–834) once turned out all the lights in his Zendo and said to the students, "I have one teaching. I'll tell it to you when a calf has been born of a bull."*
>
> *First there was silence. Then in the darkness someone called out, "A calf has been born of a bull. Why don't you say it?"*
>
> *Yaoshan called for lamps to be brought so he could see who had spoken. But whoever it was had already disappeared back into the assembly, and they couldn't find the speaker.*

A bull can't give birth to a calf. What was Yaoshan talking about?

Clearly, some impossible kind of birth. But the student who spoke recognized what the master meant. He too had been through this impossible birth—an experience whereby we go in as one thing and emerge as something else. The two sides of the equation don't fit together. They don't add up. We enter from the finite, separated side, and we emerge as infinite, unified.

Woah. What does that mean?

Well, maybe no one can *say* exactly. We just have to trust (if we're interested) and go through it, ideally with a guide to maybe hold our hand. Though really, no one can hold our hand through it. They can just say afterward, *Yes, you too.* And not just you. Look at all your companions across the ages, who also fell through. Though if it happens, then you don't even need to hear that.

This kind of experience is a single, decisive shift, which changes us forever. That's the promise.

4. BLAZING FORTH

Once again, emptiness is neither void nor inert. It couldn't be more *full.* It is the plenum—the fullness—of Christian mysticism. It's the pleroma—the divine totality—of Neoplatonism. In spite of being nothing, it is all-creating, both the source of all *and* all.

In Taoist language, according to scholar, poet, and practitioner David Hinton, original nature is "absence." In his book *Existence*, which explores the origins of Chan Buddhism, Hinton explains that fundamental *absence* is the fabric of all existence. But it has the inherent property of *tsu-jan*, or "blazing forth." All this world is original nature's *blazing forth*, in its infinite multiplicity.

What blazes forth is utter "absence." And what it pours forth *as* is *all phenomena.*

Emptiness is infinite creative generosity—the limitless outpouring of existence. And to experience this intimately, for ourselves, is to find that we are not separate from it. In the end, it's what we are.

Our response to discovering this is a spontaneous up-welling of loving gratitude, a tidal wave of love—a creative energy that just can't stop itself from giving and giving. That is what it "loves" to do. We are its mute and floored beneficiaries.

The thirteenth-century master Wumen said, "Where the active wheel revolves, even a master fails."

In the face of the limitless capacity, power, and love of original nature, not even a master can say or do anything.

Joan Rieck Roshi used to say that her teacher had called all this world "the acrobatics of emptiness."

Juan de la Cruz, the sixteenth-century Spanish mystic, talked of a spring that never ceases to flow.

> ¡Qué bien sé yo la fonte que mana y corre, aunque es
>   de noche!
> (How well I know the spring that runs and flows,
>   though it be in the dead of night!)

The spring itself is shrouded in darkness. Yet it can be intimately known. How well Juan de la Cruz knows it, though it can't even be seen.

And some might add here, it *can* be seen. It is this very day, this very room, this sunny, blustery morning, and the shadows and dappled light stirring on the wall of this room, across from the window. Here it is, pouring forth as this moment, here and now.

Try This

Come into stillness, with your eyes open. Look straight ahead, across the space in front of you.

Keep your eyes more or less still. Now imagine that the whole field of your vision is like an illuminated stage at the front of a dark auditorium.

Let yourself start to feel what it's like to be seeing this stage while drifting backward, as if you're drawing back away from the stage, farther back over the rows of seats, back into the dark space behind you. Let yourself go still farther, behind the last row of seats. Meanwhile, there is still the lit-up stage of your field of sight in front of you. Now you're starting to see it floating in a great, dark space.

Let it be as if the stage of your sight becomes a kind of box, with light illuminating it, and you are in the darkness away from it, looking at the lit box. Feel the dark space that envelops the whole area of sight, and envelops you too. Feel the dark space all around and behind you. While being aware of the illuminated area of your sight, sense how wide the darkness all around you actually is. Maybe it's wider than we can ever know. Maybe it opens endlessly to either side and behind us.

What would it be like to recede still farther back into that darkness? To dissolve into it? What kind of deepest rest might it offer? Is it possible that some part of us knows we have a deep home in that spacious darkness?

GUIDED MEDITATION

The Nature of Awareness

Come into a comfortable seated position. Let your whole body relax.

In this meditation we are going to explore the nature of awareness.

We start by feeling the whole body at ease. Let the jaw sink a little, let the shoulders and arms be slack, and let the torso be warm, soft, and hollow. Let the buttocks, the legs, and the feet also be warm, relaxed, settled, and at ease.

Note how it is possible to be aware of the whole body as a kind of warm interior space. Feel that space within your body, as if your whole body were something like a body-shaped balloon filled with warm atmosphere, warm space. Just feel that space. Note that your awareness can also be present all through that inner space of your body. If you choose, then you can inhabit your whole body with your awareness.

Now rest in awareness of your body.

Good.

Now let's shift our awareness to the soundscape all around. Note that all sounds are arising within a kind of space that envelops you like a bubble. The soundscape itself is a space too. Let your awareness rest in the space of sounds for a while.

Now let's combine our awareness of the two spaces—the space of the body and the space of the soundscape.

It's as if there were one balloon—awareness of the body—and all around it there were another balloon, larger, which is awareness of sounds. Can you become aware of both "balloons"? Both those spaces?

Is the space of body awareness different in its nature from the space of soundscape awareness?

What if the two spaces could blend into one larger space? What if the boundary between them could become thin and even dissolve? Then they might become one single wide space.

Is the awareness of body space different from awareness of sound space? Can the two awarenesses become one? What if one single awareness pervades the body and also pervades the space in which sounds arise?

Rest in the single larger awareness. Where does this awareness end? Can you find the far edges of it? Can you be aware of the whole building you are in? Does awareness reach beyond the walls of the building? What about the whole yard around the building? The whole neighborhood? The whole town? Even the whole region?

How big is awareness? Where does it end?

Don't try too hard with these explorations. Just rest with the invitations, and let them be gently absorbed into your awareness. Just rest as you are and silently ask the question, *How big is my awareness?* Let awareness be warm and soft, and let it feel like a true home you've always known but may have forgotten. A home that has always been with you, one that you have never lacked. Allow yourself to come home to this wonderful abode, which is always here for you.

Thank you.

CHAPTER EIGHT

Integration

A REVERSAL

I remember watching a movie as a kid about a group of brave
jet pilots, back in the 1950s, who were trying to break the
sound barrier. They would climb to stratospheric heights
in their early jet planes, point the nose at the ground, and
open the throttle. The hope was to break the speed of sound
in time to pull out of the perilous dive. The problem was
that time and again, a pilot would get right up close to the
speed of sound but then be unable to pull out. The controls
would stop responding. Some of them managed to bail out,
but some hurtled to their deaths, leaving smoking craters in
the ground.

Finally, one brave pilot broke through the sound barrier,
and then found that like the others he couldn't pull out of
his dive. But instead of trying to, he reversed the controls,
pushing deeper into the dive. Miraculously, his plane came
up into straight and level flight, saving his life.

According to the movie, at that pace, beyond the speed of sound, he discovered that you had to reverse the controls. They worked backward.

Awakening can be like that. Our guidance systems for practice and life almost seem to get reversed. Things get back to front. Our dreams, desires, and ambitions were in part a beguiling smoke screen, it turns out, and as long as we believed in them, we couldn't see the truth. Perhaps they weren't in fact as good as we had thought. Being too focused on getting the things we wanted may actually have been one of the things holding us back from a larger life.

By contrast, awakening is like the Holy Grail—the chalice from which one sip fulfills us completely. It even dissolves our very hunger for fulfillment, as we disappear into the *all* we didn't realize had been waiting here for us all along.

I later learned that the movie I'd seen as a child, made by the great British director David Lean in 1952 and titled *The Sound Barrier*, had some crucial details wrong. (When he made it, Lean had to rely on scraps of information that emerged from the shroud of secrecy surrounding the real-life sound barrier project.) Actually, once they reached the sound barrier, the pilots had to let go of the controls altogether, rather than reverse them, and the planes would then fly straight and level by themselves. But either way—reversing the controls or letting them go—the analogy is still quite apt for the process of awakening. In both cases, whether we go against our natural tendency to pursue what we think we need, or release our hold on our current understanding of our best interests, a larger truth emerges to reset our understanding.

Paradoxically, either way, in a kind of reversal, we find we may have been misguided about our wishes and fears. Our life has always been part of a larger reality than we realized. Once we see that, we may find the kinds of fulfillment we formerly chased no longer have the same allure. We may or may not choose to pursue them now. But once we have tasted a deeper and more dependable fulfillment—and not through the means we dreamed of or expected, but rather through a means we couldn't have conceived of until it happened—we are then freer to engage with our relationships and with the day-to-day joys that life offers. In other words, awakening needn't entail the loss of things we enjoy and love. Rather, it allows us to appreciate them from a place not so much of need or attachment, but of appreciation, so we can cherish them more. Our need has slackened, so our love can grow.

NATURAL AWAKENING

Some people get hit out of the blue with awakening experiences without any practice at all. This lends credence to the view that awakening is a natural state, not something devised or constructed by us, as some scholars have argued. It's an innate property of consciousness.

These "natural awakenings" are also reminders that practices are simply methods. They can do no more than increase the likelihood of our stumbling into what is already awake within and around us. It may be better not to get too attached to specific forms of practice. The important thing is what they lead us to, not the forms themselves.

Personally, I was struck by a random awakening when I was nineteen years old. Out of the blue I fell into an overwhelming intimacy with what felt like the whole universe, in which the distinction between the world and myself disappeared. I belonged and had done so since the beginning of time. It felt as though my nose were pressing against the far edge of the cosmos. Every last ounce of me belonged to every last corner of the universe. It felt like a boundless benevolence, an immemorial love. I knew my life had just been fulfilled, and I could have died happily that night.

Who knows how often something like this happens to people, unrecorded and unexplored? How rare these unprovoked experiences are is actually a matter of research. David Yaden, a professor of sociocultural studies at the University of Arizona, has estimated that 30 percent of adults have likely had some kind of "self-transcendent experience."

This term, often abbreviated to STE, has become current as a standard marker for "spiritual experience" in research centers today. It's an umbrella term that includes various kinds of experience, not all of which meet the criteria for non-dual awakening. For example, mindful witnessing and flow states both count as STEs, even though they typically are neither free of self nor non-dual. But if Yaden's (and others') research is right, then it's still encouraging to know that so many people are familiar with finding exceptional peace and joy in their being, and the numbers affirm the view that such experiences are natural and intrinsic to us.

A FRIEND OF mine was once running late to a funeral. As she raced up the steps to the church where the ceremony was being held, and pulled open the door, she was suddenly struck by something like a great wind, as she put it in conversation some years after the event. It blew right through the dark interior of the church, and right through her. Except the wind wasn't exactly physical. It was something like a "spiritual" wind, blowing away the pews, the altar, and herself. There was nothing but that mighty wind.

Shocked and confused, laughing and crying, she found herself staggering through the church toward the cluster of people up at the front gathered around the coffin. She had no idea what was happening to her, except that it had something to do with a vast benevolence that enveloped the world. That wind, whatever it was, was infinitely, fiercely loving.

After that, she continued her work as a writer and journalist, and still does. But that day also marked the start of her path to becoming an Episcopalian priest.

Awakening always happens by itself, whether in a context of deliberate practice or with barely a whisper of encouragement from any outside party. One of the great advantages of spontaneous natural awakening is that you don't have to put in long hours of meditation to taste it. Two qualifying points, however: it's utterly unreliable and it's rare. And it's rarer still for random awakenings to have enough clarity and thoroughness that no further practice is needed in order to live out their implications. Even the great twentieth-century Indian sage Ramana Maharshi, who had a momentous awakening as a teenager, needed some six months of "incubation" in a cellar afterward, followed by several years of training and guidance under a *rishi*, or master, before he could integrate and embody his awakening.

Awakening, for the majority of people, is an initial step: most of us need help in waking up further—more clearly, thoroughly, and consistently—and in integrating it into the way we live.

AN EXERCISE

Who Awakens?

The shift from dualistic to non-dual experience can be disorienting to our ordinary sense of things. The trick is not to mind. To let it be, however unfamiliar it is. The disorientation lasts only as long as the ordinary self is still trying to make sense of things.

What to do? As little as possible. Rest in how things are. Just let them be.

Right now, let your attention be drawn to awareness itself. Let awareness be what you are aware of. This instruction is a sound and long-proven approach for starting to immerse yourself in non-dual reality.

Imagine a cup of water that is slowly being submerged in a calm ocean. Let the water in the cup be floating in the midst of the wide waters of the ocean all around it.

Imagine that you are the awareness within the cup, and all around you is a greater awareness. Let your awareness fill your body. Let the wider awareness occupy the whole world around you.

Now imagine that the cup is losing its opacity. It's fading into glass. Now there's the water within the glass, and the water all around the glass. We can still distinguish between the two bodies of water—the small, defined volume within the glass and the vast one all around it. But the membrane separating the two has become see-through.

Gradually, allow that transparent membrane to release itself and dissolve. Let it disappear altogether.

Allow yourself to surrender your sense of self. Let any boundary between you and all that surrounds you disappear. Let your sense of self disappear into the great ocean of awareness.

Let your identity switch off. We no longer feel that we are a particular person. We belong to a vast awareness. And it seems to pervade all creation. We become all of creation.

This can be a profoundly pleasant experience. It washes us clean. It cleanses our senses and bathes our soul. When we emerge back into a more ordinary sense of things, we may still feel connected to an unconditional well-being. In time, we can come to see our ordinary experience of things as a beautiful mirage floating in this open vastness. It can be as if the ordinary experience becomes transparent. Just beyond the world of things, just behind it, we sense a great openness patiently waiting.

There are other ways the reality revealed in awakening can show itself.

Sometimes it's less about awareness and more about a single physical fact, almost like a single solidity, which all things are made of. Sometimes the process of identification remains active but migrates to all that is perceived, and we sense clearly that what we really are is all that we see and hear. Instead of there being an onboard witness and agent who is having our life, we feel that we are the reverse— that "agent" was a fiction, and what we actually are is all that the agent thought they were not—namely, all the objects of awareness.

One student reported getting up to go to a meeting with their teacher, deep in a meditation retreat, and as they were walking quietly across the meditation hall, it suddenly struck them that their true mind was not within their skull. Their real mind was the floor they were crossing, the walls of the room, the other people sitting there. They were walking *through* their very self.

They went into the meeting with the teacher, where they couldn't help slapping the wall next to them and the floor beneath them, saying, "This is the teacher. This is me. This is who I am."

At the time, they were visiting a somewhat daunting Japanese master, a revered and austere figure, to whom they had never spoken like this before. But to their surprise and delight, the teacher's face suddenly softened in kindness and broke into a smile, and they quietly affirmed what the student was saying.

Non-dual experience can also show up as a wild energy devoid of content. No cosmos or materiality or objects of any kind—just an unbounded, open energy.

A friend of mine, who works as a meditation teacher and a neuropsychologist, had spent a few days climbing in the California desert. On his last day, in the late light at the end of day, as he was coming down the dusty path back to the parking lot where he had left his truck, he was suddenly overtaken by a rush of blind energy. He said it was as if it blew away his conscious experience. All that was left was a wild, ungraspable openness, void of content, too dynamic to be understood or even thought about.

It left him exhilarated in a way that he had never felt before, as if he had just been touched by a creative energy at the heart of the universe.

Sometimes there is no sense of space at all. Instead, there is an emptiness of zero dimension. Sometimes there isn't even awareness—it is a kind of death, from which awareness will reemerge, purged and cleansed of clinging, the root system of desire and aversion having been dug out.

And so on. Different faces of awakening. And the various traditions value different aspects of awakening more than others. They even assess the thoroughness and stability of awakening in different ways. But all recognize that for awakening to become a real part of our life, it needs to be embodied in our day-to-day existence.

Some schools want a practitioner to consciously reside in awakened awareness. Others reckon that is too self-conscious, and self-assessment must be washed away. In some, the process isn't complete until all awareness of awakening has been completely erased, and the practitioner is leading a perfectly normal life—with the exception that their efforts and energies are joyfully directed toward the well-being of others. And they might not even be aware of their contributions, so fully has their life of compassion become second nature.

THE TEN OXHERDING PICTURES

There is an old map of the process of spiritual awakening known as the Ten Oxherding Pictures. It comes out of ninth-century Chinese Buddhism, but can be applied more broadly, to the long arc of any spiritual life, as we come to inhabit our true place in the world more fully.

In the first oxherding picture, "Seeking the Ox," an oxherder realizes that they have lost their ox and decide to search for it. That is to say, we realize that we are not whole, that we live with an underlying sense of lack and unease, and that we yearn for a more whole life. We resolve to search for it.

The second picture, "Seeing the Ox's Hoofprints," is where the oxherd picks up the trail of the ox's prints in the earth. This is us finding our way to a path of practice.

The stage seen in the second picture is equivalent to finding the loving shelter of the first wheel-rut in the cart track metaphor. We are settling into regular meditation, growing in mindful awareness, receiving some guidance and support, and reconnecting with the life of our bodies. We become more grounded in self-compassion, and we learn to live in greater harmony with our colleagues, family, and friends. We are walking the trail of love, which leads us successively through the first three inns of practice.

In the third picture, "Seeing the Ox," the oxherd has their first glimpse of the ox itself—of the boundless love inherent in non-dual reality. It's only a glimpse—they see the ox's rump in the bushes or its head or flank or tail. But it's enough to know that there is a live beast out there, a wild, awake energy. They have actual, personal, experiential confirmation that the ox is real.

This is the second rut of the cart track: unbroken, undivided, wide-open reality. It's equivalent to *kensho*—the sudden seeing of our true nature, original love. The ox is this original love. It is who we really are, beyond the cluster of assumptions, opinions, and views we commonly take ourselves to be, something wild and unnameable—open, boundless, empty, all-inclusive. It's a direct connection with original love.

Meanwhile, we return to normal activities, with a renewed vitality, a new commitment to do what we can to help alleviate suffering in the world. The further we go on the path, the more "prosocial" emotions come to the fore—compassion, empathy, and loving-kindness. This happens because we are tapping more deeply into original love, which is the primary element of the original nature we have found.

We may also have some bewilderment about what has happened and what we should do about it. Generally, the answer is simply to keep meditating, and keep working for harmony and well-being in our homes and communities.

CATCH BULL AT FOUR

The singer-songwriter Cat Stevens titled one of his albums *Catch Bull at Four*, a reference to the fourth oxherding picture. (He practiced Zen meditation for a while before finding his way to Islam.)

If the third ox picture is about plunging into original nature for a moment before withdrawing, then the fourth, "Catching the Ox," is different. Here we encounter a lasting shift in our center of gravity. Our hearts open to the boundless in such a way that they need never close again. They will at times, for sure, but access to original love is now free to seep into our daily lives. We are reorienting ourselves to openhearted living, informed by the presence of the vastness of original nature in every moment.

This is where our work in the first wheel-rut becomes so helpful. Gradually, we have been unraveling many knots and digging out root systems of attachment. Mindfulness, the recognition of support from others and our interconnectedness with all things, and the softening effects of absorption states have all given us tools to develop our clarity about the second wheel-rut. It can be invaluable, in the inn of awakening, to have easy access to the other three inns. By availing ourselves of the services of all *four* inns, we gradually wear down whatever obstructs the boundless love found in the inn of awakening. We need to work on multiple levels, with growing mindfulness, with support and perhaps "outriggers," such as therapy, somatic work, yoga, dance, and so on, and with deepening absorption, or samadhi. Here is where the multilevel approach really pays off.

When we do finally reach the fourth ox picture and stably rest in fundamental awareness, with original love freely welling up and supporting us, it usually comes about through a deeper experience, in which our resistances collapse and we break through more thoroughly. A critical piece of our machinery of "selfing" gets knocked out. In its place there's a wide, deep peace, an unnameable freedom, and sweet love, which keeps welling up in our hearts.

Thereafter practice becomes easier. We have finally come home. Nothing holds us back. It's like we wear this moment as our own body. It's not just home, it's who we are. We reside right here, in the heart of this moment. In the core of *now*, a boundless love, not separate from us, is always at work generating this moment. All our spiritual striving, all our seeking, all our efforts, have finally borne fruit.

"All shall be well, and all shall be well, and all manner of thing shall be well": these are the words of the medieval mystic Julian of Norwich. And we feel this to be true, even though we're more awake than ever to the pains and sufferings of this world, to its manifold injustices and cruelties. Somehow our new perspective encourages and energizes us to work for the relief of suffering, for the healing of the world.

FOR MOST WESTERN practitioners, the fourth ox picture may seem like the end of the trail. It represents an abiding shift in how we experience life, bringing a stable openness to the non-dual, a wild openness to every moment, and a new sense of purpose, framed around help and service.

Any territory *beyond* this would seem irrelevant. Surely our whole purpose has been to get here? Who would care about any further development? And actually, though the path does go on, the remaining pictures, five through ten, are about integrating what we have already experienced ever more thoroughly into ordinary life. They are about returning to the world with a heart full of love and an intention to serve this world the best we can.

We'll cover them more swiftly here.

TO INFINITY AND BEYOND

As of now, a growing mainstream interest in awakening in the West is focused on the stages of the third and fourth oxherding pictures—on finding and residing in "non-dual awareness." Yet the old-school explorers, the psychonauts of yore, who spent decades investigating the territories of consciousness through silence and stillness, left records and maps of their discoveries for us, such as the oxherding pictures. And they show that we can go beyond awakenings.

One of my teachers, the former Philippines Jesuit turned Zen master, Ruben Habito Roshi, now a professor of comparative religion at Southern Methodist University, has often said, "Practice is like Buzz Lightyear in *Toy Story*: 'It's to infinity—and beyond.'"

The further stages of the oxherd's journey, "beyond awakening," involve personalizing awakening, becoming less self-conscious about it—"Washing away traces of awakening," as Yamada Kōun puts it in his book *Zen: The Authentic Gate*. In the fifth ox picture, "Taming the Ox," we start to embody the implications of original love as our priorities shift away from our egoistic self toward serving the wider family of all beings. It's not always automatic. Practice is needed.

In the sixth picture, "Riding the Ox Home," our life grounded in original love is becoming second nature.

There's a well-known philosophy of four phases in skills acquisition. With any new skill, we start with *unconscious incompetence*. We don't even realize what we are doing wrong. Then we move to *conscious incompetence*, where we are aware of our errors. Then comes *conscious competence*, where we have the skills but they require conscious effort. Finally, we reach *unconscious competence*, where the training has turned the new skills into traits, and conscious effort is no longer needed. This would be equivalent to "riding the ox home"—naturally living in original love.

In the seventh, "Forgetting the Ox," the ox disappears. There is no longer an awareness of awakening. We have "washed it away." In the eighth picture, "Ox and Self Forgotten," we have forgotten all traces not just of awakening, but of any kind of self who could have awakened. In the ninth picture, "Returning to the Source," we return to this moment, knowing deep in our bones, without thinking about it, that there is nothing besides *this*. Original love is no different from exactly this.

The tenth ox picture is captioned: "Returning to the Market-place with Gift-bestowing Hands." Here we come back to ordinary life with a simple, spontaneous wish to serve this world and its beings the best we can, as servants of original love now, spreading the love however and wherever we can, the best we can. Fully human, with all our foibles and mistakes, warts and all, but in love with the world.

We just keep trying to do better while being at peace with the full range of human experience. Joy, ease, and wonder are natural—and so are sadness, fear, and irritation. In some traditions there's an ideal that the practitioner is a more or less perfect human being, free of all taint of greed or ill will. In other traditions, there's a recognition that the practitioner is a pretty ordinary person now. Yes, they try to offer the gifts of their service the best they can, putting their shoulder to the wheel of creating a more just and compassionate world, according to the needs of the people and times they find themselves in. But not in some holier-than-thou way. Instead, they are at home in the world as a fully embodied, natural human being.

Practice never requires us to abandon our lives. Instead, it allows us to experience them in new ways. It shows us that whatever we are doing, a boundless love is always present, right in the midst of things. It's there because everything is its creation. Or viewed the other way around, it's there because we only have to look closely at anything, and we can come to see that it's made of nothing but an empty, nameless creative force.

Meditation is sometimes described as a deconstructive process. It can deconstruct our cravings and aversions, and thus our sufferings. It can help to deconstruct our psychological patterns and blocks, and nudge us into releasing them. It can deconstruct unhealthy attachments. But it can also deconstruct our experience, so that we see through it to the vast, boundless source that is everywhere and nowhere all at once.

But in doing all this, it shows us ever more clearly that our deepest longing—to unify with a boundless love at the heart of things—is always available. We don't need special, sequestered circumstances to find it. It's always right here, at the tips of our fingers, at the end of our nose, staring us in the face, hidden in plain sight. All we have to do is slow down, notice, surrender our assumptions and preconceptions, and all we could ever want is right here. That's what meditation is for.

ORDINARY LIFE

The great Jewish-American novelist Isaac Bashevis Singer once wrote a short story called "Short Friday," in which an elderly Jewish couple living in an old shtetl in eastern Europe in the late nineteenth century go through a day of devout preparation for the Sabbath, which is coming the next day. They tidy up their little house, they bake the correct pies for the coming day of rest, and they utter the customary blessings.

As a reader, you sense the tender devotion that they bring to each of these tasks and the deep affection they have for one another. You can feel the quiet holiness of their lives and their gentle, loving engagement with their home and with one another. They are at peace, even as they contemplate the eternal rest that awaits them, not too far off down the road.

Gradually, by the end of the story, the reader comes to realize that in fact the couple have already died. They are already living in heaven. They didn't notice the transition, because their life on earth was already so closely aligned to the heavenly.

The message of the story might be: live well, and you can live in something like heaven on earth. And it may look rather like the ordinary life you already have.

That is also the message of the path of awakening. In

awakening, everything is just as it was before. No difference. Except for one tiny thing . . . thoughts of self have
gone, fallen back into their rightful place: in a kitchen
drawer, along with the string, the scissors, and the tape.

There's an ancient Zen poem titled "Trust in the Heart"
that says:

> One hair's breadth of difference
>   separates heaven from earth

And what that hairsbreadth of difference is, is the tiny
thought of self.

Nothing else changes. But with self gone, we see the un-
changed world in a whole new, changed way.

CAVE RETREAT

I was on a solo retreat in northern New Mexico, staying in
a cave high up a valley in the Sangre de Cristo Mountains,
a simple space with a narrow bed, a camping cooker, and a
woodstove. I carried in my water and scavenged for fire-
wood. The cave was set up for practice—a small, half-buried
chamber, a berm deep in the valley's side beneath a stand of
ponderosa pines, with a small platform for meditation.

I was having a restless time. My brain was in recovery
from a concussion, the current state of US politics was
dire, and our retreat center down in Santa Fe was having
difficulties—all of which made me uneasy, sometimes angry,
sometimes sad.

In my restless state, my eye kept getting drawn to a gorgeous Tibetan *thangka*, or icon, that hung above the meditation seat. It was an image of the Tibetan goddess Tara. A couple of extra divinities had been tucked into either corner below her. One was a voluptuous female figure (an emblem of desire?), and the other a green demon wielding a sword, engulfed in a ball of small, expertly depicted flames.

What was *that* dude, that green devil, doing in a picture that was all about sublime practice, I kept wondering. I found him fascinating and sneaked peeks at him when I thought I ought to be deepening my meditation. Suddenly, it hit me: of course, whatever else he might be, he surely represented anger, ill will, hatred, the "second poison" of Buddhism.

But why was he here, in an icon of the goddess of love and awakening?

Again, it struck me: anger was 100 percent fine, from a goddess's point of view. From the perspective of awakening, anger was no problem. It was "empty"—transparent and boundless.

You could work with anger either by trying to reduce it or by seeing clear through it—recognizing its "unborn nature." The goddess—or awakening—would kind of smile at you regardless, whichever way you went.

I couldn't help smiling myself and then grinning, until I burst out laughing. A great peace opened up. I felt myself physically stretch wide until I popped, and a boundless wildness opened up, in which all was well, in spite of my brain injury, national politics, the problems at the center, and the many struggles and sufferings of the world.

Feeling giddy, as if the seat I was sitting on, the floor

beneath it, and the land all around me were nothing but a fizzing vacancy, I got up and went outside to walk off the effervescent energy bubbling up. Outside, everything was filled with a smoky vacancy, as if the dry tussocky grass, springy underfoot, was here, just as it seemed to be, but also not here; as if the meadow, looking bleached in the fading light, were a mirage; and as if the mighty ponderosa trunks, which seemed like great temple columns in the gathering dusk, were all evanescent, fizzing, and diaphanous, made of smoke too.

And just behind that smokiness was a gulf, a nothing, an utter blankness. All this world that was appearing—it was flashing like lightning out of nothing, out of a black hole, not a space but an absolute zero. And somehow it was all made of that nothingness.

Just to see that made everything unutterably beautiful. High above, a sublime pyramid of rock floated, the highest nearby peak, and just now it was pale gold in the late light. It hung there in another world, a beacon of a higher world, a gatepost to some heaven we humans could recognize from afar but never enter.

Except that right then, in a flash, that peak and I were both pouring like lightning out of the same utter blankness, with no distance between us, as if a single force were generating both of us, as well as the trees and hillsides and grasses all around us. All of it was one single body pouring itself forth into existence.

I kept walking—going nowhere, walking on nothing, on air, on space, on emptiness, every step part of the very same wonder of creation springing forth, all made of nothing, yet all a single arising, a single body, a single cloud, a single wonder, a single flash of lightning.

Nameless. Marvelous. Empty. And here.

KOANS

We touched on koans earlier, and I want to revisit them in light of all we have been exploring.

Koan training is an ingenious method for conveying the experience of awakening, and for learning to live it more thoroughly, in a rich, deep life informed by love.

Most koans are about *things*. A dog. A tree. A bridge. A flower. Autumn leaves. Somehow, in Zen, these ordinary things of the world contain the deepest truths. If these truths are explored through koans, then the most ordinary things can awaken us.

One Zen student had been sitting with the koan *What is this?* for some time. One afternoon she was tying her shoelaces prior to going out for a run. All of a sudden, there was nothing but the shoelaces in her fingers. Everything else fell away. It was as if those very laces occupied the whole universe. There was no room left for her. Stunned, she went outside and gazed at the world, as if seeing it for the first time and finding that it was filled with astounding beauty. The clouds moved overhead like folds of gray velvet, and the trees were awake and alive, their roots plunging into the earth, their boughs seeming to embrace the sky. She had found the answer to the koan. She knew now what the koan meant by "this": the world was one marvelous co-arising of all phenomena as one single reality, with no trace of the self she normally believed herself to be.

Koans are brief excerpts from the biographies of enlightened masters in the Buddhist traditions of India and China, baffling to our ordinary reasoning mind. It's said that they are dark to the mind but radiant to the heart. They can trigger powerful experiences, but prior to any awakening, they can also settle and deepen our sitting. And afterward, they can help to integrate awakening into our lives. They actually cover the whole sweep of the path.

What is the sound of one hand? Stop the sound of the distant bell. Make Mount Fuji take three steps. A meditator runs a koan through their mind as they sit, until they become absorbed in the phrase.

Someone using a simple koan—for example, as above, *What is this?*—will find it can relax and expand their awareness. The koan is speaking from a different register of being, and something in us feels recognized and goes gratefully quiet.

What is the sound of one hand? A nonsense question. Yet if we refrain from going into problem-solving mode, and don't try to unravel it like a puzzle, then we can allow the strange question to hover in our minds, like a full moon rising in the evening sky as sunset is darkening into night. There the hazy moon is, floating low in the sky. So the koan floats in the mind. We wait and see—does it awaken a calm, an ease, a quiet? Does it spark curiosity?

Over time, koans can become a means for entering the territory of awakening. "The sound of one hand"—some Zen masters say you won't find that sound until you "hear

it with your eyes and see it with your ears." What on earth
do they mean?

Perhaps they mean that only the eyes and ears of the heart
can apprehend what the koan is trying to share. Maybe it
wants us to experience a hand in a way that we never have
before. Maybe even this ordinary hand at the end of my arm,
which I take so much for granted, actually has something to
teach me about my life, which the flash of *kensho* may reveal.

But koans also take us beyond *kensho*. If *kensho* is a lurch
into the boundless, selfless universe of enlightenment, then
afterward we still need to gradually cultivate our embodi-
ment of what we have experienced. One way to do this is
to train with koan after koan, gradually integrating the experience into ordinary life. More "openings" may befall us,
which shake us to our core and blow even our core away.

As Dōgen put it in the thirteenth century, "Body and
mind fall away." In other words, all experience vanishes.
And then reappears. We lose nothing except what bound us
and made it harder to experience the original love inherent
in every moment. Now we are liberated and every last thing
can be a gift, a treasure, a miracle.

Yamada Kōun sometimes offered metaphors for awakening that drew on his background in mathematics. He invited
students to think of a fraction. Every fraction consists of
a *numerator*, the number above the fraction bar, and a *denominator*, the number below the fraction bar. We have been
living in the world of numerators only. Each thing we experience, we see as a separate entity, not realizing that every
phenomenon is in fact a fraction. Each thing is both the nu-

merator we normally see and the denominator underneath it. In awakening, the denominator shows itself.

What is the denominator? Zero. Infinity. Unity. All three at once.

A koan helps us glimpse that denominator. And because all phenomena share the same denominator, we join all things in that shared denominator. Hence all is experienced as one.

In time, with ongoing practice, we come to see the *entire* fraction: because the *real* nature of things is neither just their separate multiplicity (the numerator level) nor just the empty boundlessness (the denominator), but *both*. The two halves of the fraction are actually *one*. They were never separate at all.

In one koan, Yunmen Wenyan (864–949 CE) is asked, "How do you go beyond awakening?"

He answers, "Rice cake."

That's the end of the koan.

Yunmen is trying to answer the question as clearly as he can. What happens after awakening? He's not striving for some kind of bathos, nor is he kidding around. He's not trying to undermine highfalutin ideas we might be suffering from about "Buddha nature" or "awakening." He is simply presenting his experience.

The answer to the deep question, "How do you go beyond awakening?" really is, "Rice cake." Let's remember to enjoy it the next time we reach into the cupboard and open up a pack.

The point of these strange little nuggets of story is that there surely are paths to awakening. There truly is an inn where ways of approaching non-dual reality continue to be offered. Many traditions are devoted to keeping their doors open, offering "rooms at the inn." Not only is original love alive and well, but paths to it are alive and well too.

SELFLESS

One final word here: the path isn't about a self-conscious effort to be "good." Sometimes adepts who reach the later phases of the path don't look too much like adepts anymore. There was Ryokan, a kind of holy fool in nineteenth-century Japan, who lived as a beggar in a straw hut on the edge of a village, playing ball games with the local children. There was Ikkyū in fourteenth-century Japan, who abandoned his position as abbot of a monastery to live with a blind singer-courtesan near the docks of his local town, supporting her with whatever money he had. There was Patacara, who through long practice with the Buddha, healed from her grief at losing her two young children in a flood, and became a sublimely untroubled guide to others. There was Patrul Rinpoche, who after lengthy training, ambled through the mountains and towns of Tibet dressed in rags, chiding himself about his inadequacies. And there was the fourth-century Egyptian saint Isidora, berated by the other nuns for her apparent insanity, who took all their abuse with patience, responding only with kindness. When the revered hermit Saint Pitirim visited their convent, he fell to his knees before her, recognizing her holiness, to the shock of the other nuns.

One more example, from late twentieth-century Britain:

Brother Guy, a Frenchman who left his career in France to join the Order of Little Brothers of Jesus in the Algerian Sahara. After several years, the order sent him to Leeds in the north of England, where immigrants from Pakistan were having a hard time, their lives blighted by poverty and discrimination. Like them, he went to work in a local steel mill. Despite losing three of his fingers to the machinery, he still did what he could to comfort the workers and alleviate the hardship of their lives. In his spare time, he worked in a shelter for homeless addicts, rolling cigarettes for them with his diminished hands.

The standard here might seem like a thoroughgoing self-lessness few of us could ever attain, or even aspire to. But for each of them, it came naturally. They lived without conscious enlightenment. And we can hold them up as inspiring ideals, the scope of whose work was small. Like them, we can find our own small ways to do what we can to heal the wounds of this world.

Try This

An Exercise in Loosening Self

Relax, settle in. Now say to yourself, *I am [your name].*
(For example, *I am Henry.*)

Now imagine seeing your name in lights against a night sky. See your name there for a moment. Now imagine the lights going out, until your name disappears. There is nothing left but the dark sky. Check in with how it feels to watch your name disappearing. Perhaps there is a sense of unfamiliarity or possibly a sense of peace or freedom. Or something else.

Now imagine a voice saying your name.

Let the voice get quieter and quieter. Let it be just a whisper. Let it get even quieter still . . . and then let it vanish into silence.

What is it like to hear the sound of your name disappear into silence? What is it like to taste the silence it leaves in its wake?

Is there a kind of openness? Perhaps a peace? Or perhaps something else: a subtle clenching or tightness? Whatever it is, let yourself rest with it. Take your time. Breathe gently, into and around whatever your experience is.

When you feel ready, try the next invitation.

Now see yourself in your mind's eye. Bring up an image of yourself. Imagine a photograph of yourself. Take a moment to see this image.

Now imagine that the corner of the photograph is being held to a candle. See the flame spread across the photograph. See the image blacken and curl and flake apart. See your image disappearing.

What is it like for you to disappear like that?

Imagine your face in perfectly still water, reflecting like a mirror. Gaze at your face for a while.

Now imagine ripples in the water. See your image break up in the disturbance and then vanish altogether.

Again, how does it feel to have your image vanish?

Now explore whether you can find a trace in your body of what it feels like to be you. For some, there might be a faint sense of contraction in the chest or the belly or the throat—some sensory signature telling you that you are you. Explore this until you find some faint, subtle muscular sense of you being you.

Feel that subtle sensation. Now let it get fainter . . . and weaker . . . until it too is fading away . . . and now it's gone.

Your body is clear, open, spacious. Where you could "feel" yourself, there is now no trace of any contraction or tension, just peaceful openness.

What is it like for that space within to be free?

Exploring a Koan

In this meditation we'll explore sitting with a classic koan. This one actually has two formulations: "This" and "What is this." We'll try out both in this sit. A key aspect of meditating with a koan is not to try to answer or resolve it. It may seem paradoxical, but instead of seeking a response, see if you can just state the koan in your mind and simply observe what effect the word or phrase has on the quality or clarity of your meditation.

As with any other sit, start by finding a comfortable seated position. Let your whole body relax. Let your body be balanced, so all parts can relax downward around the central column of the upper body. (If you're reclining, then give yourself entirely to the support beneath you.) The spine has its own intrinsic capacity to hold itself upright. Let it do that by itself. Let your body be balanced around it, so everything else can drape and hang, like rigging gone slack on a tall ship at rest in a bay.

Feel the swells of breath rolling gently through you, slightly lifting and lowering the hull of your lower trunk. Let the rise and fall of the breath soothe you.

Now sense the space within which your body sensations are appearing.

Tune into the space within which sounds are arising. Note that they are really one space, one great space.

Now, as presence starts to develop and you begin to inhabit your experience here and now, gently bring in the koan. Start by saying in your mind the word *This* . . . *This* . . . on each exhalation.

Let the word come gently, quietly. You inhale . . . and then exhale, and in your mind you add the word *This* . . . to the longer, relaxing release of the exhalation.

This . . . *This* . . . *This* . . .

Don't try to do anything special. Don't seek anything special. Just imagine that there is truly nothing more to be found. All that there is, is here right now. There is nothing but *This* . . . *This* . . .

Again, don't look for anything. Just rest in exactly what is happening right now. *This* . . . *This* . . .

How does it feel to hear the word *This*? Notice when you say it whether the word has any effect on you that you can detect. *This* . . .

If this practice is feeling interesting or is arousing curiosity or appreciation, then stay with the feeling and continue as you are. *This* . . . *This* . . .

If the practice is not particularly engaging, or if you feel like you have done enough of it for now, then we can shift to a different formulation.

Now, in the same way as before, on each exhalation, add the words *What is this.* . . .

Don't think of the words as a question to which you need to find an answer. Imagine that there is no answer and that the words are only a phrase. *What is this.* . . .

Gently, quietly, and tenderly, pour this little phrase into the stream of your exhalation.

Inhale . . . and exhale: *What is this.* . . .

What is this. . . . *What is this.* . . .

No seeking, no striving, no answering. Just the words. Just the phrase. *What is this.* . . .

Once again, see how it feels in your body and mind when you add this question into the space of your meditation. Utter the phrase in your mind, and taste any aftereffects of saying it.

What is this. . . .

And when you feel ready, drop the phrase and rest in silence and stillness for a few moments. Then bring some movement into your toes and fingers, your limbs, and your spine. Open your eyes and stretch. Come back to the space you're in, ready for whatever is next.

Thank you for being open to trying this.

The Answer

A

This book began with a question. One of the great Buddhist scriptures is just one letter long.

A.

Some consider it the supreme teaching of Buddhism. But how can an entire wisdom tradition possibly be summed up in a single letter?

A is a prefix of negation in Sanskrit, like our English *a-*. As in apathy—no feeling. Or atheism—no god.

It's like the *in-* of *incomplete*. The *un-* of *unlikely*. The *im-* of *impossible*.

In.

Un.

Im.

A.

How could a single negative syllable encapsulate all human wisdom and love? What really is *A*?

Yamada Kōun once wrote a letter to a friend describing his experience of "great enlightenment." All evening he was captivated by a quotation from a sutra. Finally, he went to bed. But in the middle of the night he woke up.

At midnight I abruptly awakened. At first my mind was foggy, then suddenly that quotation flashed into my consciousness: "I came to realize that Mind is no other than mountains, rivers, and the great wide earth, the sun and the moon and the stars." And I repeated it. Then all at once I was struck as though by lightning, and the next instant heaven and earth crumbled and disappeared. Instantaneously, like surging waves, a tremendous delight welled up in me, a veritable hurricane of delight, as I laughed loudly and wildly. "Ha, ha, ha, ha, ha, ha! There's no reasoning here, no reasoning at all! Ha, ha, ha!" The empty sky split in two, then opened its enormous mouth and began to laugh uproariously: "Ha, ha, ha!" Later one of the members of my family told me that my laughter had sounded inhuman.

I was lying on my back. Suddenly I sat up and struck the bed with all my might and beat the floor with my feet, as if trying to smash it, all the while laughing riotously. My wife and youngest son, sleeping near me, were now awake and frightened. Covering my mouth with her hand, my wife exclaimed, "What's the matter with you? What's the matter with you?" But I wasn't aware of this until told about it afterward. My son told me later he thought I had gone mad.

"I've come to enlightenment! Shakyamuni and the ancestors haven't deceived me! They haven't deceived

me!" I remember crying out. When I calmed down, I apologized to the rest of the family, who had come downstairs frightened by the commotion.

Even now my skin is quivering as I write.

That morning I went to see Yasutani-roshi and tried to describe to him my experience of the sudden disintegration of heaven and earth. "I am overjoyed! I am overjoyed!" I kept repeating, striking my thigh with vigor. Tears came which I couldn't stop. I tried to relate to him the experience of that night, but my mouth trembled and words wouldn't form themselves. In the end I just put my face in his lap. Patting me on the back he said: "Well, well, it is rare indeed to experience to such a wonderful degree. You are to be congratulated."

"Thanks to you," I murmured, and again wept for joy. Repeatedly I told him: "I must continue to apply myself energetically to zazen." He was kind enough to give me detailed advice on how to pursue my practice in the future, after which he again whispered in my ear, "My congratulations!" and escorted me to the foot of the mountain by flashlight.

For Yamada, the world collapsed and disappeared. And out of that nothing, boundless joy burst forth, a well-being and a goodness beyond anything he had known before. The marvel of unconditional, empty original love had filled the world for him. His life was irrevocably changed.

And yet it also wasn't. He still carried on his work as chief manager of a hospital and cared for his family just as before. Meanwhile, he continued his daily meditation. He reassured his family the next day that he hadn't in fact gone mad, and was perhaps more sane now than he had ever been.

In time, he became an internationally appreciated Zen teacher, who inspired many Europeans and Americans to take up meditation. And it all came from that one night when he lost his self as he'd known it, and found a boundless self that was one with a universal love. Those who came to know him in his subsequent life, such as the Buddhist author David Loy and the Zen teacher Sister Elaine MacInnes, described sitting with him as like being in the presence of a mountain of compassion.

MU

One of the best-known Zen koans is also a single syllable: *Mu*. Just that one word. *Mu*.

Mu means "not."

Mu, "not," "no."

A.

These monosyllables—they can take us back to the source, suck us back down into the origin point of all creation. That origin contains everything. It is limitless power, potentiality, energy, love. If we somehow drop everything, and fall back into it, then we cannot but "blaze forth" along with everything else, knowing for the first time exactly what we are.

We have found, firsthand, the original love of the universe.

So we go about our ordinary lives—pulling into the grocery store parking lot, ambling up the shopping aisles with a cart, driving to work, greeting colleagues at the office, seeing clients, making sales calls, and grabbing a bite of lunch with a friend. All this is the functioning of that original love. It loves us, it loves all this so much that it *is* all this.

The rocket scientist Konstantin Tsiolkovsky led the Soviet Union's rocket program in the 1920s, and is still recognized as a pioneer of astronautics. He had an oddly mystical bent. He believed that the universe created itself "so that atoms could experience joy."

And yes, he was a rocket scientist.

And what are *we* if not atoms? Could it be that we, when we awaken to original love, are also the purpose of the universe? And to know it for ourselves—that's when the purpose of the universe is fulfilled. Original love becomes terminal love. It has reached its destination. It has been recognized. It has been unmasked.

Right here, right now.

Here.

Now.

As you.

Epilogue

A MEDITATION

Let's review what it's like to slip into original love in our meditation. Let's bring it all together into one single sit, as if we're now in one vast new inn, where all the formerly separate inns have been combined under one roof, one sky.

Within this new, greater "inn," there are the different windows onto original love, different eaves beneath which original love can shelter us, and different chambers where that love welcomes us.

So I sit and settle, and soon, perhaps, I'm lost in thought. I notice. I hear talk in the mind and see images in the mind. *Hear . . . hear*, I tell myself. And I repeat, *See . . . see*, softly in my mind, until I'm consistently aware of the presence of thinking, broken down now into speech in the mind and images in the mind.

Is there a feeling? Yes.

So I say silently, *Feel . . . feel*. I find a knot, a contraction, a tightness, in my lower chest. I rest with it. I soften around it. Become open to it. Welcome it . . . and it starts to soften in response, to become easier, to feel more welcome.

I keep at it. And soon I realize I'm noticing sounds outside, in the space around me. And perhaps some inner ear sounds too. A soft hiss. A gentle hum. A kind of hearing different from the words that had been arising in the mind. These sounds are peaceful, lovely.

I also feel my hands now and then my feet, twin areas of warmth and tingling.

And I notice the easy, lovely rise and fall of the breath.

I'm coming alive once more, alive to this moment. I'm alive again in the here and now.

Then something flips. It's like a switch. Suddenly, there's an ease, a peace. It's almost like water flowing all through my experience. It's wonderful, it's easy, as if everything becomes transparent, glassy, watery. It's like being underwater, and as if I'm barely there, totally see-through, and the currents of the water can drift right through me.

Whatever this sense of flow is, it's as if it's aware by itself. It's aware of all this experience, and it freely drifts around it and through it, sensing it all.

At the same time, it's not caught up in any of it. It's free. It's a kind of flowing, easy, transparent awareness, which flows all through the elements of sense experience without being caught by any of them, and also goes much wider than my normal scope of awareness.

Peace. Energy. Clarity. And it has tenderness in it too. It loves. It loves this experience. It loves me. I'm enough. It's all enough.

Yes, it says to me. And I say back, *Yes*.

It's mindfulness. It's support. It's absorption. It's beyond the duality of self and other.

It's all of the preceding, and yet it also is its very own thing—a thing-that-is-no-thing. It actually doesn't quite fit any of the categories. It's both in them and beyond them. It's alive. It's free. It's inside. It's outside. It's everywhere. And it's also outside space and time. As well as inside them. It can't be contained. It's utterly free. And it's utter peace.

Peace. Peace. Peace.

It's pure love. Love with every last trace of anything else extracted out of it.

Pure love. Clear as air. Empty. Pure.

And there's simply nothing else.

THE FUTURE OF AWAKENING PRACTICE

To track the exponential growth of interest in awakening in globalized Western culture is heartwarming. It has to be one of the most positive cultural phenomena of recent decades, beginning with the Beats in the 1950s, and accelerating at an electrifying pace now, in the twenty-first century. Several trends have driven it, such as the massive spread of mindfulness as a foundational meditation practice, and the growing need for a fresh, personal spirituality as the old religious structures wane. But in addition, the recent revival of research into psychedelics has been a major factor.

The relationship of psychedelic experience to meditative awakenings is a complex topic. But here are a few considerations. Much psychedelic experience happens in the "imaginal realm." Trips can often be somewhat like extended dreams—firings of the imagination that take a user on a profound, transformational journey. Usually, there is a certain amount of "noise" in which the true "signal" may be harder to detect: sensory distortions, hallucinations, confusion, and so on. There may also be cathartic emotional releases, which can lead to profound healing. And sometimes, especially with the compound DMT, or with high doses of psilocybin, users also report experiences that are more like classic awakenings: opening to boundlessness, to no-self, to unsurpassable oneness, even emptiness.

Whether these chemically driven experiences "land" in people's lives as thoroughly as awakenings that are the fruit of long, patient practice is hard to gauge. It could be that there's no replacing long-term practice. There's something particularly powerful about an opening that occurs right in the midst of ordinary experience, to a non-intoxicated consciousness. It's as if we can't help but recognize this kind of awakening as an insight into the nature of our ordinary mind, rather than requiring some rarefied, non-ordinary state of mind. But on the other hand, to have shifts in consciousness become more reliably available through the compounds is a major benefit. New models of practice are already emerging that involve some combination of the two, such as the joint ayahuasca-and-meditation retreats offered by dharma teacher and shaman Spring Washam.

Spring told me that after years of teaching "pure" meditation, she felt it was invaluable for many of her students to be exposed to the disruptions of psychological patterning that ayahuasca (which contains DMT) could produce. And at the same time, she feels, these breakthroughs need the ongoing practice of meditation in order to be integrated.

Either way, the new interest in and research into psyche-delics is invaluable—first, in the terrain of mental health, where studies are showing psychedelics can be profoundly helpful for depression and anxiety, and also, in throwing open entrenched mindsets. They can shake loose fixed pre-conceptions and reveal how much vaster the territory of consciousness is than we would ever have guessed. They can reveal unimaginable dimensions, and disrupt our fixed ideas about time, space, and self. And finally, they are generating new research into awakening itself.

At last, researchers have templates and inventories of the qualities of mystical experience. They have indexes for measuring changes in life priorities. They are beginning to grapple with the complex matter of personality change, and the ways that powerful spiritual experiences can help with it.

All of this is clearly beneficial for the study of meditation too. We are starting to develop tools with which to gauge how and why meditative experiences can be so effective in chang-ing priorities and personalities, and what they could poten-tially do in a collective, even global, way. Truly, it seems like the culture has crossed a threshold into a new world of un-derstanding the human potential that awakening represents.

BUT AT THE same time, a word of caution is in order. Is it right to think that awakening is simply there for the taking, like a medicine on a shelf? Here's the problem—*suffering*. And there's the solution—*awakening*. Cool, I'll take two.

But it's not like that. It's more like the way Amazonian villagers are cognizant of the great constricting snake, the anaconda. Awakening is a force of nature that could turn our lives upside down.

To regard awakening as a feature it would be nice to hang over the bed, or an item that we can add to the daily regime— microdose, keto diet, flow-inducing work practice, and oh yes, getting my non-dual mind on—is beside the point. It's not like that. That would be like the difference between switching on a bedside light in the middle of the night in order to pad to the bathroom—versus hanging on a ledge in the high Himalayas as a mind-warping storm lashes in, pinning you to the cliff for three days, so you daren't even unzip the tent flap to pee outside.

Real awakening can't be tamed. And it's not really something we see. *Ah look, the view has changed*. Rather, it's a mind-eradicating change. It's a sea change. It's the discovery that our life has been a kind of hoax. A cosmic joke. Me and all my troubles, however seriously on some level I must take them, because others depend on my doing so, at the same time are no more substantial than clouds in the sky. There the clouds are—beautiful white plains when viewed from the Boeing crossing the continent, puffy white circus animals when seen from the suburban lawn, and lowering thunderheads when observed from the sea-lashed pier—yet get right up to one, and its shape is gone, it is only mist.

Liberation is not exactly what we might think. It's not a matter of: everything we know, but all free. It's nothing we know. Kyogen, a ninth-century Chinese master, said on his awakening, "One knock, and everything I knew has been forgotten." He had been sweeping a yard, and accidentally flicked a pebble against a nearby bamboo. When it struck—*tock*—he heard that knock and the whole world fell away. Who knows why? Why then exactly? Yes, he'd been practicing. Yes, he'd heard of this turnaround that was possible. But what the turnaround is, no one can know. In a way, not even those who have been through it can know. The very going through it is the extraction of the part that could know. Do we really want that?

The answer is yes, some really do.

But there's a problem here too. If you can get what you want without really having to wear yourself down, to prostrate yourself before the forces of creation, to deny yourself externally and internally; if you can just *get* it, or at least a glimpse of it, through a retreat, a course, or perhaps a dose—if it's really that easy to get, just the way you want, then isn't there something somehow wrong with this picture? If it's a genuine yearning, a longing, yet it can truly be easily satisfied simply by signing up for a course, then can you *really* be getting what it *really* is? When what it *really* is, is a revelation about the real nature of our life. Which in a sense devours and pulverizes some part of us (or can, in time), leaving us servants of a greater love. And to have that operation happen at our beck and call—it seems like it's the wrong way around.

In the meditation hall, in the long years of quiet, patient sitting, the patience is all about letting the wish for self-transcendence quiet down, letting it settle, letting it go quiet, letting it quietly die its own sweet death, until all that is left is the silence of the hall, the candle on the altar, the soft breathing of the fabric of the other sitters' clothing, the occasional rustle of breath, the stillness, the sublime stillness that seems to melt the very walls, that sometimes erases the roof beams, so the hall opens up to the entire night sky. This kind of stillness, one that gently develops, and slowly envelops its quiet-hearted witness, bears them off, opens them up, spreads their heart wide, and shows them the whole wide field of the cosmos—how can this kind of slow, transformative invitation from the very force of creation itself, to come and bear you to its bosom, which may take decades, be compared with a transactional acquisition of an hour of weirdness bought for a thousand dollars from a cashed-up start-up selling "enlightenment"? Even if it "works." In a way, that's almost worse.

To barter for awakening as if it were a commodity—it's as bewildering as trying to buy a taste of the beauty of the ocean. As if someone could sell you a taste of that beauty. It's you, before the mystery of creation. You, begging the vast mystery to make you worthy to know it more intimately. And if after many years, it agrees, just a little bit, it's like the mortal who saw the face of Apollo and died on the spot—it kills you. Maybe just one small part of you, maybe more. But if you keep at it, if your contemplative quest is earnest, and carries on, more and more of you is killed off, until perhaps you get what you really wanted, only none of you is left to enjoy it.

And weirdly, nothing could be better. The one who sought, the one who wanted—they are gone. And all is well. In getting it, they lost themselves. And nothing could be better. Love consumed them.

Yet at the same time, we *are* children of the universe. Literally. How could we not be? So why should it after all be such a tricky and fraught undertaking to take a peek under the hood and see something of our miraculous genesis? It's surely built into us anyway. That's precisely what Taoism, Chan, Zen and other branches of Buddhism, and yogic, Vedic, and Advaita Vedanta practices have been saying for generations. And some rare Abrahamic practitioners too, the ones with the particular disposition for it. All it takes in the end is the right longing. But let's just not forget that part of the preparation is the long denial of what we want. The learning to be okay with things as they are. And once we truly are, then revelation may strike, when, in a sense, we finally no longer need it.

From this perspective, it's also easier to see why ongoing practice beyond deep awakenings is so critical—however much an experience may release us from our narrower sense of self, we still need a way to ground it and integrate it, and meditation is a primary means of doing that.

ANOTHER VALLEY

This journey we've been on—the journey of a lifetime, into what life *is* and toward what we *are*—is a wonder. The vessel on which we embark, which ferries us across the seas of trouble and beauty—that's a wonder too. It's just our sitting.

All we do is sit still. Every day. For a little while, whether half an hour, an hour, or two hours. That's more than enough. Stillness is our vessel. Apparently, it can take us further than any known form of transport.

We come to see that what we thought of as "life" is a weave of stories. We live in stories. Stories are what make our human world.

Is this journey just another story? Perhaps. But perhaps not: after all, it's made by letting go of stories. As we let them go, as we release the strands of narrative, of understanding, of consequence, which have constituted our life as we've known it, we open to something wider, wilder, and ultimately boundless, and in the end not even a thing of any kind. Yet it turns out to be our very selfless self.

PRACTICE IS A long project. And its sheer length can be oddly comforting. To get a glimpse of the empty infinite may be protracted work. Then it's another thing to know it sustainably. Who knows how long that may take? Then to rest in it throughout all circumstances—that's yet a further piece of work. A lifetime really isn't very long for this project.

The Tibetan master Milarepa said this:

In the beginning nothing comes, in the middle nothing stays, in the end nothing goes.

But even if we do "get there"—well, congratulations to us. And we still need to personalize it, make it ordinary, and come right back to the marketplace, where normal life happens.

And then—lest we get caught in some form of spiritual materialism, in which we inadvertently think of practice as a means to "get" certain kinds of experience—at last it's clear that all our practice has really been is a way of escaping enthrallment to a misguided sense of self. All we're doing is getting closer to being clear about the true way of things. And from that somewhat clearer basis, we start to see what the *real* project has been all along.

It's as if we grew up in a small valley and didn't know it. We assumed that our little view was the whole world. Then finally, we started to realize that the slopes and hillsides around us weren't the end of the world: they were geographical features in a bigger world. And it was possible to hike up and over them.

Except that the valley sides are choked with gorse and briar. Not so easy to get out after all. But with effort and guidance, we finally find a snarled old path that just might lead to the ridge at the top—and sure enough, one day we crest the steep slope, we get out of the gulley, and a great vista opens up.

We've tasted escape from the world of separation. A great empire reaches beyond the brow. That empire has a name: *other beings*.

That's where we belong. Our concern shifts. We break free of the pull of the magnetic ego. It's a liberation to conquer the citadel of self. Now we discover our real work: to help that great world of beauty and suffering beyond, the empire of other beings.

In some views, the true project is the awakening of the whole cosmos: that all beings discover their participation in one boundless consciousness.

The deeper we go, the greater the work ahead. It's project upon grand project.

But there is a treasure in such vast conceptions, namely, that we will never finish the massive task.

Could there be any better project than helping all beings maximally? The fact that it never ends recommends it. All our ordinary projects are kind of child's play by comparison. At the same time, any sense of grandiosity such a project might induce is thwarted by its scale.

And it serves as a reminder for course correction. Whatever we may engage in, we can assess whether it's worthwhile by checking this: does it help in the overarching project of liberation for all?

To dedicate our efforts not to ourselves, but to other beings, turns out to be the most liberating thing we can do for ourselves. What an ironic twist of fate for the old self-server within. The only way to satisfy the self is to forget the self.

ONE WATER SYSTEM

The same way this world is wrapped and threaded through with water systems, so our life is threaded through with the water system of original love.

Just as streams and small rivers nourish the high valleys, and puddles moisten the fields, and ponds grace the woodlands, so in practice we first open up to *mindfulness*, to the capacity to be still in the midst of restlessness, to sit attentively and kindly with our unease, anxieties, and discomforts. We become kinder toward ourselves. Then we open up our sense gates to the world, and start to notice its gifts of beauty, its need for help.

This starts to open more secret sluices of love, like tapping into unknown water sources. Trickles of loving *support* start to seep into our life.

As practice develops, we taste deeper stirrings of well-being—we catch glimpses of a river of practice, a force for good in the world, a wholesomeness different from the kinds of success we might previously have sought. We are being carried by a prior current of love, as if life has an intrinsic wholeness that makes it an act of love in itself. This is the flavor of a mutual support we can trust.

The river emerges into a broad lake. We float, entranced by the deep stillness of samadhi, of absorption—the wondrous awareness with which we are preinstalled, rich with the intrinsic well-being of existence, which does not need to be earned or won.

Then in time we catch a glimpse of the great ocean. All of a sudden, it becomes clear that we aren't what we thought. Rather than being isolated and alone, we fall back into a wholeness that was always here. We are that ocean. It formed itself into a shape—the little stream of our life—but now that stream knows it is inseparable from all water. We were never apart from the ocean.

The clouds, the rains, the springs and aquifers, the storms and water tables, the brooks and torrents, the ponds and lakes—they are all one water system. Every part of this life is fully irrigated, fully alive with the loving energy of the ocean. Nothing is apart from the ocean. The water reaches everywhere.

AN OLD HASIDIC Jew called Zosya once said, "When I die, the Father won't ask me why I wasn't more like Moses while I lived. He'll ask why I wasn't more like Zosya."

Your greatest gift to the universe is yourself. It's time to be you in a whole way.

Gloria enim Dei vivens homo, said Irenaeus of Lyon, the second-century Greek Christian bishop. "The glory of God is the fully alive human being." Or as Simone Weil suggested: deep within we will find what we most want. In a sense, we can trust ourselves more deeply than we might think.

What is it that most lights you up, that you would be most happy to have given your vital energies to, before you die? As Cat Stevens asks, "What will you leave us this time?"

How to discern this? Love is the guide. Are we experiencing love, here and now? Our full aliveness as humans is impossible without love. The great purpose of human beings may be just to experience love—and then act accordingly, to spread that love the best we can.

Yamada Kōun used to say, "This world may all be a dream, but we must still work to make it a happy dream."

We are slowly becoming more bodhisattva-like: beings who work for the welfare of all.

ORIGINAL LOVE IS not a story. It is one totality, so there can *be* no story. It is existence itself, an "origin" that is none other than what it produces. Origin and product, cause and effect, are one.

One day, physics will identify this intrinsic creative force, right where emptiness becomes energy, and energy seems to turn into matter. One day, we'll know what it is. For now, we can wonder how all this comes into being. And hear a few wild mystics or practitioners claim that they have tasted the origin point of existence, and it's mind-blowing and beautiful beyond measure. And we might think, *What a lot of claptrap.*

But many sane, high-functioning people have done their time on the cushion, and still work in mainstream professions—in academia, health care, research, administration, finance, retail, industry, tech, or construction—and raise functional families the best they can. They don't join cults and aren't misfits subsisting on wild honey and locusts. That's hardly a pledge of scientific reliability. But nevertheless, some of the wilder existential experiences that meditation can bring us to, attested to by records over the millennia, and these days supported by evidence-based, university-funded research into "self-transcendent" experience, are not delusional or dangerous. On the contrary, they may just show us truer levels of reality and consciousness, and deeper levels of mental health, than any previously known. And at some point, perhaps we will all find the boundless force just behind conscious experience, which seems to be intrinsically, impersonally benevolent—the original love of our cosmos.

Acknowledgments

Preparing the list of people who helped bring this work into being has brought delight and a little unease. My memory is not what it used to be, and so many supported this book's creation that I just can't be sure whom I may have forgotten. One way or another, I hope everyone who ought to be here on this list is, and to anyone inadvertently omitted, my sincere apologies.

First and foremost, thanks to Clare Dunne, who has done so much to see this through. Thank you, my enduring love!

Great thanks to selfless readers of early drafts: Rick Hanson, who with his copious, compassionate wisdom was a dream cheerleader and incisive critic; also Michael Taft, Rodger Kamenetz, Bill Broyles, Andrew Mitchell, Christy Hengst, Jack Shukman, Ann Shukman (thank you for the course correction, mum), Will Francis, Lisa di Mona, and Sarah Giffin: you all helped this tract become itself.

Much gratitude to Tom Melk and Sarah Potter for the crucial weeks up at the cabin under the Brazos Cliffs, where this book wrote its own first draft. And profound thanks to Roshi Joan Halifax, for such companionable and kind guidance and for the precious weeks up at the cave under San Leonardo lake. Also to Scott Manfredi of Canyon Ranch, Costa Mesa, who provided a haven for incubation when it was most needed.

For people who inspired and supported the project in other ways: many thanks to Conrad Freiburg, Bill St. Cyr, Joel Monk, Tias Little, Guy Zimmerman, Pierre Philippon, Aaron Sugarman, Caroline Sugarman, Teo Biele ("back to self" indeed!), Fred McDaniel, and the brilliant Polly Young-Eisendrath.

Thank you to my teachers and mentors: Joan Rieck, Yamada Ryōun, John Gaynor, and Ruben Habito—roshis all! And to Shinzen Young, Roshi Joan, Stephen Snyder, Scott Kiloby, Stevie Shukman and Saul Shukman.

To people who helped with background support, great thanks—especially to Rachel Belash, Scott Lalonde, Johanna Sindelar (who took down the first foundational notes), Valerie Forstman, Sara Ross, and Mark Petrick. And Jeremy Riesenfeld: brilliant co-conspirator and manager.

Finally and also foremost, to key people who have helped steward this book's journey into the world, boundless thanks: wise and insightful Leslie Meredith, gifted Julie Mosow, and spectacular Emma Varvaloucas. And once again, to Natalie Goldberg—thank you, Nat! And to the exceptional, visionary Gabriella Page-Fort (first minister in the church of the ubiquity of love in the universe, for sure!), and to the tirelessly helpful and gifted Ryan Amato.

Further Reading

This book's main wellspring is the wisdom of ancient meditation practices. But it has also drawn inspiration from contemporary research on meditation and its wider context. For readers who would like to explore some topics further, I have compiled the following list of works—mostly in contemporary science, scholarship, and thought—that in one way or another helped to inspire this book.

Science and Philosophy

Dawkins, Richard. *The Extended Phenotype: The Long Reach of the Gene.* Oxford, 2016.

———. *The Selfish Gene: 40th Anniversary Edition.* New York, 2016.

Dennett, Daniel C. *From Bacteria to Bach and Back: The Evolution of Minds.* New York, 2017.

Doidge, Norman. *The Brain's Way of Healing: Remarkable Discoveries and Recoveries from the Frontiers of Neuroplasticity.* New York, 2015.

Eagleman, David. *The Brain: The Story of You.* New York, 2017.

Goleman, Daniel, and Richard Davidson. *Altered Traits: Science Reveals How Meditation Changes Your Mind, Brain, and Body.* New York, 2017.

Gray, John. *Straw Dogs: Thoughts on Humans and Other Animals.* London, 2002.

Hanson, Rick. *Hardwiring Happiness: The New Brain Science of Contentment, Calm, and Confidence.* New York, 2016.

Hanson, Rick, with Richard Mendius. *Buddha's Brain: The Practical Neuroscience of Happiness, Love, and Wisdom.* Oakland, 2009.

Hoffman, Donald. *The Case Against Reality: Why Evolution Hid the Truth from Our Eyes.* New York, 2019.

Kingsland, James. *Siddhartha's Brain: Unlocking the Ancient Science of Enlightenment.* New York, 2016.

Kotler, Steven, and Jamie Wheal. *Stealing Fire: How Silicon Valley, the Navy SEALs, and Maverick Scientists Are Revolutionizing the Way We Live and Work.* New York, 2018.

Levin, Janna. *How the Universe Got Its Spots: Diary of a Finite Time in a Finite Space.* New York, 2003.

Mack, Katie. *The End of Everything (Astrophysically Speaking).* New York, 2021.

Reich, David. *Who We Are and How We Got Here: Ancient DNA and the New Science of the Human Past.* New York, 2018.

Rosenblum, Bruce, and Fred Kuttner. *Quantum Enigma: Physics Encounters Consciousness.* Oxford, 2011.

Rovelli, Carlo. *Helgoland: Making Sense of the Quantum Revolution.* New York, 2021.

———. *Seven Brief Lessons on Physics.* New York, 2016.

Sapolsky, Robert M. *Behave: The Biology of Humans at Our Best and Worst.* New York, 2018.

Seth, Anil. *Being You: A New Science of Consciousness.* New York, 2021.

Walker, Matthew. *Why We Sleep: Unlocking the Power of Sleep and Dreams.* New York, 2018.

Psychology and Philosophy

Burke Harris, Nadine. *The Deepest Well: Healing the Long-Term Effects of Childhood Trauma and Adversity.* Boston, 2018.

Corbin, Henri. *Mundus Imaginalis, or the Imaginary and the Imaginal.* Ipswich, 1976.

Csikszentmihalyi, Mihaly. *Finding Flow: The Psychology of Engagement with Everyday Life.* New York, 1997.

Duhigg, Charles. *The Power of Habit: Why We Do What We Do in Life and Business.* New York, 2014.

Ellis, Albert. *How to Stubbornly Refuse to Make Yourself Miserable about Anything: Yes Anything!* New York, 2003.

Godfrey-Smith, Peter. *Other Minds: The Octopus, the Sea and the Deep Origins of Consciousness.* New York, 2016.

Hadot, Pierre. *The Inner Citadel: The Meditations of Marcus Aurelius.* Cambridge, MA, 1998.

———. *What Is Ancient Philosophy?* Cambridge, MA, 2002.

Hillman, James. *The Dream and the Underworld.* New York, 1979.

———. *The Soul's Code: In Search of Character and Calling.* New York, 1997.

Holden, Robert. *Loveability: Knowing How to Love and Be Loved.* Carlsbad, CA, 2013.

Irvine, William B. *Aha!: The Moments of Insight that Shape Our World.* Oxford, 2015.

———. *On Desire: Why We Want What We Want.* Oxford, 2006.

Jenkinson, Stephen. *Die Wise: A Manifesto for Sanity and Soul.* Berkeley, 2015.

Kahneman, Daniel. *Thinking, Fast and Slow.* New York, 2013.

Kamenetz, Rodger. *The History of Last Night's Dream: Discovering the Hidden Path to the Soul*. New York, NY, 2007.

Maté, Gabor. *When the Body Says No: Exploring the Stress-Disease Connection*. Hoboken, NJ, 2011.

McGilchrist, Iain. *The Master and His Emissary: The Divided Brain and the Making of the Western World*. New Haven, CT, 2019.

Mitchell, Andy. *Ten Trips: The New Reality of Psychedelics*. New York, 2023.

Moore, Thomas. *Care of the Soul: How to Add Depth and Meaning to Your Everyday Life*. New York, 1998.

Safran, Jeffrey, ed. *Psychoanalysis and Buddhism: An Unfolding Dialogue*. Boston, 2003.

Shaw, Martin. *The Snowy Tower: Parʒival and the Wet, Black Branch of Language*. Ashland, OR, 2014.

Unno, Mark, ed. *Buddhism and Psychotherapy Across Cultures: Essays on Theories and Practices*. Boston, 2006.

Van der Kolk, Bessel. *The Body Keeps the Score: Brain, Mind, and Body in the Healing of Trauma*. New York, 2015.

Watson, Gay, Stephen Batchelor, and Guy Glaxton, eds. *The Psychology of Awakening: Buddhism, Science, and Our Day-to-Day Lives*. York Beach, ME, 2000.

Wellwood, John. *Toward a Psychology of Awakening: Buddhism, Psychotherapy, and the Path of Personal and Spiritual Transformation*. Boston, 2000.

Wilber, Ken. *Eye to Eye: The Quest for the New Paradigm*. Boston, 2001.

History and Religion

Anthony, David. *The Horse, the Wheel, and Language: How Bronʒe-Age Riders from the Eurasian Steppes Shaped the Modern World*. Princeton, 2007.

Armstrong, Karen. *The Great Transformation: The Beginning of Our Religious Traditions*. New York, 2006.

Augustine. *The Confessions of St. Augustine*. New York, 1963.

Bryson, Bill. *A Short History of Nearly Everything*. New York, 2005.

Buber, Martin. *Tales of the Hasidim*. New York, 1991.

Carson, Anne. *Economy of the Unlost: Reading Simonides of Keos with Paul Celan*. Princeton, NJ, 1999.

Chapman, John. *The Spiritual Letters of Dom John Chapman*. London, 1935.

Chitty, Derwas J. *The Desert a City: An Introduction to the Study of Egyptian and Palestinian Monasticism under the Christian Empire*. Oxford, 1966.

Fields, Rick. *How the Swans Came to the Lake: A Narrative History of Buddhism in America*. Boston, 1992.

Goldberg, Philip. *American Veda: From Emerson and the Beatles to Yoga and Meditation: How Indian Spirituality Changed the West*. New York, 2010.

Gosden, Chris. *Magic: A History: From Alchemy to Witchcraft from the Ice Age to the Present*. New York, 2021.

Hatto, A. T., ed. *Traditions of Heroic and Epic Poetry: Volume 1: The Traditions*. London, 1980.

Kamenetz, Rodger. *The Jew in the Lotus: A Poet's Rediscovery of Jewish Identity in Buddhist India*. New York, 2007.

Kuzminski, Adrian. *Pyrrhonism: How the Ancient Greeks Reinvented Buddhism*. Lanham, MD, 2008.

Laird, Martin. *Into the Silent Land: A Guide to the Christian Practice of Contemplation*. Oxford, 2006.

McEvilley, Thomas. *The Shape of Ancient Thought: Comparative Studies in Greek and Indian Philosophies*. New York, 2002.

Reader, John. *Africa: A Biography of the Continent*. New York, 1998.

Seraphim, Metropolitan. *Chronicles of Seraphim-Diveyevo Monastery in the Ardatov Region of the Nizhegorod Province: Including the Lives of Its Founders St Seraphim and Schema-Nun Alexandra.* Cambridge, 2018.

Buddhist Scholarship

Bielefeldt, Carl. *Dōgen's Manuals of Zen Meditation.* Berkeley, 1988.

Broughton, Jeffrey L. *The Bodhidharma Anthology: The Earliest Records of Zen.* Berkeley, 1999.

Cole, Alan. *Fathering Your Father: The Zen of Fabrication in Tang Buddhism.* Berkeley, 2009.

Collins, Steven. *Selfless Persons: Imagery and Thought in Theravāda Buddhism.* Cambridge, 1982.

Faure, Bernard. *Chan Insights and Oversights: An Epistemological Critique of the Chan Tradition.* Princeton, NJ, 1993.

Forman, Robert K. C., ed. *The Problem of Pure Consciousness: Mysticism and Philosophy.* New York, 1990.

Garfield, Jay L. *Losing Ourselves: Learning to Live without a Self.* Princeton, NJ, 2022.

Gombrich, Richard F. *What the Buddha Thought.* London, 2009.

Hershock, Peter D. *Chan Buddhism.* Honolulu, 2005.

Hinton, David. *China Root: Taoism, Ch'an, and Original Zen.* Boulder, CO, 2020.

————. *Existence: A Story.* Boulder, CO, 2016.

Loy, David. *Money, Sex, War, Karma: Notes for a Buddhist Revolution.* Boston, 2008.

————. *Nonduality: In Buddhism and Beyond.* Somerville, MA, 2019.

Mitchell, Donald W. *Buddhism: Introducing the Buddhist Experience.* New York, 2008.

Rudy, John G. *Wordsworth and the Zen Mind: The Poetry of Self-Emptying.* Albany, NY, 1996.

Stevens, John. *Three Zen Masters: Ikkyū, Hakuin, Ryōkan.* Tokyo, 1993.

Wright, Robert. *Why Buddhism is True: The Science and Philosophy of Meditation and Enlightenment.* New York, 2017.

Dharma and Related

Abram, David. *Becoming Animal: An Earthly Cosmology.* New York, 2011.

———. *The Spell of the Sensuous: Perception and Language in a More-Than-Human World.* New York, 1997.

Anālayo. *Compassion and Emptiness in Early Buddhist Meditation.* Glasgow, 2015.

App, Urs, ed. *Zen Master Yunmen: His Life and Essential Sayings.* Boulder, CO, 2018.

Ash, Joel. *Tetralemma: A Buddhist Entertainment.* Pennsauken, NJ, 2020.

Batchelor, Stephen. *After Buddhism: Rethinking the Dharma for a Secular Age.* New Haven, CT, 2015.

———. *The Art of Solitude: A Meditation on Being Alone with Others in This World.* New Haven, CT, 2020.

———. *Confession of a Buddhist Atheist.* New York, 2010.

Bennett, Francis. *I Am That I Am: Discovering the Love, Peace, Joy and Stability of the True Self.* Oakland, CA, 2013.

Bodhi, Bhikku. *In the Buddha's Words: An Anthology of Discourses from the Pāli Canon.* Boston, 2005.

Brach, Tara. *Radical Acceptance: Embracing Your Life with the Heart of a Buddha.* New York, 2003.

————. *Radical Compassion: Learning to Love Yourself and Your World with the Practice of RAIN*. London, 2020.

Caplan, Mariana. *Halfway Up the Mountain: The Error of Premature Claims to Enlightenment*. Prescott, AZ, 1999.

Caplow, Florence, and Susan Moon, eds. *The Hidden Lamp: Stories from Twenty-Five Centuries of Awakened Women*. Boston, 2013.

Chayka, Kyle. *The Longing for Less: Living with Minimalism*. New York, 2020.

Chinmayananda. *Mandūkya Upanisad with Gaudapāda's Kārikā: Truth: Witness of Waking, Dream and Deep Sleep*. Mumbai, 2015.

Cleary, Thomas, and J. C. Cleary, trans. *The Blue Cliff Record*. Boulder, CO, 2005.

Culadasa (John Yates), Matthew Immergut, and Jeremy Graves. *The Mind Illuminated: A Complete Meditation Guide Integrating Buddhist Wisdom and Brain Science for Greater Mindfulness*. New York, 2019.

Desmond, Tim. *How to Stay Human in a F*cked-Up World: Mindfulness Practices for Real Life*. San Francisco, 2019.

Ehrenreich, Barbara. *Living with a Wild God: A Nonbeliever's Search for the Truth about Everything*. New York, 2014.

Ferguson, Andy. *Zen's Chinese Heritage: The Masters and Their Teachings*. Boston, 2000.

Goldberg, Natalie. *The Great Failure: My Unexpected Path to Truth*. New York, 2005.

————. *The Great Spring: Writing, Zen, and This Zigzag Life*. Boston, 2017.

Goldstein, Joseph. *Insight Meditation: The Practice of Freedom*. Boston, 1993.

————. *Mindfulness: A Practical Guide to Awakening*. Boulder, CO, 2013.

Gunaratana, Bhante Henepola. *Mindfulness in Plain English*. Somerville, MA, 2015.

Habito, Ruben L. F. *Living Zen, Loving God*. Boston, 2008.

Halifax, Joan. *The Fruitful Darkness: A Journey Through Buddhist Practice and Tribal Wisdom*. New York, 2007.

———. *Standing at the Edge: Finding Freedom Where Fear and Courage Meet*. New York, 2019.

Hanh, Thich Nhat. *The Miracle of Mindfulness: An Introduction to the Practice of Meditation*. Boston, 1987.

Harris, Sam. *Waking Up: A Guide to Spirituality Without Religion*. New York, 2014.

Hixon, Lex. *Coming Home: The Experience of Enlightenment in Sacred Traditions*. Garden City, NY, 1978.

———. *Mother of the Buddhas: Meditations on the Prajna Paramita Sutra*. Wheaton, IL, 1993.

Isherwood, Christopher. *My Guru and His Disciple*. Minneapolis, 2001.

Iyer, Pico. *The Half Known Life: In Search of Paradise*. New York, 2023.

———. *The Man Within My Head*. New York, 2012.

Little, Tias. *Yoga of the Subtle Body: A Guide to the Physical and Energetic Anatomy of Yoga*. Boston, 2017.

Kapleau, Philip, ed. *The Three Pillars of Zen: Teaching, Practice, and Enlightenment*. New York, 1989.

Kelly, Loch. *The Way of Effortless Mindfulness: A Revolutionary Guide for Living an Awakened Life*. Boulder, CO, 2019.

Khema, Ayya. *Who Is My Self?: A Guide to Buddhist Meditation*. Boston, 1997.

Kornfield, Jack. *After the Ecstasy, the Laundry: How the Heart Grows Wise on the Spiritual Path*. New York, 2000.

Maa, Amoda. *Falling Open in a World Falling Apart: The Essential Teaching of Amoda Maa*. Lanham, MD, 2020.

MacInnes, Elaine. *The Flowing Bridge: Guidance on Beginning Zen Koans*. Somerville, MA, 2007.

Maharaj, Nisargadatt. *I Am That: Talks with Sri Nisargadatta Maharaj.* Durham, NC, 2012.

Manuel, Zenju Earthlyn. *The Shamanic Bones of Zen: Revealing the Ancestral Spirit and Mystical Heart of a Sacred Tradition.* Boulder, CO, 2022.

Moore, Meido. *The Rinzai Zen Way: A Guide to Practice.* Boulder, CO, 2018.

Morinaga, Soko. *From Novice to Master: An Ongoing Lesson in the Extent of My Own Stupidity.* Boston, 2004.

O'Neill, Eugene. *Long Day's Journey Into Night.* New Haven, CT, 2014.

Red Pine. *The Platform Sutra: The Zen Teaching of Hui-neng.* London, 2009.

Ricard, Matthieu. *Enlightened Vagabond: The Life and Teachings of Patrul Rinpoche.* Boulder, CO, 2017.

Rinpoche, Yonge Mingyur, with Helen Tworkov. *In Love with the World: A Monk's Journey Through the Bardos of Living and Dying.* New York, 2021.

Salzburg, Sharon. *A Heart as Wide as the World: Stories on the Path of Lovingkindness.* New York, 1999.

Schumacher, E. F. *Small Is Beautiful: Economics as if People Mattered.* New York, 2010.

Snyder, Stephen, and Tina Rasmussen. *Practicing the Jhanas: Traditional Concentration Meditation as Presented by the Venerable Pa Auk Sayadaw.* Boston, 2009.

Spira, Rupert. *A Meditation on I Am.* Oxford, UK, 2021.

Suzuki, Shunryu. *Zen Mind, Beginner's Mind: Informal Talks on Zen Meditation and Practice.* Boston, 2011.

Taft, Michael W. *The Mindful Geek: Secular Meditation for Smart Skeptics.* Kensington, CA, 2015.

Ta Hui. Cleary, Christopher, trans. *Swampland Flowers: The Letters and Lectures of Zen Master Ta Hui.* New York, 1977.

Tanahashi, Kazuaki, ed. *Moon in a Dewdrop: Writings of Zen Master Dōgen*. San Francsico, 1995.

———. *Treasury of the True Dharma Eye: Zen Master Dogen's Shobo Genzo*. Boston, 2010.

Thompson, Evan. *Why I Am Not a Buddhist*. New Haven, CT, 2020.

Tisdale, Sallie *Women of the Way: Discovering 2,500 Years of Buddhist Wisdom*. San Francisco, 2006.

Tolle, Eckhart. *The Power of Now: A Guide to Spiritual Enlightenment*. Novato, CA, 2004.

Warner, Brad. *Sex, Sin, and Zen: A Buddhist Exploration of Sex from Celibacy to Polyamory and Everything in Between*. Novato, CA, 2010.

Wellings, Nigel. *Why Can't I Meditate?: How to Get Your Mindfulness Practice on Track*. New York, 2016.

Whyte, David. *Consolations: The Solace, Nourishment and Underlying Meaning of Everyday Words*. Langley, WA, 2002.

Wilkerson, Isabel. *Caste: The Origins of Our Discontents*. New York, 2020.

Winston, Diana. *The Little Book of Being: Practices and Guidance for Uncovering Your Natural Awareness*. Boulder, CO, 2019.

Yamada, Kōun. *Zen: The Authentic Gate*. Somerville, MA, 2015.

———. *The Gateless Gate: The Classic Book of Zen Koans*. Somerville, MA, 2015.

Yang, Larry. *Awakening Together: The Spiritual Practice of Inclusivity and Community*. Somerville, MA, 2017.

Yogananda, Paramahansa. *Autobiography of a Yogi: The Classic Story of One of India's Greatest Spiritual Thinkers*. London, 2018.

Young, Shinzen. *The Science of Enlightenment: How Meditation Works*. Boulder, CO, 2018.

Credits and Permissions

Excerpt on page 297–98 from *Three Pillars of Zen* edited by Roshi Philip Kapleau, copyright © 1965 by Roshi Philip Kapleau, copyright © 1980 by The Zen Center, Inc. Used by permission of Anchor Books, an imprint of the Knopf Doubleday Publishing Group, a division of Penguin Random House LLC. All rights reserved.

About the Author

Henry Shukman has guided thousands of students from around the world through mindfulness and awakening practices in a decade and a half of teaching. He is cofounder of the meditation app The Way and is a bestselling author of poetry and fiction, with his inspirational poems appearing in the *New Yorker* and the *Guardian*, and his essays in the *New York Times*, *Outside*, and *Tricycle*. He has taught poetry at the Institute of American Indian Arts and meditation at Google and Harvard Business School, and is a Zen master in the Sanbo Zen lineage, with a master's degree from Cambridge and a master of letters degree from St Andrews. He is the spiritual director emeritus at Mountain Cloud Zen Center in Santa Fe, New Mexico.

Find out more at www.henryshukman.com
and www.thewayapp.com.